Effective
Business
Communication

Houghton Mifflin Company
Boston

Editor: Laura P. Chesterton

The two quotations from pages 200 and 3–5, respectively, of
Thomas J. Peters and Robert H. Waterman, Jr.'s book *In Search
of Excellence: Lessons from America's Best-Run Companies*
(New York: Harper & Row, 1992) that are found on pages 41
and 42 of this book have been reproduced by permission of
HarperCollins Publishers.

Library of Congress Cataloging-in-Publication Data

Effective business communication.

p. cm.

Includes index.
ISBN 0-395-61308-6
1. Business communication. 2. Business writing.
HF5718.E34 1992
658.4′5—dc20   91-32938
                                                      CIP

BP 10 9 8 7 6 5 4 3 2 1

Table of Contents

Introduction

Effective Business Communication is a comprehensive yet concise guide to writing, formatting, and transmitting all types of business documents, from letters, memorandums, and minutes to corporate reports. Its in-depth coverage of both conventional and automated systems provides essential knowledge for today's employee. With a practical, hands-on approach, this book can dramatically improve your day-to-day professional correspondence—in turn, improving your ability to communicate with grace and precision and thereby to cultivate important business relationships.

The first chapter, "Using English Effectively in Business," is a crash course in using good prose to your best advantage. This chapter features 274 Usage Notes based on *The American Heritage Dictionary, Second College Edition;* 28 rules for capitalization and 93 rules for punctuation, with examples following each rule; and guidelines for the proper styling of footnotes and bibliographies. Extensive lists of 535 clichés and 63 redundant expressions show you what to avoid in achieving fresh, original prose. Another section reviews basic grammar. Sample business letters provide useful models for the content of twelve basic types of professional correspondence.

Chapter Two, "Creating Business Document: Dictation and Transcription," begins with an overview of the workstation, explaining how to organize your space for optimal efficiency. Twelve pages discuss the best equipment and methods used to take dictation, followed by sections on transcription. The chapter concludes with material on taking and transcribing the minutes of meetings.

Chapter Three, "Styling Business Documents," provides a thorough reference for all the different acceptable formats used when actually keying or typing a document. It examines each part of a standard business letter, then illustrates seven different letter styles with letter facsimiles. Facsimiles of real memorandums, press releases, and corporate reports follow. This material is highlighted by ten tables, including ones showing standard spacing and alignment. Also included are a list of standard abbreviations for street and place names and ten pages on forms of address. The chapter then explains how to index a document and how to correct errors.

Chapter Four, "Sending Business Documents: Conventional and Electronic Mail," suggests procedures for sorting incoming mail and for handling and posting outgoing mail. It introduces the reader to electronic mail—what features to look for in a system and what types of systems are on the market. It also includes an overview of other ways to "mail" documents—namely, through facsimile services and the Telex network.

Effective Business Communication, with its numerous illustrations, examples, and tables, together with its readable text and useful information, contains all the resources that you require to produce polished, professional documents as you move forward confidently into the twenty-first century.

Laura P. Chesterton

1

Using English Effectively in Business

In business, your professional image depends upon your ability to communicate well—that is, to ensure that the message you are trying to communicate is the same message that actually gets heard. What follows is a kit of tools and a guide to their use that will help you put together the building blocks of effective communication.

GUIDELINES TO CAPITALIZATION, PUNCTUATION, ITALICIZATION, AND USE OF NUMERALS

Capitalization
Capitalization should be used in the following instances:

beginnings
1. For the first word of a sentence:

> The evening offered barbecued chicken, cornpones, and iced tea.
>
> Personal income rose 0.9% in December from November.
>
> Fabergé agreed definitively to be acquired by McGregor Corp. for $32 a share, or $179.8 million. (*The Wall Street Journal*)

2. The first word of a direct quotation (however, lowercase is used for the continuation of a split quotation or a quotation closely woven into the sentence):

> "I was there and I shook hands with the Chinese foreign minister," he said.
>
> "It is not a matter of what they want," commented one knowledgeable observer, "but a question of timing and tactics."

3. The first word of every line in a poem in traditional verse:

> My candle burns at both its ends;
> It will not last the night;

But oh, my foes, and oh, my friends—
It gives a lovely light.
(Edna St. Vincent Millay)

proper names

4. The names of people, of corporations, of organizations and their members, of councils and congresses, and of historical periods and events:

> Shirley Chisholm
> The Natural Resources Defense Council
> Environmental Protection Agency
> the Civil War
> the Industrial Revolution
> Roman Catholic Church
> a Republican
> the Democratic Party
> General Dynamics Corp.
> Delta Air Lines
> The bleak situation of the American steel industry is drawing the United Steelworkers and U.S. Steel Corp. into their sharpest conflict since the 116-day steel strike of 1959. (*Business Week*)

5. The names of places and geographic divisions, districts, regions, and locales:

Wall Street	Silicon Valley
New York	the Sunbelt
North Pole	China
the South	Greenwich Village
Pennsylvania	New England
George Washington Bridge	Division Street

> This is the Corn Belt, heart of the most efficient agriculture in the world. . ..(*Farm Journal*)

Do not capitalize words indicating compass points unless a specific region is referred to:

> Turn north onto Interstate 84.

6. The names of rivers, lakes, mountains, seas, and oceans:

Atlantic Ocean	Blue Ridge Mountains
Mississippi River	Lake Superior

> [The] ill-fated drillship, the *Glomar Java Sea*. . . [sank] in the South China Sea recently with 81 crew members. (*Oil & Gas Journal*)

7. The names of ships, airplanes, and space vehicles:

U.S.S. *Enterprise*   Lindbergh's *Spirit of St. Louis*
British Airways' *Concorde*   Skylab
the spy satellite Ferret-D

The Soviet Union launched a Progress tanker spacecraft to Salyut 7 Oct. 20 to refuel the space station that suffered a serious propulsion system problem Sept. 9. (*Aviation Week & Space Technology*)

8. The names of nationalities, races, peoples, and languages:

Americans   Caucasian
Yoruba   French
Gaelic   Old Church Slavonic

"Every time I see an Arab," says Sylvester Tinker, principal chief of Oklahoma's Osage tribe, "I don't care who he is or what he looks like. I want to run up and kiss him, because he has done more for the Osage people in 4 years than the federal government has done in 150." (*Forbes*)

9. Words that are derived from proper names, when used in their primary senses:

European cities   British royalty

But do not capitalize these if they are used as integral elements of compound words having their own distinct meaning:

chinese red (i.e., a specific shade of red)
moroccan leather (i.e., a specific kind of leather)

titles of people

10. Words indicating familial relationships when preceding a person's name and forming a title:

Aunt Millie   Uncle Ed

but:

my aunt, Millie Martin

11. Titles—civil, corporate, military, royal and noble, religious, and honorary—when preceding a name:

Chief Justice Warren Burger
General George S. Patton
Mayor Dixon
Pope John Paul II
Remington Products President Victor Kiam II
The Honorable Barbara Jordan

"There was no cash up front, no margin calls and no interest accrued on the principal," recalls Louisiana-Pacific Chairman Harry Merlo. . . .(*Forbes*)

12. All references to the President and the Vice President of the United States:

President Bush   Vice President Quayle
the President   the Vice President

titles of publications and artistic works

13. All key words in titles of literary, dramatic, artistic, and musical works:

the book *The One Minute Manager*
the short story "The Lottery"
the *Fortune* article entitled "Winners (and Losers) from IBM's PC Jr."
the poem "For My People"
the play *A Raisin in the Sun*
Van Gogh's *A Sidewalk Cafe at Night*
the Beatles' album *Sgt. Pepper's Lonely Hearts Club Band*
the movie *Gone With the Wind*

14. *The* in the title of a newspaper if considered an integral part of the publication's entire title:

The Wall Street Journal
the *Washington Post*
Missing a deadline is bad for any newspaper, but it's worse for the *Odessa* (Tex.) *American. (Editor & Publisher)*

salutations and complimentary closes

15. The first word of the salutation and of the complimentary close of a letter:

Dear Lee,   To whom it may concern:
All hands: Yours truly,
Kind regards,

epithets

16. Epithets used as substitutes for the names of people or places:

the Father of Capitalism
the City by the Bay
the Oval Office
Yes, Virginia, there finally was a Peanut, and the pint-size personal computer wearing Big Blue's [International Business Machines'] daunting logo turned out pretty much as the rumor mill had described it. (*Fortune*)

personifications

17. Words used in personification:

Because I could not stop for Death,
He kindly stopped for me.
(Emily Dickinson)

the pronoun I

18. The pronoun *I*:

> I know Sir John Gielgud does a wine commercial where he plays the butler, but I couldn't tell you whose wine it is. (*Advertising Age*)

names for the Deity and sacred works

19. Names for the Deity, for a Supreme Being, and for sacred books:

God and His blessings	the Almighty
Allah	Jehovah
the Talmud	the Koran
the Bible	the Messiah

days, months, and holidays

20. Days of the week, months of the year, holidays, and holy days:

Monday	March
Fourth of July	Passover
Ramadan	Christmas

courts

21. The names of specific judicial courts:

> The Supreme Court of the United States
>
> the United States Court of Appeals for the Seventh Circuit
>
> The New York State Supreme Court heard oral argument on the publishers' motion December 22. (*Publishers Weekly*)

treaties and laws

22. The names of treaties, pacts, accords, acts, laws, and specific amendments:

> the Fifth Amendment to the Constitution
>
> the Civil Rights Act of 1964
>
> the Strategic Arms Limitation Talks II Treaty
>
> Warsaw Pact
>
> the Equal Rights Amendment
>
> Labor Management Relations Act
>
> Truckmakers say that the recovery of sales of Class 8 rigs . . . was slowed last year by confusion over the Surface Transportation Assistance Act of 1982. (*Business Week*)

trademarks and service marks

23. Registered trademarks and service marks:

Xerox	Band-Aid
Teletype	3M Post-it

Kleenex	Ping-Pong
Plexiglas	TelePrompTer

In addition to Seven Up's Like cola, now available in more than half the country, other new caffeine-free sodas on the market are Pepsi Free, Pepper Free and Coca-Cola's caffeine-free Coke, Diet Coke and Tab. (*Chain Store Age Supermarkets*)

scientific terms

24. The names of geologic eras, periods, epochs, and strata and the names of prehistoric divisions:

Paleozoic Era	Precambrian
Pleistocene	Bronze Age

Israeli firms are watching a step-out [oil well] that awaits testing in the Zuk Tamrur area, site of the 1 Zuk Tamrur well, the country's first production from the Triassic [geologic period] formation that underlies most of Israel. (*Oil & Gas Journal*)

25. The names of constellations, planets, stars, and other celestial bodies:

the Milky Way	Earth
Pleiades	Neptune

In addition the Spacelab 1 issue has both cost and hardware implications affecting the Spacelab 2 and 3 missions, and the Astro ultraviolet telescope mission that has Halley's Comet as one target. (*Aviation Week & Space Technology*)

26. Genus—but not species—names in binomial nomenclature:

Chrysanthemum leucanthemum
Macaca mulatta
Rana pipiens

27. New Latin names of classes, families, and all groups higher than genera in botanical and zoological nomenclature:

Gastropoda	Nematoda

But do not capitalize adjectives and nouns derived from these New Latin names:

a gastropod	a nematode

abbreviations and acronyms

28. Many abbreviations and acronyms:

Dec.	Wed.
Dr. Jones	Lt. Gov. Smith

1600 Pennsylvania Ave.	IBM
FBI	CORE

During the preceding 44 years, the Civil Aeronautics Board (CAB) had exercised tight controls over the ability of new airlines to start service. . . . (*Black Enterprise*)

Punctuation

Apostrophe   '

1. Indicates the possessive case of singular and plural nouns, indefinite pronouns, and surnames combined with designations such as *Jr.*, *Sr.*, and *II*:

   Mr. and Mrs. Postman could be anyone's lovable grandparents.

   Investors also applauded XYZ Corporation's purchase of a new personal computer company.

   The partnership owns 40 per cent of Dustin Hoffman's latest triumph [*Tootsie*]. . . .(*Barron's*)

   And just what was it that woke Wall Street from its uneasy six months' sleep?

2. Indicates joint possession when used with the last of two or more nouns in a series:

   Standard and Poor's data

   Coke and Pepsi's battle

   Jane and Bob's law firm

3. Indicates individual possession when used with each of two or more nouns in a series:

   Smith's, Roe's, and Doe's reports

4. Can be used to indicate the plurals of figures, letters, or words:

   poorly formed *a*'s and *e*'s

   88's and *12*'s transposed

   the 1900's

but also possible:

   *a*s and *e*s

   *88*s and *12*s

   the 1900s

   Indeed, major companies seeking to recruit MBAs at the business schools. . . .(*Madison Avenue*)

Note: The Associated Press and United Press International stylebooks for magazines and newspapers call for an *s*, not an '*s*, as do the style guides for various publishing houses.

5. Indicates omission of letters in contractions:

> isn't (is not)
>
> it's (it is)
>
> wouldn't (would not)
>
> Tax shelters have been around "ever since we've had tax law," said William L. Raby. . . .(*Journal of Accountancy*)

6. Indicates omission of figures in dates:

> the class of '84
>
> The mistake we made in the '70s was to assume there was only one possible course. (*Canadian Business*)

Brackets **[ ]**

1. Enclose words or passages in quotations to indicate insertion of material written by someone other than the original writer:

> I don't think [increasing the Court's membership to ease the workload for each Justice] would solve the problem. (Retired Supreme Court Justice Potter Stewart, quoted in *Forbes*)

2. Enclose material inserted within matter already in parentheses:

> (The return on equity [ROE] is 35 per cent.)

Colon **:**

1. Introduces words, phrases, or clauses that explain, amplify, or summarize what has preceded:

> You know what I mean: The idea that we should all be happy all of the time. . . .(*Advertising Age*)
>
> A big question hangs over one major vocational group: clerical workers. (*Fortune*)
>
> The Buckingham Corporation . . . and a company within the Beverage Group of Beatrice Foods have announced the appointment of D'Arcy-MacManus & Masius, Inc. as the advertising agency for Finlandia as well as for its other exclusive U.S. imports: Cutty Sark and Cutty 12 Scots Whiskies. . . . (*Beverage World*)

2. Introduces a rather long quotation:

> Says Warner: "The deficit is more destructive than any enemy we face. National defense cannot be stronger than the economy on which it rests." (*Nation's Business*)

3. Introduces a list:

> The session also gives major insights into:
> * current consumption data
> * sales projections
> * the competitive situation
> (*Chemical Week*)

4. Separates chapter and verse numbers in references to biblical quotations:

> Esther 2:17

5. Separates city from publisher in footnotes and bibliographies:

> Boston: Houghton Mifflin, 1991

6. Separates hour and minute in time designations:

> 3:45 P.M.   a 7:30 meeting
>
> So when I left the mill at 9:30 and walked toward the big back door where the trucks unload, one of the millwrights said, "I hope you're not going to close the company today." (*Inc.*)

7. Follows the salutation in a business letter:

> Ladies and Gentlemen:
> To whom it may concern:
> Dear Mr. or Ms. Kane:

Comma   *,*

1. Separates the clauses of a compound sentence connected by a coordinating conjunction:

> Instead, they'll point up the good parts of the idea, and only then might they discuss a potential problem with the idea.
>
> "A lot of people are trying to catch us, but we're a moving target," says founder and [Lotus Development Corp.] President Mitchell D. Kapor. (*Industry Week*)

The comma may be omitted in short compound sentences:

> We have prepared the case and we are ready to present it.

2. Can be used to separate *and* or *or* from the final item in a series of three or more:

> Want to boost employee morale? Then give your employees a New Year's present that helps them save for: retirement, a new house, college tuition, unexpected medical expenses, or other major expenses. (*ABA Banking Journal*)

Note: In accordance with the AP and UPI stylebooks, most magazines and newspapers drop the last comma before the *and* or *or* in simple series.

3. Separates two or more adjectives modifying the same noun if *and* could be used between them:

> The short, khaki-clad guest of honor works the room like the politician he is. . . .(*The Wall Street Journal*)

but:

> a polished mahogany desk (*and* could not be placed between *polished* and *mahogany*)

4. Sets off a nonrestrictive clause or phrase (one that if eliminated would not affect the meaning of the sentence):

> Clearly, there is a fine line between editing and formatting, which is covered in the following section. (Harry Katzan, Jr.)

But the comma should not be used when the clause is restrictive (essential to the meaning of the sentence):

> One railroad that already knows what will work is the Southern. . . . (*Railway Age*)

5. Sets off words or phrases in apposition to a noun or noun phrase:

> Dennis R. Tourse, a partner in the Boston firm of Fitch, Miller and Tourse, [says] "your office has to look the way people picture a business lawyer's office." (*Black Enterprise*)

In this example, *partner* is in apposition to *Dennis R. Tourse.*

Note: The comma should not be used if such words or phrases precede the noun they modify:

> The Navy, said ex-Chief of Naval Operations Elmo (Bud) Zumwalt, assumes "that everyone below the rank of commander is immature." (Thomas J. Peters and Robert H. Waterman, Jr.)

not

> "ex-Chief of Naval Operations, Elmo (Bud) Zumwalt"

6. Sets off transitional words and short expressions that require a pause in reading or speaking:

> Unless safeguards are put in place, the computer age, at least for a while, could resurrect some of the class barriers that liberals spent much of this century trying to tear down. (Heather Menzies)

7. Sets off words used to introduce a sentence:

> Indeed, southern Florida does have warm winters.
>
> At best, commodity trading is a high risk game where the only consistent winners are the brokers who charge you commissions. (*Money*)

8. Sets off a subordinate clause or a long phrase that precedes a principal clause:

> If we state, then, that champions and systems of champions are the single most important key to sustained innovative success in the excellent companies, how do we reconcile repeated failure and overall success? (Thomas J. Peters and Robert H. Waterman, Jr.)
>
> Weighing in base form 1,630 lbs. (739 kg.), CRX has plastic fenders and lower body panels. (*Ward's Auto World*)

9. Sets off short quotations and sayings:

> "We plan to reincarnate Elvis," says Joseph Rascoff, the New York accountant who is masterminding it all. (*Forbes*)

10. Indicates omission of a word or words:

> To err is human; to forgive, divine.

11. Sets off the year from the month in full dates:

> February 6, 1991

But note that when only the month and the year are used, no comma appears:

> February 1991

12. Sets off city and state in geographic names:

> A case in point is the Panther Valley Apartments in Allamuchy, N.J. . . . (*Professional Builder*)

13. Separates series of four or more figures into thousands, millions, and so on:

> Every time bulk diesel fuel goes up a penny, it costs us $100,000.
> The plant still produces 155,000 lb/week of dyed sewing thread plus about 50,000 lb/week of dyed yarn. . . .(*Textile World*)

14. Sets off words used in direct address:

> Mr. Stone, please be ready to submit your report in one hour.
> I have received your report, Ms. Smith, and I have these comments.

15. Separates a tag question from the rest of the sentence:

> Didn't take long for Jesse Jackson to get into the political mainstream of America, did it? (*Advertising Age*)

16. Sets off any sentence elements that might be misunderstood if the comma were not used:

> Dole has already held hearings, and hopes to introduce the measure in the next month or two. (*Forbes*)

17. Follows the salutation in a personal letter and the complimentary close in a business or personal letter:

> Dear Lee,   Sincerely,

18. Sets off some titles, degrees, and honorifics from surnames and from the rest of a sentence:

> Sandra Maynard, Esq.   John Kennedy, Jr.
> Susan P. Green, MD, presented the case.

Dash ——

1. Indicates a sudden break or change in continuity:

   > Last year Presley's Graceland attracted over 500,000 people—more than Thomas Jefferson's Monticello—at $6 a head for adults. (*Forbes*)

2. Sets apart a defining or emphatic phrase:

   > Only one sector—public transit—fared badly in 1983. . . .(*Engineering News Record*)

   > More important than winning the election, is governing the nation. That is the test of a political party—the acid, final test. (Adlai E. Stevenson)

3. Sets apart parenthetical material:

   > . . . newspapers' 1982 income from retail ads was five times as much as from national ads—$15 billion vs. $3 billion. (*Advertising Age*)

4. Marks an unfinished sentence:

   > "I demand we take a vote on—" the shareholder insisted during the annual meeting before his microphone was shut off.

5. Sets off a summarizing phrase or clause:

   > Now GM, Ford, Chrysler, American Motors—it's up to you. (*Broadcasting*)

   > The vital measure of a newspaper is not its size but its spirit—that is its responsibility to report the news fully, accurately, and fairly. (Arthur H. Sulzberger)

6. Can be used to set off the name of an author or source, as at the end of a quotation:

   > "We have not given up on the U.S. small car. Despite all the statements by our competitors and the doomsayers, we did not give up."—Roger B. Smith, chairman of General Motors (*Fortune*)

Ellipses • • •

1. Indicate, by three spaced points, omission of words or sentences within quoted matter:

   > "No, I would not say things like that again, even after some of the things that have been done recently. . .I would like to convince the Soviets that no one in the world has aggressive intentions toward them." (Ronald Reagan in *Time* magazine, quoted by *Forbes*)

2. Indicate, by four spaced points, omission of words at the end of a sentence:

   > "There might be an argument for doing nothing. . . ." (Kissinger Commission on Central America, quoted by *Forbes*)

3. Indicate, when extended the length of a line, omission of one or more lines of poetry:

Come away, O human child!

. . . .

For the world's more full of weeping
Than you can understand.
(William Butler Yeats)

4. Are sometimes used as a device to catch and hold the reader's interest, especially in advertising copy:

> Sergeant Major Zack Carey believed in Truth, Justice, and the American Way. . .until a small-town sheriff set him up. (advertisement for the James Garner movie *Tank*, in *Variety*)

Exclamation Point   !

1. Terminates an emphatic or exclamatory sentence:

> "No money can buy the workers here!" (*Forbes*)

2. Terminates an emphatic interjection:

> No! I won't go.
> Encore!

Hyphen   -

1. Indicates that part of a word or more than one syllable has been carried over from one line to the next:

> . . . Chemical [Bank] and other litigants are expected to make a separate legal effort. . . .(*Dun's Business Month*)

2. Joins the elements of some compounds:

> cost-of-living index
> foot-dragging
> cost-effectiveness

3. Joins the elements of some compound modifiers preceding nouns:

> a cattle-feeding enterprise
> a heavy-duty press
> . . .disease ravaged [Jim] Power's 65-sow farrow-to-finish operation. . . .(*Farm Journal*)

4. Indicates that two or more compounds share a single base:

> three- and four-ton stamping machines
> eight- and ten-year-old foundries

5. Separates the prefix and root in some combinations:

> prefix + proper noun or adjective (an *anti-American* protestor; engaged in a *pro-capitalism* quest)

some prefixes ending in a vowel + root beginning with a vowel (presidential *re-election; co-author*)

stressed prefix + root word if absence of hyphen could cause misunderstanding of meaning (*re-form/reform; re-cover/recover; re-creation/recreation*)

6. Substitutes for the word *to* between figures or words:

   ... 33.1 per cent have owned [a home] only 1-2 years....(*Professional Builder*)

7. Punctuates written-out compound numbers from 21 through 99 (note, however, that house styles differ on this point):

   a thirty-five per cent return on equity
   fifty-seven clients
   ninety-nine computer companies

Parentheses ( )

1. Enclose material that is not an essential part of the sentence and that if not included would not alter its meaning:

   But Kansas City television (KCTV-5) anchor Wendall Anschutz said he would ask the source. . . .

   Also named as defendant in the suit (filed in federal court in San Francisco) was the San Francisco Newspaper Printing Co. . . .(*Editor & Publisher*)

2. Often enclose letters or figures to indicate subdivisions of a series:

   It seems our choices are (a) launch a counteroffensive marketing attack; (b) press ahead to get our new model out six months ahead of schedule; or (c) run like hell.

3. Enclose figures following and confirming written-out numbers, especially in legal and business documents:

   Attempts were made to get in touch with the defendant, but he hung up on the plaintiff's telephone calls twelve (12) times in a single afternoon.

4. Enclose abbreviations of written-out words when the abbreviations are used for the first time in a text and may be unfamiliar to the reader:

   According to Kevin Feeney, a practice-management official for the American Medical Association (AMA), hospitals provide another avenue for financing. (*Black Enterprise*)

Period .

1. Terminates a complete declarative or mild imperative sentence:

   A new fad in consumer stroking seems to be hotline telephone numbers.

   "Boulder Beer should be made in Boulder," claims Jerry Smart, president of Boulder Beer Company. (*Beverage World*)

   Would you please sign here.

2. Follows some abbreviations:

Inc.	etc.
a.k.a.	Ave.
Calif.	Jan.
Ltd.	F.Y.I.

Question Mark   ?

1. Terminates a direct question:

> ... why should anyone want to come to him for a service they can get through a toll-free number? (*ABA Banking Journal*)

but:

> I wonder who said, "Speak softly and carry a big stick."
> I asked if they planned to leave early.

2. Indicates uncertainty:

> Ferdinand Magellan (1480?–1521)

Quotation Marks:
" " and ' '
double quotation marks " "

1. Enclose direct quotations:

> "We discovered that we couldn't efficiently manufacture copiers at the low number of units we were producing," explains George Bradbury....
> (*Madison Avenue*)
> When advised not to become a lawyer because the profession was already overcrowded, Daniel Webster replied, "There is always room at the top."

2. Enclose words or phrases to clarify their meaning or to indicate that they are being used in a special way:

> The theme "Reaching out in new directions" was revealed in an eight-page blockbuster spread....(*Madison Avenue*)
> ALCOA is finding that it "deep discounts" its own prices even more...And common alloy grades continue to be discounted "four fives," or four progressive 5% cuts, which amounts to about 18%. (*Business Week*)

3. Set off the translation of a foreign word or phrase:

> *déjà vu*, "already seen"

4. Set off the titles of series of books, of articles or chapters in publications, of essays, of short stories and poems, of individual television and radio programs, and of songs and short musical pieces:

> "The Horizon Concise History" series
> an article entitled "Electronic Mail in the Small Business"

Chapter Nine, "Voice Mail Technology"
Pushkin's short story, "The Queen of Spades"
Tennyson's "Ode on the Death of the Duke of Wellington"
ABC's "Good Morning America"
NPR's "All Things Considered"
Schubert's "Death and the Maiden"

single quotation marks   ‘   ’
Enclose quotations within quotations:

> The blurb for the piece proclaimed, "Two years ago at Geneva, South Vietnam was virtually sold down the river to the Communists. Today the spunky little. . .country is back on its own feet, thanks to 'a mandarin in a sharkskin suit who's upsetting the Red timetable.' " (Frances FitzGerald)

Note: Put commas and periods inside closing quotation marks; put semicolons and colons outside. Other punctuation, such as exclamation points and question marks, should be put inside the closing quotation marks only if it is part of the matter quoted.

Semicolon   ;

1. Separates the clauses of a compound sentence having no coordinating conjunction:

> Some firms went bankrupt; others scrambled to leave the community development business altogether. (*Barron's*)

2. Separates the clauses of a compound sentence in which the clauses contain internal punctuation, even when the clauses are joined by a conjunction:

> Lewis reckons that each of these depressions lasted 10 years, except for the 1929 one; it lasted 12 years. (*Forbes*)

3. Separates elements of a series in which the items already contain commas:

> The issues that top security analysts favor include SmithKline Beckman (NYSE, $58) and Bristol Myers (NYSE, $42), among drug concerns; McDonald's (NYSE, $72) and Chart House (recently traded over the counter at $20) in restaurants; and retailers Associated Dry Goods (NYSE, $67) and Dayton Hudson (NYSE, $31). (*Money*)

4. Separates clauses of a compound sentence joined by a conjunctive adverb such as *nonetheless, however,* or *hence*:

> We will produce the product; however, it will cost $15, not $12.

5. May be used instead of a comma to signal longer pauses for dramatic effect:

But I want you to know that when I cross the river my last conscious thoughts will be of the Corps; the Corps; and the Corps. (General Douglas MacArthur)

Virgule /

1. Separates successive divisions in an extended date:

   the fiscal year 1984/85

2. Represents the word *per*:

   CRX achieves an awesome 51 mpg (4.6L/100km) rating in EPA city tests. . . .(*Ward's Auto World*)

3. Means *or* between the words *and* and *or* (and/or) and sometimes between other words to indicate possible options or choices:

   In working with a Chevrolet stamping plant in Cleveland, Case Western Reserve's Dr. Berrettoni found that existing "go/no go" gages were inadequate. . . .(*Industry Week*)

Italics

1. Indicate titles of books, plays and very long poems:

   the book *Ship of Fools*
   the play *The Little Foxes*
   the epic poem *Paradise Lost*

2. Indicate the titles of magazines and newspapers:

   Jeffrey Gluck, publisher of *Saturday Review* and other magazines, has signed a definitive agreement with the Newhouse family to acquire the *St. Louis Globe-Democrat*. (*Editor & Publisher*)

3. Set off the titles of motion pictures and radio and television series:

   ABC's regular Wednesday schedule of *Fall Guy, Dynasty,* and the new *Hotel* won with ease. . . .(*Broadcasting*)

4. Indicate the titles of long musical compositions:

   Messiah
   Die Götterdämmerung
   Bartok's *Concerto for Orchestra*

5. Set off the names of paintings and sculpture:

   Mona Lisa
   Pietà
   American Gothic

6. Indicate words, letters, or numbers that are referred to:

I think *don't* would be more forceful than *shouldn't*.
You form your *n*'s like *u*'s.
The *60* in an earlier memo should be a *600* instead.

7. Are used to indicate foreign words and phrases not yet assimilated into English:

garçon   *pâtissiers*
Sturm und Drang   *c'est la vie*

8. Indicate the names of plantiff and defendant in legal citations:

Franklin v. *Madison*

9. Emphasize a word or phrase:

. . . too many of those studies *weren't* being implemented. (*Inc.*)

Note: Use this device sparingly.

10. Distinguish the New Latin names of genera, species, subspecies, and varieties in botanical and zoological nomenclature:

Homo sapiens

Do not italicize phyla, classes, orders, and families in botanical and zoological nomenclature:

Gastropoda   Nematoda

11. Set off the names of ships and planes, but not space vehicles:

U.S.S. *Kitty Hawk*
Spirit of St. Louis
Apollo 11
the space shuttle Challenger
the spy satellite Ferret-D

Numerals

1. Use figures to express specific dates, measures, hours, addresses, page numbers, and coordinates:

$35 a share	p. 12
January 22, 1984	Vol. 3
80° north latitude	76 tons
4:00 P.M.	0.5 microns
30 Rockefeller Plaza	2.5 ml.
10 per cent (*or* 10%) after-tax profit margin	

2. Generally, spell out numbers from zero to ninety-nine and use numerals for numbers 100 or larger (styles can and do vary):

> forty-seven applicants
> 371 tons of iron ore

3. When a sentence begins with a number, do not use figures; spell it out:

> Fifteen thousand feet of wire was lost.

but:

> We lost 15,000 feet of wire.

Calendar years, however, are the exception:

> 1985 promises double last year's earnings.
> We expect double earnings in 1985.

4. When two or more numbers appear in one sentence, spell them out consistently or use figures regardless of whether the numbers are larger or smaller than ninety-nine:

> Fifteen thousand feet of wire was delivered on two trucks.
> About 15,000 feet of wire was delivered on 2 trucks.

Note: House styles vary considerably on this point.

5. Spell out numbers used casually:

> A thousand times No!
> Thanks a million.
> I traveled a half mile.

6. Spell out ordinals in texts:

> the nineteenth century
> the tenth meeting

Ordinals in business correspondence address blocks may be spelled out or abbreviated:

> Fifth Avenue   5th Avenue

7. Sometimes a number (or numbers) forms part of a corporate name or a set phrase; style corporate names and phrases associated with them exactly as shown on letterhead or in reference works such as *Thomas Register:*

> Ten Speed Press   20th Century-Fox Studios
> 42nd Street Photo   Pier 1 Imports
> Saks Fifth Avenue   Fortune 500

8. Rounding out large numbers is often acceptable:

$116.7 million sales (instead of *$116,698,447*)

a $200 billion federal deficit (instead of the unwieldy *$200,000,000,000* federal deficit)

9. Use numerals for all decimal fractions:

100.23 mm. (not *one hundred point twenty-three mm.* or *one hundred and twenty-three one-hundredths mm.*)

THE BASICS OF GRAMMAR AND USAGE

The most basic rules of English grammar and usage are presented here within the context of business writing.

The Verb

A verb (*perform* or *be,* for instance) is a word that expresses action or a state of being:

Action: She *performs* well under pressure.

State of Being: He *is* the chief operating officer.

A verb can indicate tense (present, past, or future, for example), person (first, second, or third), number (singular or plural), and voice (active or passive). It can also indicate mood (indicative, subjunctive, imperative).

Regular verbs are inflected by the addition of *-ed, -ing,* and *-s* or *-es* to the base form (*mix, mixed, mixing, mixes*), while irregular verbs are inflected (*do, did, done, doing, does; be, am, is, are, was, were, being, been*) by way of major changes in the base form. When you are uncertain about a particular inflected form, look up the word in *The American Heritage Dictionary,* where you will find the principal parts of all regular and irregular verbs entered.

The tense of the verb specifies the time or the nature of the action that occurs. The following chart conjugates the verb *to write* through the past, present, and future tenses.

Tense	I	He/She/It	We/You/They
present	write	writes	write
present progressive	am writing	is writing	are writing
past	wrote	wrote	wrote
past progressive	was writing	was writing	were writing
perfect	have written	has written	have written
past perfect	had written	had written	had written
future	will write	will write	will write
future perfect	will have written	will have written	will have written

A verb may be marked for person and number. For example:

I have no time for this.
You have no time for this.
He has no time for this.
We have no time for this.
They have no time for this.

Voice indicates whether the verb is active or passive. For example:

Active: The two companies *have merged.*
Passive: The two companies *have been merged.*

The mood of a verb is used to express a statement of fact, a condition contrary to fact, or a command. The indicative mood is used for statements of fact: *The two companies have merged* (i.e., they've done it and the merger is a reality). The subjunctive mood indicates a conditional situation—one contrary to what we know is the case right now: *If the two companies were to merge, managerial heads would roll* (i.e., the two companies haven't merged yet). The imperative mood expresses a command: *See that you are not late for the meeting.*

Verbs can be transitive or intransitive. A transitive verb takes an object: *The FTC issued an important ruling last week.* In this sentence, *issued* is the transitive verb and *ruling* is its object. On the other hand, an intransitive verb (or a verb used intransitively) does not take an object: *No new information issued from the press conference.* In this example, the verb *issue* has been used intransitively. The subject is *information* and there is no object for the verb.

Linking verbs connect subjects and predicate nouns, pronouns, and adjectives and express a condition or a state of being. The most common linking verb is *to be.* Also included in the linking verb category are the "sense" verbs *feel, look, smell,* and *taste* together with *appear, become, continue, grow, prove, remain, seem, stand,* and *turn* when used in specific senses. Remember to use adjectives and not adverbs after linking verbs. For example: *He felt uncomfortable about making a presentation on such short notice. Those projected figures seem erroneous to me. They became obstinate when we asked them to change their advertising copy.* This, then, is a brief description of our verb system. Now let's look at a few of the problems that can arise.

Subject/verb agreement.   The verb must agree with its subject in number and person. *The company officers were unavailable for comment* (plural subject, plural verb). *The company president was unavailable for comment* (singular subject, singular verb). However, certain words and expressions sometimes pose problems in connection with subject/verb agreement:

1. Collective nouns

   Collective nouns such as *committee, jury,* and *group* usually take singular verbs but can take plural verbs if the constituents of the collective unit are being considered individually: *The Publishing Committee has unanimously vetoed the project.* Or, *The Publishing Committee were divided about the viability of the project.* See also the discussion about collective nouns that appears under the subsection on nouns herein. (Additional information may be found in the usage notes for **number, per cent,** and **percentage.**)

2. *One* and *one of those*

   Constructions employing *one* often raise questions about whether verbs should be singular or plural. One such construction is exemplified by this sentence: *One in every ten applicants was found deficient.* Although the plural verb *were* is sometimes used in such a sentence, a singular verb, in agreement with the subject *one,* is the acceptable usage in formal writing.

   A more controversial construction involves *one of those who* or a variant: *He is one of those managers who always complain about their expense accounts.* Most experts feel that only the plural verb (in this case, *complain*) is possible, since the antecedent of *who* is a plural noun (in this example, *managers*). In other examples, however, *one* may be construed as the subject of the verb in the relative clause: *The manager is the only one of those people who has* (not *have*) *complained.*

   The construction *more than one* is always singular despite the fact that logic would seem to require a plural verb: *More than one of the applicants has failed to complete the test.* Conversely, *fewer than two* is always plural: *fewer than two have completed the test.*

3. Singular subjects, the verb *to be,* and plural complements

   The number of the verb *to be* must agree with the subject and not with the complement (a complement is a predicate noun or adjective coming after the verb): *The topic of my memorandum is fiscal irresponsibility and managerial incompetence.* In this example, *topic* is the singular subject, with which the singular verb *is* agrees. The compound phrase, *fiscal irresponsibility and managerial incompetence,* is the complement.

4. *There*

   There frequently precedes a linking verb such as *be, seem,* or *appear* at the beginning of a sentence or a clause: *There has been a great deal of uncertainty as to the exact meaning of the law.* The number of the verb is governed by the subject, which in such constructions follows the verb: *There is a storage facility across the street. There seem to be many options.* But a singular verb is also possible before a compound subject whose parts are joined by a conjunction or conjunctions, especially when the parts are singular: *There is* (or *are*) *much work and planning involved.* When the first element of such a subject is singular, a singular verb is also possible even though the other element may be plural: *There were* (or *was*) *a box and two bags in the back of the truck.* But, *There were two bags and a box in the back of the truck.*

5. Extraneous expressions
Don't be misled by the presence of plural nouns in phrases that intervene between the true subject and its verb; the subject and verb must agree in person and number. *The executive, together with two secretaries, a chauffeur, and four bodyguards, has arrived. She, and not any of her associates, is responsible for the litigation. The parent company, as well as its affiliate, was named in the indictment.* The expressions set off by commas in the previous sentences do not constitute additions to the real subject, since the elements linking them to the subject do not have the force of conjunctions. Therefore, the singular subjects in the respective sentences require singular verbs. See also the entries **together with** and **well** in the usage section.

6. Singular subjects preceded by *each, every, many a, such a,* or *no*
A singular subject preceded by *each, every, many a, such a,* or *no* takes a singular verb even when several such subjects are linked by *and: Each manager and each division chief has urged the employees to invest in the thrift plan. No department head and no divisional manager has ever commented on that.*
See also the entry **each** in the usage section.

7. *Either/or* and *neither/nor*
If the subjects so joined are both singular, use a singular verb: *Either the general manager or the publisher decides that.* If both subjects are plural, use a plural verb: *Neither the managers nor their secretaries have responded.* If one subject is singular and the other plural, the number of the verb is usually governed by the number of the subject closest to it: *Neither the supervisor nor the union members are willing to negotiate. Neither the union members nor the supervisor is willing to negotiate.*

8. Unitary compounds and singular verbs
When referring to a unit, such as an organization or corporate entity, a singular verb is correct: *Hutchins/Young & Rubicam has prepared an elaborate presentation. Little, Brown is a Boston publisher.*

Split infinitives. The split infinitive, as in *to readily accept,* is not a grammatical error, and it has ample precedent in literature. But many writers and editors still feel that it should be avoided, especially in its more extreme form. It is least desirable when *to* and its verb are separated by a succession of modifying words that slows the reader's comprehension and produces a clumsy effect: *We are seeking a plan to gradually, systematically, and economically expand our plant.* In this example (deemed unacceptable by many), placement of the adverbs at the end of the sentence would improve the clarity and style without changing the desired sense: *We are seeking a plan to expand our plant gradually, systematically, and economically.* Most splits are not so extreme, and in such cases opinion as to acceptability is often divided: *If you want to really help patients, you must respect their feelings. To better understand the miners' plight, the coal company president lived among them for a week.* The split infinitive has greatest acceptance when it expresses concisely and clearly a sense that could not be expressed so concisely and clearly by another phrasing: *We expect our output to more than double in a year.* Many writers also feel that it is better to split an infinitive than to displace an adverb from what is felt to be its natural position in the sentence, a practice that can make the sentence appear stilted or ambiguous. If the sentence *the supervisor wanted to really help the trainee* is rewritten either as *the supervisor wanted really to help the trainee* or as *the supervisor wanted to help the trainee really,* it is unclear whether *really* modifies *wanted* or *help.* Expressions involving the verbs *be* and *have,* such as *to be really sure* and *to have just seen,* are often taken to be split infinitives. They are not, because *to* is not separated from the infinitive *be* or *have.*

Participles.   When a participle is used as a modifier, there should be no ambiguity or illogicality about the element it modifies. Special care should be taken to avoid the dangling participle—a participle that is wrongly attached to (and seemingly modifies) a noun, pronoun, or other such word and thus produces an absurdity: *Turning the corner, the view was much changed.* (Since it was not the view that turned the corner, a better phrasing would be: *Turning the corner, we discovered that the view was much changed.*) Similarly: *Lacking a better candidate, it was decided to postpone the election.* This is better rewritten: *In the absence of a better candidate, it was decided. . . .* Many participlelike constructions are well established as prepositions, however, and may be used freely. These include *speaking of, owing to, concerning, failing, considering, granting,* and *judging by.* Thus, we may write: *Speaking of politics, the election has been postponed. Considering the hour, it is surprising that the morning newspaper arrived at all.*

The verbless sentence.   Not all sentences must have main verbs to be grammatically acceptable. In memos, letters, and especially in advertising copy we often see quite effective sentence fragments. The following examples are taken from a business magazine and a newspaper, respectively:

At long last, a word processing and mailing list program that might have been heaven-sent since it can do so much and yet costs so little. (Advertisement in *PC World* for Paperwork, Harris Micro Computers, Inc.)

In this example, the sentence fragment lacks a main verb, although verbs have been included in the subordinate clause beginning with the word *since*.

In the next example, the advertisement begins and ends with full sentences but all the matter in between is fragmentary:

Looking for a new job is a hassle. Expensive, too. The cost of resumes, mailings, and phone calls. The cost of wasted time; sneaking around at job fairs. And the fear that it might cost you your present job. There is an easier way. (Advertisement in *The Boston Globe* for JobLine.)

Other typical examples of verbless sentences include these:

Are you coming? *Yes.*
Hello. My name is Jane.
Encore!
These, then, are the problems. *What to do?*

The Noun

A noun is traditionally described as a word that names a person, place, thing, or abstraction. Proper nouns name specific persons, places, or things (Silicon Valley; Telex); common nouns are sometimes classified as abstract nouns that name ideas, beliefs, or qualities (capitalism); and concrete nouns that name tangible things (typewriter). Nouns can show possession (the treasurer's report) and they can show number (singular or plural).

The problem of number.   Nouns usually form their plurals by addition of -s or -es to the base form (president, presidents; box, boxes). Another large group of nouns with a final -y follows the pattern of *query, queries.* There are irregular nouns that indicate the plural by a change in the base form (mouse, mice) or that undergo no change at all (sheep, sheep). Still other nouns have variant forms in the plural, all of which are acceptable (memorandum, memorandums, or memoranda; phenomenon, phenomena, or phenomenons). When you are uncertain about a particular plural form, consult *The American Heritage Dictionary,* in which all noun plurals other than those formed by addition of -s or -es are shown. Some nouns ending in -s are plural in form but may function as either singular or plural or as both in number. By way of illustration, below is *The American Heritage Dictionary* entry for the word *politics,* in which the first four senses require use of a singular verb while the last two require use of a plural verb:

pol·i·tics (pŏl'ĭ-tĭks) *n.* **1.** *(used with a sing. verb).* The art or science of government; political science. **2.** *(used with a sing. verb).* The activities or affairs of a government, politician, or political party. **3.** *(used with a sing. verb).* **a.** The conducting of or engaging in political affairs, often professionally. **b.** The business, activities, or profession of a person so involved. **4.** *(used with a sing. verb).* The methods or tactics involved in managing a state or government. **5.** *(used with a pl. verb).* Intrigue or maneuvering within a group: *office politics.* **6.** *(used with a pl. verb).* A person's general position or attitude on political subjects: *His politics are conservative.*

When you are unsure whether words such as *acoustics, aerobics,* or *economics* take singular or plural verbs, look them up in the dictionary. *The American Heritage Dictionary* gives the appropriate information about all such words.

Collective nouns.   A collective noun denotes a collection of persons or things regarded as a unit. A collective noun takes a singular verb when it refers to the collection as a whole and a plural verb when it refers to the members of the collection as separate persons or things: *The committee was in executive session. The committee have all left for the day.* (In British usage, however, collective nouns are most often construed as plural: *The government are committed to a liberal policy.*) A collective noun should not be treated as both singular and plural in the same construction. Thus: *The company is determined to press its* (not *their*) *claim.* Among the most common collective nouns are *committee, company, clergy, enemy, group, family, flock, people,* and *team.*

Uses of nouns.   A noun can be the subject of a sentence: *The housing industry is in trouble;* the direct object of a verb: *Spiraling interest rates and inflation have softened the housing industry;* the object of a preposition: *This is one of the hottest issues in the housing industry;* or the indirect object of a verb: *Give the housing industry a chance and it may recover.*

Nouns as modifiers.   Nouns often occur as modifiers of other nouns in such terms as *office systems* management, *product* quality, *cost* analysis, *work distribution* chart, and *photodiode sensor array* scanner. In the preceding examples, the italicized words are nouns functioning as modifiers. Long strings of such modifiers can sometimes be confusing, as demonstrated by the following sentence: *Network intercommunications and intersystem address specifications have been established and implemented via a computer data transport system.* Rewriting will remove any unclarity about the subject of the sentence: *Specifications for network intercommunications and intersystem addressing have been established. These specifications are implemented via a computerized data transport network.*

The Pronoun

A pronoun is a word that substitutes for a noun and refers to a person or thing that has been named or understood in a particular context. Pronouns have grammatical case (subjective or objective), number (singular or plural), person (first, second, or third), and gender (masculine, feminine, or neuter).

Personal pronouns.   Personal pronouns refer to people or objects and must agree with their antecedents (i.e., the nouns or other pronouns that they refer to) in person, number, and gender:

Has the *supervisor* finished dictating *his* memo?

The *management* and *union negotiators* refused to budge from *their* positions.

The *Publishing Committee* has given us *its* unanimous approval.

The *CEO* has not given us *her* comments yet.

This is the general rule with regard to pronoun/antecedent agreement. But there are a large number of words and expressions in English that are singular in form but felt to be plural in sense, so that speakers are uncertain whether to use a singular or plural pronoun in referring to them. For example, strict grammarians have long insisted that it is correct to say *everyone took his coffee break,* not *their coffee break* or *their coffee breaks,* and that we must say *no one is happy when he is fired* and not *when they are fired.* Yet speakers persist in using the plural pronouns, and the most thoughtful grammarians have recognized that there is no entirely happy solution to the problem. The constructions affected fall into three classes. First, there are words formed with the word elements *-one* and *-body,* such as *anyone, somebody, everyone, nobody,* together with the two-word form *no one.* Second, there are the words *either, each, none,* and *any* used alone (as in *each found his seat*) or together with a noun (as in *each of the participants has his notebook* and *none of the notebooks has its cover intact*). Finally, there are the words *whoever, whatever,* and *whichever,* either used as indefinite pronouns (as in *whoever reveals privileged information will have his security clearance revoked,* or together with a noun, as in *whichever nation is attacked first will find itself at a disadvantage.* The traditional rule is that only a singular pronoun can be used in referring back to these constructions, as in the preceding examples of correct usage. But the rule as stated creates grammatical complications. For one thing, a pronoun outside the sentence containing the element it refers to *cannot* be in the singular. Thus, it is simply not English to say: *Everybody left in a hurry. He took his coat with him.* Nor can one say, *No one could be seen. The individual must have been hiding behind a wall.* Constructions with *whoever* are exceptions. One says: *Whoever is elected will take office in January. I am sure* *she will do a good job.* Writers who do not want to risk violation of the traditional rule will have to find other ways of expressing the meaning. One may rephrase so as to get the pronoun into the same sentence as its antecedent, saying, for example, *Everybody left carrying his raincoat with him.* One may also substitute other words, such as the plural *all,* as in *All the visitors left. They took their coats with them.*

Each presents some special problems. When it precedes the noun, a following pronoun is correctly singular: *Each of the actors has learned his* (not *their*) *part.* When *each* follows the noun, however, the pronoun is generally plural: *The actors have each learned their parts* (not *his part*). It also should be noted that *none* has for centuries been used by the best writers as if it were a plural form, taking both plural verb and plural pronouns: *None of them have learned their parts* must be considered an entirely acceptable variant of *None of them has learned his part.* Only the mixture of singular verb and plural pronoun would be considered incorrect, as in *None of them has learned their parts.* Traditional grammarians insist that the masculine singular *him* or *his* be used as a "neutral" pronoun referring to a mixed-gender group, even in sentences such as *Every one of the actors and actresses has learned his part.* But for the last century this usage has been increasingly criticized for reflecting and perpetuating gender discrimination, and its usage has declined accordingly. If you find the traditional usage distasteful, or if you think your readers may object, you may substitute a coordinate form, such as *his or her,* or simply recast the sentence (e.g., *All of the actors and actresses have learned their parts.* Some writers choose to use the plural pronoun, though technically inaccurate, for the sake of neutrality; others have proposed pronouns such as *s/he.*

Case is determined by the grammatical function of the pronoun in the sentence:

If *you* will give *me* the book, *I* can return *it* to the library.
  (subject)   (indirect object)   (subject)   (direct object)

The question as to when to use the nominative pronouns *I, he, she, we,* and *they* and when to use the objective pronouns *me, him, her, us,* and *them* has always been a source of controversy among grammarians and a source of uncertainty among speakers. When the subject of a sentence is a complex phrase in which a pronoun is joined to other elements by *and* or *or,* grammarians are unanimous in considering it a part of the subject proper, so that the nominative form must be used. *Pat and I* (not *me*) *will be there to greet you. Either Dale or he* (not *him*) *will come in first.* Some grammarians have gone so far as to extend this rule to cover the use of pronouns as one-word answers to questions that ask about the identity of the subject of a verb; that is, as an answer to *Who developed this new chemical compound?* we are supposed to say *I* (as in *I did*) rather than *Me.*

But such sentences are likely to occur only in informal speech or in written dialogue; in either case, the use here of a nominative, such as *I*, can only be viewed as pedantic.

When pronouns follow a form of the verb *to be*, the nominative is traditionally required, on the grounds that the pronoun denotes the same entity as the subject. Thus, the rules require *it is I, that must be she*, and so forth. The rules create problems, however, when the pronoun after *to be* denotes an entity that is also understood to be the object of some other verb or preposition. Shall we say *it is I she loves* or *it is me she loves?* There is no strict rule, but given the natural tendency to use objective forms like *me* rather than nominatives like *I* in uncertain cases, the use of *me* is entirely defensible here. It also should be noted that the use of the nominative following *to be* sounds stilted when the verb has been contracted. Nevertheless, a purist would say *it's I* rather than *it's me*, or *that's they* rather than *that's them*.

Mistakes in pronoun choice come in two varieties. There is a natural tendency to use objective forms like *me* and *him* where nominatives like *I* and *he* would be strictly required: *He has more seniority than me* instead of the correct *than I*. *In the end, it turned out to have been them all along* instead of the technically correct *turned out to have been they*. Strict grammarians are likely to regard such mistakes as the result of a carelessness that no one ever manages entirely to avoid. But in an effort to get the pronouns right, some people err in the opposite direction, substituting nominatives like *I* where the objective *him* would be correct. The result is constructions like *between you and I* (properly *between you and me*) or *it surprised the dealer more than the customer or I* (properly, *the customer or me*). Mistakes of this second sort are likely to be regarded as overcorrections that betray a fundamental linguistic insecurity on the part of the speaker. While there is no entirely safe course for the speaker who is in doubt as to which form to use, the difference between the risks in incorrect use of the nominative and the objective should be kept in mind. Some points to remember:

1. Do not confuse the possessive form of the pronoun with a contraction formed from a pronoun and a verb form:

Keep the calculator in *its* case.	(possession)
It's a very small calculator.	(contraction for *it is*)
Whose call did you take?	(interrogative/ possession)
Who's calling?	(interrogative/contraction for *who is*)
Their TV sets are broken.	(possession)
They're fixing their TV sets.	(contraction for *they are*)
Your book is on our list.	(possession)
You're on our list.	(contraction for *you are*)

2. *I* (or *me*) should be placed at the end of a series of names or other pronouns:

> Mr. Lee, Ms. Trilby, and *I* attended the convention together.
> Send copies to Bill, Bob, Jean, and *me*.
> Just between you and *me*, they're dead wrong.

3. Avoid vague personal pronoun constructions such as "they say" or "it indicates," as in:

> They say on the news that the economy is in trouble.
> It indicates in the study that our TV ratings are down.
> Who are *they* and *it?* Recast for greater precision and clarity:
> The UBC nightly newscast says that the economy is in trouble.
> Page 4 of the study indicates that our TV ratings are down.

Reflexive pronouns.   Reflexive pronouns are used only with the possessive case of the first and second person pronouns (*myself, ourselves, yourself, yourselves*) and with the objective case of the third person pronouns (*himself, herself, itself, themselves*). Therefore, nonstandard combinations such as *hisself* and *theirselves* are to be avoided. A reflexive pronoun is used for emphasis:

> The systems analyst himself couldn't solve the problem, so how could we be expected to deal with it?

A reflexive pronoun is also used when the subject of a verb and the receiver of the action are identical:

> He did *himself* a great disservice by being uncooperative.

Here, *himself* functions as indirect object of the verb and refers to the subject *he*. Use a reflexive pronoun only with an antecedent. In formal writing avoid sentences like *My colleagues and myself attended the meeting*, even though such constructions commonly occur in informal speech. Say instead, *My colleagues and I attended the meeting*. See also the entry **myself** in the usage section.

Indefinite pronouns.   Among the indefinite pronouns are *all, another, any, anybody, anything, both, each, each one, either, everybody, everyone, everything, few, many, much, neither, nobody, none, no one, one, other, several, some, somebody, someone,* and *something*. See the beginning of this section for a detailed discussion of the problems of number and gender in connection with the use of pronouns such as these.

Reciprocal pronouns.   Reciprocal pronouns, such as *one, another,* or *each other*, denote interaction between two or more members of a group:

> They helped *one another* with the mailing lists.
> The two secretaries answer *each other's* phones.

According to some traditional grammarians, *each other* is used of two; *one another*, of more than two. This distinction has been ignored by many of the best writers, however, and these examples are considered acceptable: *The four partners regarded each other with suspicion. A parent and child should trust one another.* When speaking of an ordered series of events or stages, only *one another* can be used: *The Caesars exceeded one another* (not *each other*) *in cruelty* means that each Caesar was crueler than the last. *Each other* cannot be used as the subject of a clause in formal writing. Instead of *we know what each other are thinking*, one should write *each of us knows what the other is thinking.* Instead of *the executives know that each other are coming*, write *each of the executives knows the other is coming.* Instead of *we are all each other has*, write *each of us is all the other has.* The possessive forms of *each other* and *one another* are written *each other's* and *one another's: The secretaries answer each other's* (not *each others'*) *phones. They had forgotten one another's* (not *one anothers'*) *names.*

Demonstrative pronouns.   The demonstrative pronouns are *this, that, these,* and *those.*

> *This* is my workstation. *That* is yours.
> *These* are my diskettes. *Those* are yours.

It is a mark of nonstandard usage to insert *here* or *there* after *this* or *that*, as in "This here pen is mine" or "That there pen is mine." Say instead, "*This* pen is mine" or "*That* pen is mine."

It is a common stylistic error to introduce a sentence with a demonstrative pronoun referring to something in a previous sentence:

unclear/vague
Audioconferencing consists of several people in two or more sites involved in simultaneous communication via microphones and speakers connected through a telephone network. *This* saves on travel expenses and enhances productivity.

What does *this* refer to? Audioconferencing itself? Simultaneous communication? Use of a telephone network? To avoid vagueness, such a passage should be rewritten:

clear/precise
Audioconferencing consists of several people in two or more sites involved in simultaneous communication via microphones and speakers connected through a telephone network. The use of audioconferencing results in savings in travel expenses and enhancement of productivity.

Relative pronouns.   The relative pronouns *who/whom/whose, which, what,* and *that* introduce dependent clauses functioning as nouns or adjectives. Some of them can be combined with *-ever* to yield *whoever,* *whomever, whichever,* and *whatever.* The next paragraphs discuss in detail two major problems of usage involving the relative pronouns.

The standard rule is that *that* should be used only to introduce a restrictive (or "defining") relative clause, which serves to identify the entity being talked about; in this use it should never be preceded by a comma. Thus, we say *the factory that we built in 1969 has been remodeled,* where the clause *that we built* tells which factory was built; or, *I am looking for a book that is easy to read,* where *that is easy to read* tells what kind of book is desired. Only *which* is to be used with nonrestrictive (or "non-defining") clauses, which give additional information about an entity that has already been identified in the context; in this use, *which* is always preceded by a comma. Thus we say, *The secretaries in the Administrative Department have been complaining about the heat, which* (not *that*) *has been deficient ever since the old boiler was replaced.* The clause *which has been deficient ever since the old boiler was replaced* does not indicate which heat is being complained about; even if it were omitted, we would know that the phrase *the heat* refers to "the heat in the Administrative Department." Similarly we say, *The product managers wanted to go to the marketing seminar entitled "The Power of Product Positioning," which* (not *that*) *I had already attended.* The title "The Power of Product Positioning," is by itself sufficient to identify the seminar that the product managers wanted to go to; the clause *which I had already attended* merely gives further information about the seminar. The use of *that* in nonrestrictive clauses like these last, while once common in writing and still frequent in speech, is now generally held to be an error that should be avoided in written prose. Some grammarians have argued that symmetry requires that *which* should be used in nonrestrictive clauses, as *that* is to be used only in restrictive clauses. Thus, they suggest that we should avoid sentences like *I need a book which will tell me all about the shipping industry,* where the clause *which will tell me all about the shipping industry* indicates which sort of book is needed. But the use of *which* in such clauses is widely supported by general usage and is in no sense incorrect. It is particularly useful where two or more relative clauses are joined by *and* or *or,* as in *It is a conclusion in which our strategic planners may find solace and which many have found reason to praise.* *Which* is also preferred to introduce a restrictive relative clause when the preceding phrase itself contains a *that,* as in *I can only give that which I don't need* (not *that that I don't need*) or *We want to use only that word processing system which will be the most cost-effective* (preferred to *that word processing system that will be the most cost-effective*).

According to traditional grammarians, *who* is the appropriate form to use in contexts where other subjective pronouns, such as *we* or *he* would also occur: *Who is in charge of this department? He who hesitates is lost.* As the subject of *is* and *hesitates* respectively, in the two sentences *who* is quite properly in the subjective case. In contexts requiring an objective form, such as *us* or *him*, then *whom* is appropriate to a formal style: *To whom did you speak? All the people whom we invited are planning to attend.* Although the rules are straightforward enough, problems can arise when the pronoun is at a distance from the elements of a phrase or sentence that determine the choice of case: *She interviewed the artist whom the committee had insisted that the mayor hire.* In constructing such a sentence, it is necessary to keep in mind the fact that *whom* will be the direct object of *hire.* Writing, which tends to be a more formal medium than speech, has the virtue of allowing a review of what has been produced in order to eliminate errors and inconsistencies. In speech or in the representation of speech, however, the distinction between *who* and *whom* is often not preserved: *"Who are you speaking of?"* (Thomas Hardy, *Far From The Madding Crowd*). When a preposition and its pronoun object are separated from each other, the latter is often in the technically incorrect subjective case. This usage is a common occurrence in the works of the best writers and has been defended by many grammarians and students of language on the grounds that rigid adherence to the rules, especially in informal contexts, yields sentences that sound stilted and pedantic. The same considerations as the foregoing apply to the choice between *whoever* and *whomever.* See also the next subsection.

Interrogative pronouns.   The interrogative pronouns include *who, whom, whose, which,* and *what.* Interrogative pronouns are used in direct questions.

Who is calling?
Which is your typewriter?
What are your feelings about this situation?
Whose is this blotter?
Who (or whom) did you travel with?

but:

With whom did you travel?

The Adjective
An adjective modifies a noun or pronoun. In modifying another word, an adjective serves to describe it, qualify it, limit it, or make it distinct and separate from something else (a *tall* building; a *reasonable* offer; a *two-story* house; a *red* fox). Most adjectives can be compared in three degrees (positive, comparative, and superlative). Adjectives can be compared by addition of the suffixes *-er* or *-est* to the unchanged base form (cold, colder, coldest); by doubling the final consonant before the addition of the suffixes (hot, hotter, hottest); by addition of *-er* or *-est* to a base form in

which a terminal -*y* becomes -*i*- (fuzzy, fuzzier, fuzziest); and by the use of *more, most, less,* or *least* before the unchanged base form (more important, most important, less important, least important). And some adjectives can be compared in two ways (clear, clearer, clearest or clear, more clear, most clear). A small class of adjectives are extremely irregular (bad, worse, worst). Still other adjectives, called *absolutes,* represent ultimate conditions and therefore are not compared. Examples of absolute adjectives are *prior, maximum, minimal, unanimous,* and *chief.* If you are unsure how to compare an adjective, consult *The American Heritage Dictionary,* where you will find regular and irregular comparisons entered.

Avoid making double comparisons:

wrong	**right**
the more commoner flu symptoms	the commoner flu symptoms
	or
	the more common flu symptoms
the most riskiest venture ever contemplated	the riskiest venture ever contemplated
	or
	the most risky venture ever contemplated

Incomplete comparisons (i.e. comparisons that are not directly expressed or that are understood) are often used in advertising and promotional writing. The famous slogan "Ford has a better idea" is a prime example. While such usage is effective in special contexts, it is often considered inappropriate in formal writing.

Some adjectives, because they are derived from proper names, are capitalized (*Machiavellian* judicial politics; *Churchillian* prose; *Russian* emigrés). To find out whether a particular adjective should be capitalized, look it up in the dictionary.

The Adverb

An adverb modifies a verb (read *fast*), an adjective (a *very* fast reader), or another adverb (read *very* fast). Most adverbs, like adjectives, can be compared in three degrees (positive, comparative, superlative). Many adverbs are compared by insertion of the words *more, most, less,* or *least* before the base form (*more soundly, most soundly, less soundly,* or *least soundly*). Others can be compared two ways (*loud, more loud, most loud* or *loud, louder, loudest*). Still others can't be compared (*extremely, very, there*).

Adverbs specify time (Please come into the office *now*); duration (I plan to stay here *indefinitely*); place (They are employed *here*); direction (Press the print key *downwards*); manner (The production line moves the cars *fast*); and degree (*Extremely* humid air can damage word processing equipment). Some adverbs can be used to link clauses (We automated the office; *nevertheless* some tasks must still be performed manually). See the section on conjunctions for full discussion of these conjunctive adverbs.

Remember that adverbs modify verbs: the salesperson talked *smoothly* (not *smooth*). Remember also that the linking and sense verbs discussed earlier take adjectives, not adverbs: Stock prices remain *erratic* (not *erratically*). And adverbs, not adjectives, modify adjectives and other adverbs: I feel *awfully* (not *awful*) tired.

The double negative.   A double negative is properly used when it makes an affirmative statement: *The doctor cannot just do nothing* (that is, the doctor must do something). An affirmative meaning is also found when *not* is used before an adjective or adverb having a negative sense: *a not infrequent visitor; a not unwisely conceived plan*. In these expressions the double negative is used deliberately to convey a weaker affirmative sense than would the adjective *frequent* or the adverb *wisely*.

A double negative is generally considered unacceptable when it is intended to convey or reinforce a negative meaning, especially in a short sentence: *The inspector didn't say nothing* (meaning the inspector said nothing). *We aren't going neither* (meaning we aren't going). Such constructions were once common in good writing as a form of intensified meaning. An example is Hamlet's advice to the players: *"Be not too tame neither, but let your discretion be your tutor."* A double negative is still occasionally acceptable when it reinforces a negative: *I will not resign, not today, not tomorrow.*

The Preposition

A preposition is used to indicate relationships between a noun or pronoun and another word or expression in a sentence. Prepositional phrases can indicate accompaniment (Joe attended the meeting *with several colleagues*); cause (The trip was canceled *because of bad weather*); support (Those who are not *for us* are *against us*); destination (We drove *to the city*); exception (I have everything *but a private office*); possession (The arrogance *of that official* defies description); constituency or makeup (I want a desk *of polished mahogany*); means or instrument (I worked out the problem *with my personal computer*); manner (Treat all vistors *with courtesy*); direction (I ran *across the hall* to find you); location (Jane is *in the office*); purpose or intention (They'll do anything *for a quick profit*); the goal of an action (Don't take pot shots *at me*); origin (The new manager is *from Chicago*); and time (Call me *at noon;* He arrived *on Monday*).

Between and among.   These are two prepositions that are often confused. *Between* is the only choice when just two entities are involved:

between (never *among*) *good and evil; the rivalry between* (never *among*)
Ford and General Motors. When more than two entities are involved, the
choice of *between* or *among* depends on the intended meaning. *Among* is
used to indicate that an entity has been chosen from the members of a
group: *the first among* (not *between*) *equals; Among* (not *between*) *the
three executives, Pat seems most likely to become the next president.
Among* is also used to indicate a relation of inclusion in a group: *She is
among the best engineers of our time; He took his place among the
clients waiting outside the door. Between,* on the other hand, is used to
indicate the area bounded by several points: *We have narrowed the search
to the area between* (not *among*) *Philadelphia, New York, and Scranton.*
In other cases, either *between* or *among* may be used; one may speak of *an
agreement between* (or *among*) *several merchants,* and one may say
either that *the telephone pole was lost among the trees* (in the area of the
trees) or *between the trees* (in which case we infer that the trees had
hidden the pole from sight).

Between and the objective case.   Note that all pronouns that follow
between must be in the objective case: *Between you and me* (not *I*), *the
problem is hopeless. This conflict is strictly between him and me* (not
he and I).

Prepositions in phrases.   When two or more phrases used together share
the same preposition, you need not repeat the preposition: *The testimony
is equal and tantamount to perjury.* However, if two different prepositions are required, retain both of them: *Our interest in and concern for the
welfare of our employees has led us to take steps to improve their working conditions.*

The Conjunction

A conjunction links words, phrases, or clauses. Coordinating conjunctions such as *and, or, but, nor, for,* or *so* link words, phrases, or clauses of
equal rank.

> The staff includes a secretary, an assistant, and a receptionist.
> My life is busy but lonely.
> You can go or you can stay.

Remember to link equal elements with coordinating conjunctions: adjectives with adjectives, adverbs with adverbs, clauses with other clauses of
equal rank, and so on:

unbalanced sentence
You are an organized person and your time well spent.
(faulty coordination between independent clause and phrase)

balanced sentence
You are an organized person and your time is well spent.
(two independent clauses linked by and)

Avoid excessive coordination, however, which often results in strung-out, monotonous sentences in which precise relationships are obscured, and varying degrees of emphasis are needlessly clouded:

strung-out
XYZ Corporation is a multinational petrochemical producer and has its corporate headquarters in Los Angeles and ten subsidiary offices in the United States, South America, and the Middle East.

tightened
XYZ Corporation, a multinational petrochemical producer with head-quarters in Los Angeles, has ten subsidiary offices throughout the United States, South America, and the Middle East.

The comma fault.   The comma fault occurs when two independent clauses are separated by a comma instead of being linked by a coordinating conjunction:

The chemical industry in the United States has contributed much to our economy, it should not be condemned on the basis of isolated instances of pollution.

The following sentences illustrate ways of eliminating the comma fault:

The chemical industry in the United States has contributed much to our economy, and it should not be condemned on the basis of isolated instances of pollution.
The chemical industry in the United States has contributed much to our economy. It should not be condemned on the basis of isolated instances of pollution.
The chemical industry in the United States has contributed much to our economy; it should not be condemned on the basis of isolated instances of pollution.
The United States chemical industry, having contributed much to our economy, should not be condemned on the basis of isolated instances of pollution.

The run-on sentence.   The failure to use proper punctuation or the appropriate coordinating conjunction between independent clauses will result in a run-on sentence:

run-on
The automobile had faulty brakes it was therefore recalled.

correct

The automobile had faulty brakes and it was therefore recalled.

The automobile had faulty brakes; therefore, it was recalled.

The automobile, having faulty brakes, was recalled.

Since the automobile had faulty brakes it was recalled.

Correlative conjunctions.   Correlative conjunctions work in pairs to link equal or parallel sentence elements. Correlative conjunctions include *either. . .or, neither. . .nor, whether. . .or, both. . .and,* and *not only. . .but also.* Correlative conjunctions should appear as close as possible to the equal elements that they link. In *either. . .or* constructions, the two conjunctions should be followed by parallel elements. The following is held to be incorrect: *You may either have the ring or the bracelet.* (properly, *you may have either the ring or the bracelet*). The following is also incorrect: *He can take either the examination offered to all applicants or ask for a personal interview* (properly, *he can either take . . .*).

When all the elements in an *either. . .or* construction are singular, the verb is singular: *Either the executive or the assistant is coming.* When one element is singular and the other plural, it is sometimes suggested that the verb should agree with whichever element is closest to it: *Either the department head or the line managers are going.* But: *Either the line managers or the department head is going.* Some traditionalists, however, insist that such constructions should be avoided entirely, and that substitutes must be found for them. For example: *Either the department head is going or the line managers are.* There is no generally accepted rule in these cases.

Neither is suposed to be followed by *nor,* not *or: Neither prayer nor curses brought relief* (not *or curses*). When *neither. . .nor* connects two singular elements, the following verb is singular: *Neither the executive nor the assistant is coming.* When both elements are plural, the verb is plural: *Neither the line managers nor the department heads have read the report.* When one element is singular and the other is plural, many have suggested that the verb should agree with the element closest to it. Thus we would write: *Neither the line managers nor the department head has read the report.* But: *Neither the department head nor the line managers have read the report.* Other grammarians, however, have held that these sentences must be avoided entirely and that one must instead seek a paraphrase in which the problem does not arise. For example: *The line managers have not read the report, and neither has the department head.*

Not only. . .but also constructions should be used in such a way that each of the elements is followed by a construction of the same type. Instead of *She not only bought a new car but a new lawnmower,* write *She bought not only a new car but also a new lawnmower.* In the second version, both *not only* and *but also* are followed by noun phrases. In the *not only* construction, *also* is often omitted when the second part of the sentence merely intensifies the first: *She is not only smart but brilliant. He not only wanted the promotion but wanted it desperately.*

Similarly, when *both* is used with *and* to link parallel elements in a sentence, the words or phrases that follow them should correspond grammatically: *in both India and China* or *both in India and in China* (not *both in India and China*).

Subordinating conjunctions.   Subordinating conjunctions introduce dependent clauses. Subordinating conjunctions include terms such as *because* and *since; although, if,* and *unless; as, as though,* and *however; in order that* and *so that; after, before, once, since, till, until, when, whenever,* and *while; where* and *wherever;* and *that.* Examples:

> *Since* the Management Committee has approved the plan, we can move forward.
>
> *If* you don't have the facts straight, your argument is worthless.
>
> Keep the text in memory *so that* you can make corrections later.
>
> *After* he was promoted, he spent all his time in meetings.
>
> Do you have any idea *where* they have gone?
>
> It is hard to tell *whether* the market will really take off as predicted.
>
> The newscaster said *that* John Green has been nominated for Governor's Council.

The use of subordinating conjunctions can help to achieve emphasis as well as variety. Put your main ideas into independent clauses and your less important ideas into subordinate clauses: *Although market predictions are bullish, stock prices continue to drop.*

Conjunctive adverbs.   A conjunctive adverb can be used to connect and relate two independent clauses separated by a semicolon: *Market predictions are bullish; nevertheless, stock prices continue to drop.* A semicolon precedes the conjunctive adverb, and a comma often follows it. *I proofread the letter carefully; therefore, the typos were detected.* Commas always separate the conjunctive adverb *however* from the rest of the sentence:

> I proofread the letter; however, I did not catch all the typos.
>
> I proofread the letter. I did not, however, catch all the typos.

Do not use commas with *however* when it means "no matter how": *However hard you try, management won't let you succeed.*

The interjection

An interjection is an independent sentence element that can express a sound (Ouch!), and emotion (Oh, rats!). Interjections can be used alone (Bravo!) or with other words (Oh, you've got to be kidding!).

Phrases, Clauses, Sentences, and Paragraphs

The phrase.   A phrase is a group of words that does not have both a subject and verb:

> *Having addressed the sales force,* we then took questions from the floor.
>
> *Approaching that issue* was tricky.
>
> We will be delighted *to attend.*

The clause.   A clause is a group of words with a subject and predicate. A dependent, or subordinate, clause usually functions as part of a sentence:

> Those *who have signed their performance reviews* will receive their salary adjustments on schedule (modifies *those*).
>
> *When the fourth quarter ends* our books will be closed (modifies *closed*).
>
> *That you have performed unsatisfactorily* is reflected in your performance review (subject of sentence).

The sentence.   A sentence is usually defined as a group of words having a subject and a verb; in writing, the sentence begins with a capital letter and ends with a period, question mark, or exclamation point: *The Board of Directors has unanimously voted a dividend increase.* As we have seen in the section on verbs, a sentence may be fragmentary as long as it makes sense and is idiomatic.

A sentence may be declarative (it makes a statement), interrogative (it asks a question), imperative (it requests or commands), or exclamatory (it expresses strong feeling):

> The applicants signed the forms.
>
> Did you sign the form?
>
> Sign the form here.
>
> I wish they'd sign the forms and shut up!

Grammatically speaking, there are four kinds of sentences: simple, compound, complex, and compound-complex. Examples of each follow:

simple sentence

Some people complain.

Some people complain because of dissatisfaction on the job.

compound sentence

Some people complain, and others don't.

Some people complain, some people brood, and others don't care at all.

complex sentence

When people become dissatisfied with their jobs, they often complain.

compound-complex sentence

When people become dissatisfied with their jobs, they often complain; and then management has a problem that it must address.

Sentence style.   From the standpoint of style, there are two types of sentences—the periodic and the cumulative. The periodic sentence places the main idea at the very end, so that the previous matter serves as a buildup. A good example of a periodic sentence is this one, taken from page 374 of Leonard Shatzkin's book *In Cold Type* (Boston: Houghton Mifflin, 1982):

Meeting the economic pinch by cutting overhead and
publishing programs has brought temporary relief here   ← buildup
and there, but some publishers have already passed
through that palliation to realize that *they are now*   ← main point
worse off than before.

Here is an example of a very short periodic sentence, quoted from page 200 of Thomas J. Peters and Robert H. Waterman Jr.'s book *In Search of Excellence: Lessons from America's Best-Run Companies* (New York: Harper & Row, 1982):

The most discouraging fact of big corporate life is the   ← buildup
loss of what got them big in the first place: innovation.   ← main point

In the last example, everything up to the last word in the sentence is really a buildup to the punch line or main point—*innovation.*

In the cumulative sentence the writer states the main point first, followed by supporting data: This example, also taken from Leonard Shatzkin's *In Cold Type* (page 3 this time), exemplifies a cumulative sentence:

No other consumer industry produces 20,000 different,   ← main point
relatively low-priced products each year, each with its
own personality, requiring individual recognition on   ← supporting ideas
the market.

The paragraph.   A paragraph is a distinct division of a written work that expresses a thought or point relevant to the whole but complete in itself; it may consist of a single sentence or several sentences. A paragraph should contain a topic sentence expressing the main thought, which is developed and supported by the other sentences of the paragraph. While it is possible for the topic sentence to be placed anywhere within the paragraph, it is most often found at the beginning as a statement that is enlarged upon by the sentences that follow. A topic sentence at the end of a paragraph usually functions as a cohesive summation of the ideas and arguments in the sentences leading up to it. The topic sentence is the cement binding a paragraph together into a coherent whole.

Paragraphing can be rather easy if you follow a few simple guidelines. First, keep your paragraphs unified: every sentence therein should be related to the main topic. Avoid needless digressions from the main point; irrelevancies can muddy the prose and destroy unity. Second, avoid overly short or overly long paragraphs. A short paragraph will not give sufficient scope to cover a topic adequately, while a long paragraph is uninviting to the reader and is often difficult to assimilate. It is important to keep this point in mind especially when preparing business reports and memos. Sometimes it is possible to split long paragraphs into shorter ones and, conversely, short paragraphs can be collapsed into a single longer one. A third, and very important issue has to do with transition. Transitional words and phrases (such as conjunctions, conjunctive adverbs, and demonstratives) are an invaluable aid in guiding the reader from one sentence to another. The following example of the use of smooth, logical transition comes from Peters and Waterman's *In Search of Excellence* (pages 3–5):

> Early in 1977, a general concern with the problems of management effectiveness . . . *led us to* . . . .
>
> *A natural first step was to talk* extensively *to executives* around the world who were known for their skill, experience, and wisdom . . . .
>
> *In fact, the most helpful ideas were coming* from . . . .
>
> *But as we explored the subject* . . . .
>
> *Our next step in 1977 was* . . . .

As you can see from the italicized terms in the example, each new paragraph is tied in with the one preceding it so as to provide smooth transition from one topic to another.

Another way of achieving smooth transition is repetition of key words. The key words serve as guides to the reader. A good example of the use of this technique occurs in Harry Katzan, Jr.'s book *Office Automation: A Manager's Guide* (New York: AMACOM, a division of American Management Associations, 1982, p. 18):

> The term *word processing* refers to *text* preparation through the use of a computer or its equivalent. Historically, it referred to . . . .
>
> The concept of *word processing* originated with . . . .
>
> Modern *word processing* systems permit textual information to be . . . .
>
> The key element in the *word processing* cycle is the output functions . . . .
>
> The hardware components that make up a modern *word processing* unit are . . . .

Notice the repetition of the central term *word processing* throughout the first sentences of each paragraph. Keeping the vocabulary limited to a finite number of terms that are used over and over again reinforces the message and enables the reader to understand the material more easily.

You can develop your own paragraphs in any number of other ways that will make them lucid and effective. For example, you can start off with a definition, as Harry Katzan, Jr., does on page 6 of *Office Automation: A Manager's Guide:*

> The term "office automation" refers to the use of a computer in an office environment to faciliate normal operating procedures. The impact of office automation upon work flow can be very small or very great, depending on the extent to which organizational structures are affected.

The first sentence defines *office automation*. The second sentence in the paragraph then goes on to talk about the impact of office automation in the workplace.

Another way of paragraph development is the use of comparison, contrast, and analogy. For example, you can make two points, and discuss one and then the other from comparative and/or contrastive standpoints. Or you can use analogy to explain one thing in terms of another, similar, thing. Still another technique is the use of cause and effect: you describe a given state of affairs and then discuss its underlying causes. Alternatively, you can set out the underlying causes and then build up to the result or consequence.

Still another useful technique is inclusion of examples by way of support or illustration for an idea or point of view that you have already expressed. Finally, you can set down classes, sets, or categories relating to a topic and then sort them for the reader. For example, a writer wishing to explain the secretary's role as an information broker could categorize the various aspects of information management first. These categories might be described as generation of information, modification of information, collection of information, storage of information, retrieval of information, analysis of information, communication of information, and output/distribution of information. When each category has been defined and distinguished, the writer could then go on to discuss the secretary's managerial roles with respect to each of these broad categories and activities.

A CONCISE GUIDE TO USAGE

The following notes are intended to help you with usage problems commonly encountered in writing. They are entered in alphabetical order according to key words.

a

A is used before a word beginning with a consonant (*a building*) or a consonant sound (*a university*); *an* is used before a word beginning with a vowel (*an earphone*) or a vowel sound (*an hour*). *An* should not be used before words like *historical* and *hysterical* unless the *h* is not pronounced, a practice now uncommon in American speech.

about

The construction *not about to* is often used to express determination: *We are not about to negotiate with strikebreakers.* Many consider this usage acceptable in speech but not in formal writing.

above

The use of *above* as an adjective or noun in referring to a preceding text is most common in business and legal writing. In general writing its use as an adjective (*the above figures*) is acceptable, but its use as a noun (*read the above*) is often objected to.

acquiesce

When *acquiesce* takes a preposition, it is usually used with *in* (*acquiesced in the ruling*) but sometimes with *to* (*aquiesced to management's wishes*).

admission

Admission has a more general meaning than *admittance*, which is used only to denote the obtaining of physical access to a place. To *gain admittance to the board* is to enter its chambers; to *gain admission to the board* is to become a member. One pays *admission* to a theater (to become a member of the audience) in order to be allowed *admittance* (physical entry to the theater itself).

adopted

One refers to an *adopted* child but to *adoptive* parents.

advance

Advance, as a noun, is used for forward movement (*the advance of our salespeople into the new market*) or for progress or improvement in a figurative sense (*a sales advance of 35% this year*). *Advancement* is used mainly in the figurative sense (*career advancement*). In the figurative sense, moreover, there is a distinction between the two terms deriving from the transitive and intransitive forms of the verb *advance.* The noun *advancement* (unlike *advance*) often implies the existence of an agent or outside force. Thus, *the advance of research and development* means simply the progress of the company's R & D efforts, whereas *the advancement of research and development* implies progress resulting from the action of an agent or force: *The addition of $1.5 million to last year's budget has resulted in the advancement of our research efforts.*

advise

Advise in the sense of "to inform" or "to notify" is generally acceptable in business contexts: *All retailers are hereby advised that our deluxe product line has been expanded.* Avoid this usage in formal general writing.

affect

Affect and *effect* have no sense in common. As a verb, *affect* is most commonly used in the sense of "to influence" (*how bad weather affects* deliveries). *Effect* means "to bring about or execute" (*layoffs designed to effect savings*).

affinity

Affinity may be followed by *of, between,* or *with* —thus, *affinity of persons, between two persons,* or *with another person.* In technical writing, *affinity* (meaning "a chemical or physical attraction") is followed by *for* (*a dye with an affinity for synthetic fabrics*). In general usage *affinity* retains some sense of the mutual relationship, and therefore its use with *for* is less widely accepted (e.g., *Even in school he had an affinity for politics,* but not *The product manager's affinity for living in California resulted in his rejecting a chance to return to the New York office*).

affirmative

The expressions *in the affirmative* and *in the negative,* as in *The client answered in the affirmative,* are generally regarded as pompous. *The client answered yes* would be more acceptable even at the most formal levels of style.

agenda

Agenda, meaning "list" or "program," is well established as a collective noun taking a singular verb.

ago

Ago may be followed by *that* or *when: it was a week ago that* (or *when*) *I saw the invoice.* It may not be followed by *since: It was a week ago since the order arrived. Since* is properly used without *ago,* as in *It has been a week since the order arrived.*

ain't

Ain't has acquired such a stigma over the years that it is beyond rehabilitation, even though it would serve a useful function as a contraction for *am not* and even though its use as an alternative form for *isn't, hasn't, aren't,* and *haven't* has a good historical justification. In questions, the variant *aren't I* is acceptable in speech, but in writing there is no generally acceptable substitute for the stilted *am I not.*

alibi

Alibi (noun) in its nonlegal sense of "an excuse" is acceptable in written usage, but as an intransitive verb (*they never alibi*), it is generally unacceptable in writing.

all

Constructions like *all us employees* are somewhat more informal than the corresponding *all of us employees.* The construction *all that* is used informally in questions and negative sentences to mean "to the degree expected" as in *The annual meeting was not all that exciting this year.* Many people find examples like this unacceptable in formal writing.

alleged

An *alleged burglar* is someone who is said to be a burglar but against whom no charges have yet been proved. An *alleged incident* is an event that is said to have taken place but which has not yet been verified. In their zeal to protect the rights of the accused, newspapers and law enforcement officials sometimes misuse *alleged.* A man arrested for murder may be only an *alleged murderer*, for example, but he is a real, not an *alleged, suspect* in that his status as a suspect is not in doubt. Similarly, if a murder is known to have taken place, there is nothing alleged about the crime.

all right

It is still not acceptable to write *all right* as a single word, *alright*, despite the parallel to words like *already* and *altogether* and despite the fact that in casual speech the expression is often pronounced as if it were one word.

allude

Allude and *allusion* are often used where the more general terms *refer* and *reference* would be preferable. *Allude* and *allusion* apply to indirect reference that does not identify specifically. *Refer* and *reference*, unless qualified, usually imply direct, specific mention.

alternative

Alternative is widely used to denote simply "one of a set of possible courses of action," but many traditionalists continue to insist that its use be restricted to situations in which only two possible choices present themselves. In this stricter sense, *alternative* is incompatible with all numerals (*there are three alternatives*), and the use of *two*, in particular, is held to be redundant (*the two alternatives are life and death* would be unacceptable to traditionalists). Similarly, traditionalists reject as unacceptable sentences like *there is no other alternative* on the grounds that it is equivalent to the simpler *there is no alternative.*

altogether

Altogether should be distinguished from *all together. All together* is used of a group to indicate that its members performed or underwent an action collectively: *The seven unions stood all together. The new computers were stored all together in an empty office. All together* can be used only if it is possible to rephrase the sentence so that *all* and *together* may be separated by other words: *All of the unions stood together. The new computers were all stored together.*

alumni

Alumni is generally used to refer to both the *alumni* (masculine plural) and *alumnae* (feminine plural) of a coeducational institution.

and

Although frowned upon by some, the use of *and* to begin a sentence has a long and respectable history: "And it came to pass in those days . . ." (Luke 2:1)

and/or

And/or is widely used in legal and business writing. Its use in general writing to mean "one or the other or both" is also acceptable.

ante meridian

In general, *12 A.M.* denotes midnight and *12 P.M.* denotes noon, but there is sufficient confusion over them to make it advisable to use *12 noon* and *12 midnight* where absolute clarity is required.

anticipate

Some traditionalists hold that *anticipate* should not be used simply as a synonym for *expect.* They would restrict its use to senses in which it suggests some advance action, either to fulfill (*anticipate my desires*) or to forestall (*anticipate the competition's next move*). Others accept its use in the senses of "to feel or realize beforehand" and "to look forward to" (often with the implication of foretasting pleasure): *They are anticipating a sizable dividend increase.*

any

The phrase *of any* is often used in informal contexts to mean "of all," as in *That scientist is the best of any living authority on the subject.* Many find this construction unacceptable. *Any* is used to mean "at all" before a comparative adjective: *Are the field office reports any better this month?* This use is entirely proper, but the related use of *any* all by itself to mean "at all" is considered informal. In writing, one should avoid sentences like *It didn't hurt any* or *It didn't matter any to the supervisor.*

anyone

The one-word form *anyone* is used to mean "whatsoever person or persons." The two-word form *any one* is used to mean "whatever one (person or thing) of a group." *Anyone may join* means admission is open to everybody. *Any one may join* means admission is open to one person only. When followed by *of,* only *any one* (two words) can be used: *Any one of them could do the job. Anyone* is often used in place of *everyone* in sentences like *Dale is the most thrifty person of anyone I know.* Such usage is generally unacceptable in formal writing.

apparent

Used before a noun, *apparent* means "seeming": *For all its apparent wealth, the company was leveraged to the hilt.* Used after a form of the verb *to be,* however, *apparent* can mean either "seeming" (as in *the virtues of the deal were only apparent*) or "obvious" (as in *the*

effects of the drought are apparent to anyone seeing the parched fields).
Writers should take care that the intended meaning is clear from
the context.

as

Traditionally, a distinction has been drawn between comparisons using
as. . .as and comparisons using *so. . .as*. Comparisons with *as. . .as* may be
used in any context, as in *Their marketing is as good as ours*. The *so. . .as*
construction is restricted to use in negative contexts (as in Hamlet's *'Tis
not so deep as a well*), in questions (*Is it so bad as all that?*), and in clauses
introduced by *if* or similar words (as in *If it is so bad as all that, why don't
you leave?*). The distinction between the two types of comparison is fast
disappearing in American usage, however, as the *so. . .as* construction
becomes increasingly rare. The *as. . .as* comparison may be considered
correct in any context. • In a comparison involving both *as. . .as* and *than*,
the second *as* should be retained in written style. One writes *he is as
bright as, or brighter than, his brother*, not *he is as bright or brighter than
his brother*, which is unacceptable in formal style. • In many dialects, *as*
is used instead of *that* in sentences like *we are not sure as we want to go*
or *it's not certain as she left*. This construction is not sufficiently established to be used in writing. • In comparisons, a pronoun following *as* may
be either nominative (*I, she*) or objective (*me, her*). Traditionally, the
nominative is used when the pronoun would be the subject of an
"understood" verb that has been omitted; we should say *Pat is as happy
as I* because the sentence has an equivalent version *Pat is as happy as I
am*. By the same token, we should say *It surprised her as much as me*,
using the objective pronoun, on the grounds that there is an equivalent
sentence *It surprised her as much as it surprised me*. In sentences like
these, the use of *me* where *I* would be considered correct is regarded as
careless by traditionalists. The use of *I* where *me* would be correct, however, is likely to be regarded as a pretentious overcorrection. • *As* should
be preceded by a comma when it expresses a causal relation, as in *He
won't be coming, as we didn't invite him*. When used to express a time
relation, *as* is not preceded by a comma: *She was finishing the painting as
I walked into the room*. When a clause introduced by *as* begins a sentence,
care should be taken that it is clear whether *as* is used to mean "because"
or "at the same time as." The sentence *As they were leaving, I walked to
the door* may mean either that *I walked to the door because they left* or
at the same time that they were leaving. The connectives *since* and *while*
can be ambiguous in the same way, as in examples like *Since she has been
living abroad, she has been speaking a lot of French* and *While your
income is low, you should buy insurance*. When these clauses are moved
to the end of the sentence, the proper placement of commas will serve to
distinguish the meanings.

assure

Assure, ensure, and *insure* all mean "to make secure or certain." Only *assure* is used with references to a person in the sense of "to set the mind at rest": *They assured the leader of their loyalty.* Although *ensure* and *insure* are generally interchangeable, only *insure* is now widely used in the commercial sense of "to guarantee persons or property against risk."

averse

Averse and *adverse* are often confused. *Averse* indicates opposition or strong disinclination on the subject's part: *The graduate was averse to joining the company. Adverse* is used to mean something that opposes or hinders progress: *an adverse economy; adverse circumstances.*

awhile

Awhile, an adverb, is never preceded by a preposition such as *for,* but the two-word form *a while* may be preceded by a preposition. In writing, each of the following is acceptable: *stay awhile; stay for a while; stay a while* (but not *stay for awhile*).

back

The expression *back of* is an informal variant of *in back of* and should be avoided in writing: *There was a small loading dock in back of* (not simply *back of*) *the factory.*

backward

The adverb may be spelled *backward* or *backwards,* and the forms are interchangeable; *stepped backward; a mirror facing backwards.* Only *backward* is an adjective: *a backward view.*

badly

The adverb *badly* is often used idiomatically as an adjective in sentences like *I felt badly about the ruined press run,* where grammar would seem to require *bad.* This usage is parallel to the use of the adverb *well* in sentences like *you're looking well* and is acceptable. The use of *bad* and *good* as adverbs, while common in informal speech, should be avoided in writing. Formal usage requires: *My tooth hurts badly* (not *bad*). *He drives well* (not *good*).

bait

The word *bait* is sometimes used improperly for *bate* in the phrase *bated breath.*

baleful

Baleful and *baneful* overlap in meaning, but *baleful* usually applies to that which menaces or foreshadows evil (*a baleful look*). *Baneful* is used most often of that which is actually harmful or destructive (*the baneful effects of government regulations*).

because

Because is the most direct of the conjunctions used to express cause or reason. It is used to state an immediate and explicit cause: *The company went bankrupt because the management was incompetent. Since, as,* and *for* are all less direct than *because;* they often express the speaker's or writer's view of the causal relation between circumstances or events. The clause introduced by *since* most frequently comes first in the sentence: *Since they stayed behind, they must have had something more important to do* (their staying behind leads the speaker to conclude that they must have had something important to do). *As,* like *since,* often indicates that what follows is the speaker's basis for coming to a certain conclusion: *As I have something more important to do, I would prefer to stay behind. For* is a coordinating conjunction, linking two independent statements. It expresses the speaker's reason for having said or concluded the previous statement: *The messenger definitely arrived at 11:30, for I was there and I saw him walk in. As* and *for* are now used primarily in formal levels of style. • *Because* is sometimes used in informal speech to mean "just because," as in *Because there's snow on the roof doesn't mean the fire is out in the furnace.* This use of *because* should be avoided in writing. Traditional grammar holds that the expression *the reason is because* is redundant and so should be avoided at all levels. This usage is well established, however, and has perfectly acceptable equivalents in expressions like *the time was when.* • When *because* follows a negative verb or verb phrase, it should be preceded by a comma when the *because* clause gives the subject's reason for not doing something: *I didn't leave, because I was busy* means roughly "I stayed because I had a lot of work to do." When no comma is used, the *because* clause is understood as part of what is being negated. *I didn't leave because I was busy* means "My reason for staying was not because of work, but because of something else." The conjunctions *since, as,* and *for,* when used to express a causal relation, must be preceded by commas: *She had a hurried breakfast, since she had to go to the office. I must have this phone repaired, as I have a lot of sales calls to make tomorrow. Everything at headquarters stopped, for the snowstorm had forced everyone home early.*

behalf

In behalf of and *on behalf of* have distinct senses and should not be used interchangeably. *In behalf of* means "in the interest of" or "for the benefit of": *We raised money in behalf of the United Way. On behalf of* means "as the agent of" or "on the part of": *The lawyer signed the papers on behalf of the client.*

besides

In modern usage the senses "in addition to" and "except for" are conveyed more often by *besides* than *beside.* Thus: *We had few options besides the course we ultimately took.*

better
Better is normally used in a comparison of two: *Which accounting firm does the better job?* However, *best* is used idiomatically with reference to two in certain expressions: *Put your best foot forward. May the best man or woman win!* The phrase *had better* is accepted, so long as the *had* or its contraction is preserved: *You had better do it* or *you'd better do it,* but not *you better do it.* The use of *better* for *more,* as in *the distance is better than a mile,* should be avoided in writing.

bias
Bias has generally been defined as "uninformed or unintentional inclination"; as such, it may operate either for or against someone or something. Recently *bias* has been used in the sense of "adverse action or discrimination": *Congress included a provision in the Civil Rights Act of 1964 banning racial bias in employment.*

bimonthly
Bimonthly and *biweekly* mean "once every two months" and "once every two weeks." For "twice a month" and "twice a week," the words *semimonthly* and *semiweekly* should be used. But there is a great deal of confusion over the distinction, and a writer is well advised to substitute expressions like "every two months" or "twice a month" whenever possible. However, the words with *bi-* are unavoidable when used as nouns to denote "a publication that appears every two months."

black
The preferred term for a person today is *black.* Another acceptable term is *African-American.* The noun and the adjective *black* are usually but not invariably lowercased: "Together, blacks and whites can move our country beyond racism." (Whitney Young, Jr.)

blatant
Blatant and *flagrant* are often confused. In the sense that causes the confusion, *blatant* has the meaning of "outrageous" or "egregious." *Flagrant* emphasizes wrong or evil that is glaring or notorious. Therefore, one who blunders may be guilty of a *blatant* (but not a *flagrant*) error; one who intentionally and ostentatiously violates a pledge commits a *flagrant act.*

born
In its literal sense the past participle *born* is used only of mammals and only in construction with *to be: The baby was born.* (It may also be used figuratively: *A great project was born.*) *Borne,* said of the act of birth, refers only to the mother's role, but it can be used actively or passively: *She has borne three children. Three children were borne by her* (but *born to her*). In all other senses of *bear* the past participle is *borne: The soil has borne abundant crops. Such a burden cannot be borne by anyone.*

borrow

In many American English dialects, the expression *borrow off* is used in place of *borrow from*. This usage is not sufficiently established to be used in writing, however; one writes *Gale borrowed $500.00 from* (not *off*) *the bank.*

both

Both is used to underscore that the activity or state denoted by a verb applies equally to two entities, where it might have been expected that it would apply only to one. *Both the employees have exasperated me,* for example, emphasizes that neither employee escapes my impatience. As such, *both* is improperly used with a verb that can apply only to two or more entities. It is illogical to say *they are both alike,* since neither could be "alike" if the other were not. Similarly, *both* is unnecessary in a sentence like *they both appeared together,* since neither one can "appear together" by himself. • The expression *the both,* as in *the office manager gave it to the both of them,* should be avoided in formal writing and speech. • In possessive constructions, *of both* is usually preferred: *the shareholders of both companies* (rather than *both their shareholders*); *the fault of both* (rather than *both their fault* or *both's fault*).

bring

In most American English dialects, *bring* is used to denote movement toward the place of speaking or the point from which the action is regarded: *Bring the letter to me now. The Wall Street Journal brought good news about the economy. Take* denotes movement away from such a place. Thus, one normally *takes* checks to the bank and *brings* home cash, though from the banker's point of view, one has *brought* her checks in order to *take* away cash.

burgeon

The verb *burgeon* and its participle *burgeoning,* used as an adjective, are properly restricted to the actual or figurative sense of "to bud or sprout," or "to newly emerge" (*the burgeoning talent of the young attorney*). They are not mere substitutes for the more general *expand, grow,* or *thrive.*

but

But is used to mean "except" in sentences like *No one but a compnay officer can read it.* Some traditionalists have suggested that *but* is a conjunction in this use and so should be followed by nominative pronouns like *I* and *he* when the phrase in which it occurs is the subject of the sentence. But this use of *but* is perhaps better thought of as a preposition, since the verb always agrees with the subject preceding *but;* we say *no one but the middle managers has left* (not *have left*), and traditionalists themselves do not say *everyone but I am leaving,* which is clearly ungrammatical. Accordingly, this use of *but* should properly be accompanied by pronouns in the objective case, like *me* and *him: Everyone but me has received an answer. But* is redundant when used in combination with *however*, as in *But the division, however, went on with its own plans* (eliminate either *but* or *however*). *But* is often used in informal speech together with a negative in sentences like *It won't take but an hour*. The construction should be avoided in formal style; write *It won't take an hour. But what* is informal in sentences like *I don't know but what we'll get there before the boys do*. In writing, substitute *whether* or *that* for *but*. *But* is also informal when used in place of *than* in sentences like *It no sooner started but it stopped* (in writing use *than*). *But* is usually not followed by a comma. Write *Kim wanted to go, but we didn't want to*, not *Kim wanted to go, but, we didn't want to*, which is incorrect. *But* may be used to begin a sentence, even in formal style. But it should not be followed by a comma here, either.

callous
The noun is spelled *callus* (*a callus on my foot*), but the verb and adjective are spelled *callous* (*calloused skin; a callous disregard for human rights*).

can
Generations of grammarians and schoolteachers have insisted that *can* should be used only to express the capacity to do something, while *may* must be used to indicate permission. Technically, correct usage therefore requires: *The supervisor said that anyone who wants an extra day off may* (not *can*) *have one. May* (not *can*) *I have that pencil?* In speech, however, *can* is used by most speakers to express permission, and the "permission" use of *can* is even more frequent in British English. The negative contraction *can't* is frequently used in coaxing and wheedling questions like *Can't I have the car tonight?* Avoid *mayn't*, for it is awkward and unnatural.

cannot
In the phrase *cannot but*, which is sometimes criticized as a double negative, *but* is used in the sense of "except": *One cannot but admire the takeover strategy* (that is, "one cannot do otherwise than admire the strategy"). Thus, the expression is not to be classed with the double negative that occurs when *but* in the sense of "only" is coupled with a negative. Alternative phrasings are *can but admire, can only admire, cannot help admiring*.

capital
The term for a town or city that serves as a seat of government is spelled *capital*. The term for the building in which a legislative assembly meets is spelled *capitol*.

celebrant

Celebrant should be reserved for an official participant in a religious ceremony or rite (*the celebrant of a Mass*). In the general sense of "participant in a celebration" (*New Year's Eve celebrants*) it is unacceptable to many. *Celebrator* is an undisputed alternative.

center

Center as an intransitive verb may be used with *on, upon, in,* or *at.* Logically, it should not be used with *around*, since the word *center* refers to a point of focus. Thus: *The discussion centered on* (not *around*) *the meaning of the law* (with a possible alternative being *revolved around*).

ceremonial

Ceremonial (adjective) is applicable chiefly to things; *ceremonious*, to persons and things. *Ceremonial* means simply "having to do with ceremony": *ceremonial occasions; ceremonial garb. Ceremonious,* when applied to a person, means "devoted to forms and ritual" or "standing on ceremony": *a ceremonious chief of protocol.*

certain

Although *certain* appears to be an absolute term, it is frequently qualified by adverbs, as in *fairly certain.* An acceptable sentence is *Nothing is more certain than death and taxes.*

close

Strictly speaking, the expression *close proximity* says nothing that is not said by *proximity* itself.

commentate

The verb *commentate* has been in use for several hundred years in the sense of "to give a commentary." But in the sense "to provide a running commentary on," as in *Howard Cosell commentated the Super Bowl,* it is usually unacceptable.

compare

Compare usually takes *to* when it denotes the act of stating or representing that two things are similar: *They compared the odor from the smokestack to the smell of rotten eggs.* It usually takes *with* when it denotes the act of examining the ways in which two things are similar. *The painter compared the new batch of red paint with the old one. The investigators compared the forged will with the original.* When *compared* means "worthy of comparison," *with* is used: *The plastic imitation can't be compared with the natural wood cabinet.*

complement

Complement and *compliment*, though quite distinct in meaning, are sometimes confused because of the context. *Complement* means "something that completes or brings to perfection": *The thick carpet was a perfect complement to the executive suite. Compliment* means "an expression of courtesy or praise": *We paid them a supreme compliment at the testimonial banquet.*

complete

Complete is sometimes held to be an absolute term like *perfect* or *chief*, which is not subject to comparison. It can be qualified by *more* or *less*, however, when its sense is "comprehensive, thorough," as in *A more complete failure I could not imagine.* Also acceptable: *That book is the most complete treatment of the subject available today.*

comprise

The traditional rule states that the whole *comprises* the parts; the parts *compose* the whole. In strict usage: *The Union comprises fifty states. Fifty states compose* (or *constitute* or *make up*) *the Union.* While this distinction is still maintained by many writers, *comprise* is increasingly used, especially in the passive, in place of *compose: The Union is comprised of fifty states.* That use of *comprise* should be avoided, especially in formal prose.

continuance

Continuance, except in its legal sense, is sometimes interchangeable with *continuation. Continuance,* however, is used to refer to the duration of a state or condition, as in *the president's continuance in office. Continuation* applies especially to prolongation or resumption of action (*a continuation of the board meeting*) or to physical extension (*the continuation of the railroad spur beyond our plant*). *Continuity* is used to refer to consistency over time; one speaks of *the continuity of foreign policy.* The *continuity of a story* is its internal coherence from one episode to the next; *the continuation of a story* is that part of the story that takes up after a break in its recitation.

convince

According to a traditional rule, one *persuades* someone to act but *convinces* someone of the truth of a statement or proposition: *By convincing me that no good could come of continuing the project, the director persuaded me to shelve it altogether.* If the distinction is accepted, then *convince* should not be used with an infinitive: *They persuaded* (not *convinced*) *me to go.*

council

Council, counsel, and *consul* are never interchangeable as such, though their meanings are related. *Council* and *councilor* refer principally to a deliberative assembly (such as a city council or student council), its work, and its membership. *Counsel* and *counselor* pertain chiefly to advice and guidance and to a person who provides it (such as an attorney). *Counsul* denotes an officer in the foreign service of a country.

couple

Couple, when used to refer to two people together, may take either a singular or a plural verb, but the plural is more common. Whatever the choice, usage should be consistent: *The couple are now finishing their joint research* (or *the couple is now finishing its joint research*).

criteria

Criteria is a plural form only, and should not be substituted for the singular *criterion.*

critique

Critique is widely used as a verb (*critiqued the survey*), but is still regarded by many as pretentious jargon. The use of phrases like *give a critique* or *offer a critique* will forestall objections.

data

Data is the plural of the Latin word *datum* (something given) and traditionally takes a plural verb: *These data are nonconclusive.* In casual speech the singular construction is acceptable but should be avoided in formal writing.

debut

Debut is widely used as a verb, both intransitively in the sense "to make an appearance" (*The play debuts at our new downtown theater tonight.*) and transitively in the sense "to present for the first time": *We will debut a new product line next week.* However, both of these usages are widely objected to.

depend

Depend, indicating condition or contingency, is always followed by *on* or *upon,* as in *It depends on* (or *upon*) *who is in charge.* Omission of the preposition is typical of casual speech.

deprecate

The first and fully accepted meaning of *deprecate* is "to express disapproval of." But the word has steadily encroached upon the meaning of *depreciate.* It is now used, almost to the exclusion of *depreciate,* in the sense "to belittle or mildly disparage": *The cynical employee deprecated all of the good things the company had to offer.* This newer sense is acceptable.

dilemma

Dilemma applies to a choice between evenly balanced alternatives, most often unattractive ones. It is not properly used as a synonym for *problem* or *predicament.* A sentence such as the following, therefore, is unacceptable: *Highjacking has become a big dilemma for our trucking subsidiary.*

disinterested

According to the traditional rule, a *disinterested* party is one who has no stake in a dispute and is therefore presumed to be impartial. By contrast, one is *uninterested* in something when one is indifferent to it. These two terms should not be used interchangeably despite an increasing tendency among some writers to do it.

distinct

A thing is *distinct* if it is sharply distinguished from other things (*a distinct honor*); a property or attribute is *distinctive* if it enables us to distinguish one thing from another. *This carpeting has a distinctive feel to it* means that the feel of the carpet enables us to distinguish it from other carpets. *Thick-pile carpeting is a distinct type of floor covering* means that the thick-pile carpeting falls into a clearly defined category of floor coverings.

done

Done, in the sense of "completely accomplished" or "finished," is found most often, but not exclusively, in informal usage. It is acceptable in writing in the following example: *The entire project will not be done until next year.* In some contexts this use of *done* can be unclear, as in *The work will be done next week*. Alternatives, dependent on the meaning, would be: *The work will get done next week. The work will be done by next week.*

doubt

Doubt and *doubtful* are often followed by clauses introduced by *that, whether,* or *if.* A choice among the three is guided by the intended meaning of the sentence, but considerable leeway exists. Generally, *that* is used when the intention is to express more or less complete rejection of a statement: *I doubt that they will even try* (meaning "I don't think they will even try"); or, in the negative, to express more or less complete acceptance: *I don't doubt that you are right.* On the other hand, when the intention is to express real uncertainty, the choice is usually *whether: We doubt whether they can succeed. It is doubtful whether our opponents will appear at the hearing.* In fact, *whether* is generally the only acceptable choice in such examples, though some experts would accept *if* (which is more informal in tone) or *that. Doubt* is frequently used in informal speech, both as verb and as noun, together with *but: I don't doubt but* (or *but what*) *they will come. There is no doubt but it will be difficult.* These usages should be avoided in writing; substitute *that* or *whether* as the case requires.

dove

Dove as a past tense of the verb *dive* is actually a more recent form than the historically correct *dived*. *Dove* is widely used in speech.

drunk

Drunk (adjective) is used predicatively; *The guard was drunk*. For attributive use before a noun, the choice is usually *drunken: a drunken guest*. The attributive use of *drunk*, as in *drunk driver*, is generally unacceptable. But in its legal sense it is supported by usage and statute to the extent that the two expressions *drunk driver* (one who has exceeded the legal limit of alcohol consumption while driving) and *drunken driver* (one who is inebriated) are not synonymous.

due

The phrase *due to* is always acceptable when *due* functions as a predicate adjective following a linking verb: *Our hesitancy was due to fear*. But objection is often made when *due to* is used as a prepositional phrase: *We hesitated due to fear*. Such a construction is unacceptable in writing, though it is widely used. Generally accepted alternatives are *because of* or *on account of*.

each

When the subject of a sentence begins with *each*, it is traditionally held to be grammatically singular, and the verb and following pronouns must be singular as well: *Each of the designers has* (not *have*) *his or her* (not *their*) *distinctive style*. When *each* follows a plural subject, however, the verb and following pronouns generally remain in the plural: *The secretaries each have their jobs to do*. The expression *each and every* is likewise followed by a singular verb and singular pronouns in formal style: *Each and every packer knows what his or her job is supposed to be*.

each other

According to some traditional grammarians, *each other* is used of two, *one another* of more than two. This distinction has been ignored by many of the best writers, however, and the following examples are considered acceptable: *The four partners regarded each other with suspicion. A husband and wife should confide in one another*. When speaking of an ordered series of events or stages, only *one another* can be used: *The Caesars exceeded one another* (not *each other*) *in cruelty* means that each Caesar was crueler than the last. *Each other* cannot be used as the subject of a clause in formal writing. Instead of *we know what each other are thinking*, one should write *each of us knows what the other is thinking*. Instead of *the individuals know that each other are coming*, write *each of the individuals knows that the other is coming*. Instead of *we are all each other has*, write *each of us is all the other has*. The possessive forms of *each other* and *one another* are written *each other's* and *one another's*:

The machinists wore each other's (not *each others'*) *hard hats. The district managers had forgotten one another's* (not *one anothers'*) *names.*

either

Either is normally used to mean "one of two," although it is sometimes used of three or more: *either corner of the triangle.* When referring to more than two, *any* or *any one* is preferred. • *Either* takes a singular verb: *Either plant grows in the shade.* Sometimes it is used informally with a plural verb, especially when followed by *of* and a plural: *I doubt whether either of them are available.* But such use is unacceptable to many in formal writing.

elder

Elder and *eldest* apply only to persons, unlike *older* and *oldest,* which also apply to things. *Elder* and *eldest* are used principally with reference to seniority: *elder statesman; Pat the Elder.* Unlike *older, elder* is also a noun (*the town elders; ought to listen to your elders*).

else

Else is often used redundantly in combination with prepositions such as *but, except,* and *besides: No one* (not *no one else*) *but that witness saw the accident.* • When a pronoun is followed by *else,* the possessive form is generally written thus: *someone else's* (not *someone's else*). Both *who else's* and *whose else* are in use, but not "*whose else's*": *Who else's appointment book could it have been? Whose else could it have been?*

errata

The plural *errata* is sometimes employed in the collective sense of a list of errors. Nevertheless, *errata* always takes a plural verb: *The errata are* (not *is*) *noted in an attached memo.*

everyplace

Everyplace and *every place* used adverbially for *everywhere* are appropriate principally to informal writing or speech: *Everyplace* (or *every place*) *I go, I hear raves about our product* (in formal writing, preferably *everywhere I go*). *Every place* as a combination of adjective and noun is, of course, standard English: *I searched in every place possible.*

everywhere

The only acceptable word is *everywhere* (not *everywheres*). The use of *that* with *everywhere* (*everywhere that I go*) is superfluous.

except

Except in the sense of "with the exclusion of" or "other than" is generally construed as a preposition, not a conjunction. A personal pronoun that follows *except* is therefore in the objective case: *No one except them knew it. Every member of the committee was called except me.*

excuse

The expression *excuse away* has no meaning beyond that of *excuse* (unlike *explain away,* which has a different meaning from *explain*). *Excuse away* is unacceptable: *The general manager's behavior cannot be excused* (not *excused away*).

explicit

Explicit and *express* both apply to something that is clearly stated rather than implied. *Explicit* applies more particularly to that which is carefully spelled out (*the explicit terms of ownership contained in the licensing agreement*). *Express* applies particularly to a clear expression of intention or will: *The corporation made an express prohibition against dealers' selling cars below list prices.*

farther, further

According to many traditional grammarians, the historical distinction between *farther* ("more far") and *further* ("more to the fore") should be preserved. In that case *farther* should be used only for physical distance as in *The freight train went farther down the line. Further* should be used in most other senses, especially when referring to degree, quantity, or time (*further in debt; further steps to advertise our product*). In some cases, however, either word is acceptable; one may say *further from the truth* or *farther from the truth.*

fatal

Although the senses of *fatal* and *fateful* have tended to merge in recent times, each has a different core of meaning. The contrast between *fatal,* in the sense of "leading to death or destruction," and *fateful,* in the sense of "affecting one's destiny or future," is illustrated by the following sentence: *The fateful decision to relax safety standards led directly to the fatal car crash.*

fault

Fault as a transitive verb meaning "to criticize or find fault with" is attested as far back as the 16th century but has recently come into much wider use. This usage is acceptable: *One cannot fault management's performance. To fault them is grossly unfair.*

few

Few and *fewer* are correctly used in writing only before a plural noun (*few cars; few of the books; fewer reasons; fewer gains on the stock market*). *Less* is used before a mass noun (*less music; less sugar; less material gain*). *Less than* is also used before a plural noun that denotes a measure of time, amount, or distance (*less than three weeks; less than sixty years old; less than $400.00*).

finalize

Finalize is frequently associated with the language of bureaucracy and so is objected to by many writers. The sentence *we will finalize plans to remodel twelve stores this year* is considered unacceptable. While *finalize* has no single exact synonym, a substitute can always be found among *complete, conclude, make final,* and *put in final form.*

firstly

Firstly may be used in a sequence: *firstly, secondly, thirdly,* and so on. However, it has fallen into disuse among many writers, who prefer this sequence: *first, secondly, thirdly.* Another alternative, since all these ordinal numbers can be used adverbially, is the somewhat more forceful *first, second,* or *third.*

fit

Either *fitted* or *fit* is correct as the past tense of *fit: the title fitted* (or *fit*) *my job responsibilities perfectly a year ago.* When the verb is used to mean "to cause to fit," only *fitted* is used as the past tense: *The maintenance worker fitted* (not *fit*) the file cabinet right into the space between my desk and the wall.

flammable

Flammable and *inflammable* are identical in meaning. *Flammable* has been adopted by safety authorities for the labeling of combustible materials because the *in-* of *inflammable* was understood by some people to mean "not." *Inflammable* is nevertheless widely used by writers, even though *flammable* is now established as a substitute.

flaunt

Flaunt and *flout* are often confused. *Flaunt* as a transitive verb means "to exhibit ostentatiously": *The manager flaunted a corporate credit card and expense account.* To *flout* is "to defy openly": *They flouted all social proprieties.*

follow

As follows (not *as follow*) is the established form of the phrase, no matter whether the noun that precedes it is singular or plural: *The new operating procedures are as follows* (or *procedure is as follows*).

forbid

Forbid may be used with an infinitive: *I forbid you to smoke in the elevators;* or a gerund: *I forbid your smoking;* but not with *from: I forbid you from smoking.*

forceful

Forceful, forcible, and *forced* have distinct, if related, meanings. *Forceful* is used to describe something that suggests strength or force (*a forceful marketing campaign*). *Forceful* measures may or may not involve the use of actual physical force. *Forcible,* by contrast, is most often used of actions accomplished by the application of physical force: *There had clearly been a forcible entry into the storeroom. The suspect had to be forcibly restrained. Forced* is used to describe a condition brought about by control or by an outside influence (*forced labor; a forced landing; a forced smile*).

former

The former is used when referring to the first of two persons or things mentioned. It is not used when referring to the first of three or more. For that purpose one may use *the first* or *the first-named* or repeat the name itself.

fortuitous

Fortuitous is often confused with *fortunate. Fortuitous* means "happening by chance." A *fortuitous* meeting may have either fortunate or unfortunate consequences. In common usage, some of the meaning of *fortunate* has rubbed off on *fortuitous* so that even when it is properly used, *fortuitous* often carries an implication of lucky chance rather than unlucky chance. But the word is not synonymous with *fortunate* and should not be used unless it refers to something that came about by chance or accident. The following example is unacceptable: *The meeting proved fortuitous; I came away with a much better idea of my responsibilities.*

forward

Forwards may be used in place of *forward* only in the adverbial sense of "toward the front" (*move forward* or *move forwards*). In specific phrases the choice of one or the other is often idiomatic (*look forward; from that day forward; backwards and forwards*).

founder

The verbs *founder* and *flounder* are often confused. *Founder* comes from a Latin word meaning "bottom" (as in *foundation*) and originally referred to a ship's sinking; it is now used as well to mean "to fail utterly, collapse." *Flounder* means "to move clumsily; thrash about" and hence "to proceed in confusion." If *the railroad's business between Chicago and Peoria is foundering,* expect that the line will be shut down. If *the run is floundering,* improved operating procedures and pricing policies may still save the service.

fulsome

Fulsome is often misused, especially in the phrase *fulsome praise,* by those who think that the term is equivalent merely to *full and abundant.* In modern usage *full* and *abundant* are obsolete as senses of *fulsome.* The modern sense of *fulsome* is "offensively flattering or insincere"; hence, *fulsome praise* really means insincere, unctuous compliments.

get

Get has a great number of uses, some of which are acceptable at all levels and others of which are generally felt to be informal (though never incorrect). Some uses to be avoided in writing are (1) the use of *get* in place of *be* or *become* in sentences such as *The executive got promoted;* (2) the use of *get* or *get to* in place of *start* or *begin,* as in *Let's get* (or *get to*) *working now;* and (3) the use of *have got to* in place of *must* in sentences like *I have got to go now.*

gift

Gift (verb) has a long history of use in the sense "to present as a gift; to endow": *We gifted the charity with a $1,000 donation.* In current general use, however, *gift* in this sense is sometimes regarded as affected and should be avoided.

good

Good is properly used as an adjective with linking verbs such as *be, seem,* or *appear: The future looks good. The soup tastes good.* It should be used as an adverb with other verbs: *The plant runs well* (not *good*). Thus: The designer's new suits fit well and look good.

government

In American usage *government* always takes a singular verb. In British usage *government,* in the sense of a governing group of officials, is usually construed as a plural collective and therefore takes a plural verb: *The government are determined to maintain strict reigns on industry but not on labour.*

group

Group as a collective noun can be followed by a singular or plural verb. It takes a singular verb when the persons or things that make up the group are considered collectively: *The planning group is ready to present its report. Group* takes a plural verb when the persons or things that make it up are considered individually: *The group were divided in their sympathies.*

hail

The first word of the phrase *hail fellow well met* is often misspelled *hale* in the mistaken belief that it means "sound," as in *hale and hearty.* It was originally part of a greeting, *Hail, fellow!*

half

The phrases *a half, half of,* and *half a* are all correct, though they may differ slightly in meaning. For example, *a half day* is used when *day* has the special sense "a working day," and the phrase then means "four hours." *Half of a day* and *half a day* are not restricted in this way and can mean either four or twelve hours. When the accompanying word is a pronoun, however, the phrase with *of* must be used: *half of them.* The phrase *a half a,* though frequently heard, is held by some to be unacceptable.

hanged

Hanged, as the past tense and past participle of *hang,* is used in the sense of "put to death by hanging." In the following example *hung* would be unacceptable: *Frontier courts hanged many a prisoner after a summary trial.* In all other senses of the word, *hung* is the preferred form as past tense and past participle.

hardly

Hardly has the force of a negative; therefore, it is not used with another negative: *I could hardly see* (not *couldn't hardly see*). *They listened to the presentation with hardly a smile* (not *without hardly a smile*). • A clause following *hardly* is introduced by *when* or, less often, by *before: We had hardly merged with one restaurant chain when* (or *before*) *a second chain made us an attractive offer.* Such a clause is not introduced by *than* in formal style: *Hardly had I walked inside when* (not *than*) *the downpour started.*

harebrained

The first part of the compound *harebrained* is often misspelled "hair" in the belief that the meaning of the word is "with a hair-sized brain" rather than "with no more sense than a hare." Though *hairbrained* has a long history, this spelling is not established usage.

head

The phrase *head up* is sometimes used in place of the verb *head: The committee is headed up by the city's most esteemed business leader.* The use of *head up* is unacceptable to many, and should be avoided.

headquarter

The verb *headquarter* is used informally in both transitive and intransitive senses: *Our European sales team will headquarter in Paris. The management consulting firm has headquartered its people in the New York Hyatt.* Both of these examples are unacceptable in formal writing.

headquarters

The noun *headquarters* is used with either a singular or a plural verb. The plural is more common: *Corporate headquarters are in Boston.* But the singular is sometimes preferred when reference is to authority rather than to physical location: *Headquarters has approved the purchase of desktop computers for our engineers.*

help

Help in the sense "avoid" or "refrain from" is frequently used in an expression such as *I cannot help but think.* In formal writing, use either

I cannot help thinking or *I cannot but think*. • Another common use of *help* is exemplified by the sentence *Don't change it any more than you can help* (that is, any more than you have to). Some grammarians condemn this usage on the ground that *help* in this sense means "avoid" and logically requires a negative. But the expression is a well-established idiom.

here
In formal usage *here* is not properly placed before a noun in a phrase such as *this here house*. In constructions introduced by *here is* and *here are* the number of the verb is governed by the subject, which appears after the verb: *Here is the annual report. Here are the quarterly reports.*

historic
Historic and *historical* are differentiated in usage, although their senses overlap. *Historic* refers to what is important in history (*the historic first voyage to outer space*). It is also used of what is famous or interesting because of its association with persons or events in history (*Edison's historic lab*). *Historical* refers to whatever existed in the past, whether regarded as important or not: *a historical character*. Events are *historical* if they happened, *historic* only if they are regarded as important. *Historical* refers also to anything concerned with history or the study of the past (*a historical society; a historical novel*). The differentiation between the words is not complete, though: they are often used interchangeably, as in *historic times* or *historical times*.

hopefully
The use of *hopefully* to mean "it is to be hoped," as in *hopefully we'll exceed last year's sales volume*, is grammatically justified by analogy to the similar uses of *happily* and *mercifully*. However, you may want to avoid using this word because it is objected to by so many people.

how
How is often used in informal speech where strict grammar would require *that*, as in *The president told us how he was penniless when he started in this business*. The use of *as how* for *that* in sentences like *they said as how they would go* is informal and should be avoided in writing. Similarly, one should avoid in writing the expressions *seeing as how* and *being as how*.

however
However is redundant in combination with *but*. One or the other but not both should be used in the following examples: *We had an invitation but didn't go. We had an invitation; however, we didn't go.* The use of *however* as the first word of sentence is now generally considered to be acceptable.

identical

Some authorities on usage specify *with* as the preferred preposition after *identical*. But either *with* or *to* is now acceptable: *a model identical with (or to) last year's*.

idle

Idle is now accepted in the transitive sense of "to make idle." The following example is accepted on all levels of speech and writing: *The dock strike had idled many crews and their ships*.

if

Either *if* or *whether* may be used to introduce a clause indicating uncertainty after a verb such as *ask, doubt, know, learn,* or *see: We shall soon learn whether (or if) it is true*. *If* should be avoided when it may be ambiguous, as in the following: *Let me know if the vice-chairman is invited*. Depending on the meaning, that could be better phrased: *Let me know whether the vice-chairman is invited*. *Let me know in the event that the vice-chairman is invited*. Often the phrase *if not* is also ambiguous: *The discovery offered persuasive, if not conclusive, evidence*. This could mean "persuasive and perhaps conclusive" or "persuasive but not conclusive." A clause introduced by *if* may contain either a past subjunctive verb (*if I were going*) or an indicative verb (*if I was going*) depending on the meaning intended. Traditionally, the subjunctive is used to describe a situation that is known to be contrary to fact, as in *if America were still a British colony* or *if Napoleon had been an Englishman*. The main clause of such a sentence must then contain the modal verb *would* or (less frequently) *should: If America were still a British colony, we would drink more tea than we do. If I were the President, I should (or would) make June 1 a national holiday*. When the situation described by the *if* clause is not known to be false, however, that clause must contain an indicative verb, and the choice of verb in the main clause will depend upon the intended meaning: *If Hamlet was really written by Marlowe, as many have claimed, then we have underestimated Marlowe's genius. If the main switchboard was out all day, as you say, then I understand why we didn't get any responses to our advertisement*. The indicative is also required when the situation described by the *if* clause is assumed to be true: *If I was short with you a moment ago, it is only because I wasn't paying attention. If Rome is the loveliest city in Italy, Milan is the most elegant*. When an *if* clause is preceded by *ask* or *wonder*, only the indicative should be used: *He asked if Napoleon was* (not *were*) *a great general. I wonder if the tax attorney was* (not *were*) *serious*. There is a growing tendency to use *would have* in place of the subjunctive in contrary-to-fact *if* clauses, but this usage is considered incorrect. Instead of *if I would have been promoted two years earlier*, write *if I had been promoted;* instead of *if I would have been president*, write *if I were*.

impact

Impact (verb) has ben used principally in the sense of "to pack together": *Traffic impacts the area during rush hour.* Recently it has come into more general use in the sense of "to have an impact on." Sometimes it is used transitively: *These taxes impact small businesses.* At other times it is used intransitively (with *on*): *Social pathologies, common to the inner city, impact most heavily on a plant operating in such a location.* The preceding example is unacceptable to many.

important

The following sentence may be written with the adjective *important: The shareholders' opinion is evident; more important, it will prevail.* It also may be written with an adverb: *The shareholders' opinion is evident; more importantly, it will prevail.* Most grammarians prescribe the adjective form, in which *important* stands for "what is important." But the adverbial form is also acceptable.

impracticable

Impracticable applies to that which is not capable of being carried out or put into practice: *Building a highway to the moon is impracticable. Impractical* refers to that which is not sensible or prudent: *Your suggestion that we use balloons to convey messages across town is impractical.* A plan may be impractical if it involves undue cost or effort and still not be impracticable. The distinction between these words is subtle, and *impractical* is often used where *impracticable* would be more precise.

infer

Infer is sometimes confused with *imply*, but the distinction is a useful one. To *imply* is "to state indirectly." To *infer* is "to draw a conclusion." The use of these two terms interchangeably is entirely unacceptable. One should write: *The quarterly report implies* (not *infers*) *that sales are down because of the recession. Because of that implication, investors have inferred* (not *implied*) *that we have something to hide, and our stock has fallen three points.*

input

Input has gained currency in senses not related to physics or computer technology. Example: *The report questioned whether, in such a closed administration, a president thus shielded had access to a sufficiently varied input to have a realistic picture of the nation* (*input* here meaning "a flow of information"). Example: *The nominee declared that he had no input, so far as he knew, in the adoption of the plank on abortion* (*input* here meaning "an active role, a voice in policy making"). These newer uses are unacceptable to many.

inside

Inside and *inside of* have the same meaning. *Inside* is generally preferred, especially in writing, when the reference is to position or location (*inside the warehouse*). *Inside of* is used more acceptably when the reference is to time: *The 300-page report was photocopied inside of* (not *inside*) *10 minutes.*

intend

Intend may be followed by an infinitive (*intended to go*) or a gerund (*intended going*), by a *that* clause with a subjunctive verb (*intended that he be present*), or by a noun and an infinitive (*intended him to receive the prize*).

intensive

Intensive is often used interchangeably with *intense*. However, it has the special meaning of "concentrated" (the opposite of *extensive*). Thus, one speaks of *intense heat* but *intensive study*.

intrigue

Intrigue is fully established as a noun and as a verb in all meanings except that of "to arouse the interest or curiosity of." In that sense it has been resisted by writers on usage, who regard it as an unneeded French substitute for available English words such as *interest, fascinate, pique,* or *puzzle.* Nevertheless, it has gained increasing acceptance because no single English word has precisely the same meaning. The following example is therefore acceptable: *The announcement of a special press conference intrigued the financial writers in the manner of a good suspense novel.*

its

Its, the possessive form of the pronoun *it,* is never written with an apostrophe. The contraction *it's* (for *it is* or *it has*) is always written with an apostrophe.

kind

The use of the plurals *these* and *those* with *kind* as in *these kind of films,* has respectable literary antecedents and has often been defended as a sensible idiom by British grammarians. But the usage will raise the hackles of those who go strictly by the rules and probably should be avoided in writing, if only to avoid offending the sensibilities of traditionalists. It is easy enough to substitute *this* (or *that*) *kind of* or *these* (or *those*) *kinds of* and see that the following nouns and verbs agree in number with *kind: This kind of film has had a lot of success in foreign markets. Those are the kinds of books that capture the public imagination.* When *kind of* is used to mean "more or less," it is properly preceded by the indefinite article *a* in formal writing: *a kind of genius* (not *kind of a genius*). • The use of *kind of* to mean "somewhat," as in *we were kind of sleepy,* is generally regarded as informal.

kudos

Kudos is one of those words, like *congeries,* that look like plurals but are historically singular, and so it is correctly used with a singular verb: *Kudos is due the committee for organizing a successful company picnic.*

lack

As an intransitive verb, *lack* is used chiefly in the present participle with *in: You will not be lacking in support from the finance committee.* As a transitive verb it requires no preposition but is sometimes used with *for: You will not lack* (or *lack for*) *support from the finance committee.* In that example, *lack* is preferred over *lack for.* In some cases, however, the two phrasings can convey different meanings: *The millionaire lacks nothing* (the millionaire has everything). *The millionaire lacks for nothing* (the millionaire has everything needed).

latter

Latter, as used in contrast to *former,* refers to the second of two: *Jones and Smith have been mentioned for transfer to our London office, but the latter may decline the post. Latter* is not appropriate when more than two are named: *Jones, Smith, and Kowalski have been nominated.* Kowalski should then be referred to as *the last, the last of these, the last named,* or simply *Kowalski.*

lay

Lay ("to put, place, or prepare") and *lie* ("to recline or be situated") are frequently confused. *Lay* is a transitive verb and takes an object. *Lay* and its principal parts (*laid, laying*) are correctly used in the following examples: *The messenger laid* (not *lay*) *the computer printouts on the desk. The executive dining room table was laid for four. Lie* is an intransitive verb and does not take an object. *Lie* and its principal parts (*lay, lain, lying*) are correctly used in the following examples: *The founder of the company often lies* (not *lays*) *down after lunch. When I lay* (not *laid*) *down, I fell asleep. The rubbish had lain* (not *laid*) *in the dumpster for a week. I was lying* (not *laying*) *in bed when I received the call. The valley lies to the east.* There are a few exceptions to these rules. The idioms *lay low, lay for,* and the nautical sense of *lay,* as in *lay at anchor,* though intransitive, are well established.

learn

Learn in modern usage is nonstandard in the sense of "to teach": *The instructor taught* (not *learned*) *them cardiopulmonary resuscitation.*

leave

Leave alone is acceptable as a substitute for *let alone* in the sense of "to refrain from disturbing or interfering." The following examples are acceptable: *Leave the secretaries alone and they will produce. Left alone, they were quite productive.* Those who do not accept these examples

generally feel that *leave alone* should be restricted to the sense of "to depart and leave one in solitude": *They were left alone in the wilderness.*
• In formal writing *leave* is not an acceptable substitute for *let* in the sense "to allow or permit." Only *let* is acceptable in these examples: *Let me be. Let us not quarrel. Let matters stand.*

let's

In colloquial speech *let's* has increasingly come to be used as a mere indicator that a suggestion is being proffered, and its connection with the more formal *let us* has become correspondingly attenuated, so that one hears usages like *let's us go, don't let's get all excited,* and *let's get yourself ready for the doctor.* These usages are to be avoided in formal writing.

lighted

Lighted and *lit* are equally acceptable as past tense and past participle of *light.* When used as an adjective, *lighted* is usual (*a lighted window*), but *lit* is the regular combining form (*a moonlit sky; starlit nights*).

like

Like has been used by the best writers as a conjunction since Shakespeare's time. But the usage has been so vehemently attacked by purists in recent times that the sensible writer will avoid it lest the readers pay more attention to the words than to the content. Prudence requires *The machine responds as* (not *like*) *it should.* Constructions such as *looks like, sounds like,* and *tastes like* are less likely to offend, but *as if* is better used in formal style: *It looks as if* (not *like*) *there will be no action on the bill before Congress recesses.* There can be no objection to the use of *like* as a conjunction when the following verb is not expressed: *The new senator took to politics like a duck to water.* This usage is acceptable.

likewise

Likewise, not being a conjunction, cannot take the place of a connective such as *and* or *together with,* as in *The mayor risked his credibility, likewise his honor.* Properly, *The mayor risked his credibility and* (or *and likewise*) *his honor.*

literally

Literally means "in a manner that accords precisely with the words." It is often used to mean "figuratively" or "in a manner of speaking," which is almost the opposite of its true meaning. Thus, it is not correct to say *The boss was literally breathing fire* unless, of course, the person in question is a dragon.

loan

Loan has long been established as a verb, especially in business usage, though some hold that *lend* is the preferred form, in general as well as formal writing. *Lend* is preferred over *loan* in the following examples: *One who lends* (not *loans*) *money to a friend may lose a friend. When I refused to lend* (not *loan*) *my car, I was kicked out of the carpool.* Many phrases and figurative uses require *lend* (*lend an ear; distance lends enchantment*).

lost
The phrase *lost to* can sometimes be ambiguous, as in *As a result of poor preparation, the court battle was lost to the defense attorney* (lost by the defense attorney or lost by the plaintiff's attorney to the defense attorney?) Unless the context makes the meaning clear, the sentence should be reworded.

majority
When *majority* refers to a particular number of votes, it takes a singular verb: *Her majority was five votes.* When it refers to a group of persons or things that are in the majority, it may take either a plural or singular verb, depending on whether the group is considered as a whole or as a set of people considered individually. So we say *the majority elects* (not *elect*) *the candidate it wants* (not *they want*), since the election is accomplished by the group as a whole; but *the majority of our employees live* (not *lives*) *within five miles of the office,* since living within five miles of the office is something that each employee does individually. • *Majority* is often preceded by *great* (but not by *greater*) in expressing, emphatically, the sense of "most of": *The great majority has decided not to throw good money after bad.* The phrase *greater majority* is appropriate only when considering two majorities: *A greater majority of the workers has accepted this year's contract than accepted last year's.*

man
The use of *man* to mean "a human being, regardless of sex" has a long history, but is now much less generally accepted. For many people, its use in the primary sense of "adult male human being" has made it no longer broad enough to serve as the superordinate term: *the men who settled America's frontier were a sturdy race. Twentieth-century man has made great strides in improving health care. The man of the future will eat his meals in tablet form.* Many people feel that in such cases the sense of "male" is predominant over that of "person." Other means of expressing the idea while avoiding this possible confusion are *men and women, humans,* and *human beings. Man* in the sense of "mankind" is also sometimes felt to be too exclusive. Its use in phrases such as *the evolution of man* can be avoided with similar substitutions: *the evolution of humans.* Many occupational titles in which *man* occurs as an element are being replaced, sometimes officially, by terms considered neutral. For example, *firefighter* is used instead of *fireman,* or *Members of Congress* instead of *Congressmen.*

masterful

Masterful has the undisputed meaning of "strong-willed, imperious, domineering." It is widely used also as a substitute for *masterly* in the sense of "having the skill of a master." However, many feel that the distinction between the two words should be respected, as in *a masterly* (not *masterful*) *sales presentation.*

materialize

Materialize as an intransitive verb has the primary sense of "to assume material form" or, more generally, "to take effective shape": *If our plans materialize, we will be ready to corner the market.* Though it is widely used in the sense of "appear" or "happen," as in *Three more witnesses testified, but no new evidence materialized,* such a usage is still considered unacceptable.

means

In the sense of "financial resources," *means* takes a plural verb: *Our means are quite adequate for this acquisition.* In the sense of "a way to an end," it may take a singular or plural verb; the choice of a modifier such as *any* or *all* generally determines the number of the verb: *Every means was tried. There are several means at our disposal.*

meantime

Meantime serves principally as a noun: *In the meantime we made plans for an unfavorable Federal Communications Commission ruling.* In expressing the same sense as a single adverb, *meanwhile* is more common than *meantime: Meanwhile, we made plans for an unfavorable ruling.*

might

In many Southern varieties of English, *might* is used in the "double modal" construction with *could,* as in *We might could build over there.* Less frequently, one hears *may can* and *might should.* These constructions are not familiar to the majority of American speakers and are to be avoided in formal writing.

migrate

Migrate is used with reference to both the place of departure and the destination and can be followed by *from* or *to.* It is said of persons, animals, and birds and sometimes implies a lack of permanent settlement, especially as a result of seasonal or periodic movement. *Emigrate* pertains to a single move by a person, and implies permanence. It refers specifically to the place of departure and emphasizes movement from that place. If the place is mentioned, the preposition is *from: Since many people have emigrated from the Soviet Union, we see a new demand for Russian-language books.* *Immigrate* also pertains to a single move by persons and likewise implies permanence. But it refers to destination, emphasizes movement there, and is followed by *to: Many illegal aliens have immigrated to the United States in recent months.*

minimize
According to traditional grammar, *minimize* can mean only "to make as small as possible" and is therefore an absolute term, which cannot be modified by *greatly* or *somewhat*, which are appropriately used only with verbs like *reduce* and *lessen*. The newer use of *minimize* to mean "to make smaller than before," which can be so modified, is best avoided in formal writing.

most
The adverb *most* is sometimes used in the sense of "almost": *Most all the clients accepted the provisions in the contract.* However, this usage is generally considered unacceptable in formal writing. • In the sense of "very," as an intensive where no explicit comparison is involved, *most* is acceptable both in writing and in speech: *a most ingenious solution.*

mostly
Mostly is used at all levels of style to refer to the largest number of a group: *The trees are mostly evergreens. The police arrested mostly juveniles.* In speech and informal writing, it is also used to mean "in the greatest degree" or "for the most part," but this usage is to be avoided in formal writing: *Those most* (not *mostly*) *affected are the lathe operators in Building C. For the most part* (not *Mostly*), *Northern Telecom is the supplier of our communications equipment.*

movable
Something is *movable* if it can be moved at all (*movable office furniture; a movable partition*); it is *mobile* if it is designed for easy transportation (*a mobile electric generating unit*) or if it moves frequently (*a mobile drilling rig*).

mutual
Mutual is usually used to describe a relation between two or more things, and in this use it can be paraphrased with expressions involving *between* or *each other*. Thus, *their mutual relations* means "their relations with each other" or "the relations between them." *Common* describes a relationship shared by the members of a group to something else, as in *their common interest in accounting* or in the expression *common knowledge*, "the knowledge shared by all." The phrase *mutual friend*, however, has been used since Charles Dickens to refer to a friend of each of the several members of a group: *The business partners were originally introduced by a mutual friend. Reciprocal*, like *mutual*, applies to relations between the members of a group, with an added suggestion that an exchange of goods or favors is involved, as in *reciprocal trade. Joint* is usually used to

describe an undertaking in which several partners are involved, as in *The joint efforts of federal and local officials will be required to eradicate acid rain.*

myself

In informal speech, reflexive pronouns like *myself* and *yourself* are often used for emphasis in compound subjects and objects: *The utility's board of directors and myself are undecided about the cost benefits of building a nuclear reactor. I would assign the new project to either Pat or yourself.* Both constructions are to be avoided in writing.

nauseous

Traditionally, *nauseous* means "causing nausea"; *nauseated* means "suffering from nausea." The use of *nauseous* in the sense of *nauseated* is unacceptable to many and should be avoided in writing.

need

When combined with another verb, *need* has two forms, one regular and one irregular. The regular form is marked for person and is followed by the infinitive with *to: He needs to go. Does she need to go?* The irregular form occurs only in questions, negations, and *if* clauses. Like the "modal verbs" (*must, can,* etc.), it is not marked for person and is followed by a bare verb with no *to;* moreover, its negated and questioned forms are not formed with *do.* Thus we say *he need not go,* not *he doesn't need go, he need not to go,* or *he needs not go.* Similarly, the questioned form with the irregular *need* would be *Need it be done in a hurry?* rather than *Does it need be done?* or *Need it to be done?* • The two forms of *need* are subtly different in meaning. The irregular form is roughly equivalent to "to be obliged to" and is generally reserved for situations in which there is some question as to whether its subject is under an externally imposed obligation to perform the action named by the accompanying verb. Thus *you needn't come* means "you are under no obligation to come." Where the subject is under no external compulsion to perform the action of the accompanying verb, the regular form of *need* is used. Thus, we would say: *Since I was there at the site of the accident, I don't need to read the newspaper accounts* (not *needn't read,* since the decision not to read the newspaper is entirely the subject's own). But a product safety commission might say, *If the auto company has sent letters to all owners of the defective car, has notified the press, and has alerted state motor vehicle departments about the models in question, it needn't take any further steps to get in touch with those owners who have not yet brought their cars in for free repair of the problem* (not *doesn't need to take,* since it is the company's obligations by law and not its interests that are at issue).

neither

According to the traditional rule, *neither* should be construed as singular when it occurs as the subject of a sentence: *Neither of the reports is* (not *are*) *finished.* Accordingly, a pronoun with *neither* as an antecedent also must be singular: *Neither of the doctors in the lawsuit is likely to reveal his or her* (not *their*) *identity.*

no

When *no* introduces a compound phrase, its elements should be connected with *or* rather than with *nor.* Thus we write: *The candidate has no experience or interest in product development* (not *nor interest*). *No modification or change in operating procedures will be acceptable to them* (not *nor change*).

nominal

Nominal in one of its senses means "in name only." Hence a *nominal payment* is a token payment, bearing no relation to the real value of what is being paid for. The word is often extended in use, especially by sellers, to describe a low or bargain price: *We acquired 600,000 barrels of new oil reserves at a nominal extra cost.*

not

Care should be taken with the placement of *not* and other negatives in a sentence in order to avoid ambiguity. *All issues are not speculative* could be taken to mean either "all of the issues are not speculative" or "not all of the issues are speculative." Similarly, the sentence *We didn't sleep until noon* could mean either "We went to sleep at noon" or "We got up before noon."

nothing

Nothing takes a singular verb, even when it is followed by a phrase containing a plural noun or pronoun: *Nothing except your fears stands* (not *stand*) *in your path.*

number

As a collective noun, *number* may take either a singular or a plural verb. It takes a singular verb when it is preceded by the definite article *the: The number of skilled workers is small.* It takes a plural verb when preceded by the indefinite article *a: A number of the workers are unskilled.*

numerous

Numerous is not used as a pronoun in standard English. In writing, expressions like *numerous of the firefighters* should be avoided.

obligate

Obligate has fewer meanings than *oblige. Obligate* is used chiefly to mean "to bind, compel, or constrain." In that sense it is often but not always interchangeable with *oblige.* When the constraint is from the outside, either is appropriate: *I am obliged* (or *obligated*) *to fulfill the terms of the contract.* When the constraint is in one's mind, *oblige* is the choice: *I feel obliged to give two weeks' notice.* • *Obligate* used to be

interchangeable with *oblige* in the sense of "to put under debt of grati-
tude." Although this meaning is not wholly obsolete, *oblige* is preferred
in that sense: *I am obliged* (better than *obligated*) *to you for all you
have done.*

odd

Odd, when used to indicate a few more than a given number, should
be preceded by a hyphen in order to avoid ambiguity: *thirty-odd salespeople in the showroom. Odd* in that sense is used only with round
numbers.

off

Particularly in written usage, *off* should not be followed by *of* or *from: The
speaker stepped off* (not *off of* or *off from*) *the platform.* Nor should *off* be
used for *from* to indicate a source in a sentence such as: *I got a loan from*
(not *off*) *the credit union.*

on

To indicate motion toward a position, both *on* and *onto* can be used: *The
guard dog jumped on the counter. The dog jumped onto the desk. Onto*
is more specific, however, in indicating that the motion was initiated
from an outside point. *The child wandered onto the field* means that the
child began wandering at some point off the field. *The child wandered on
the field* may mean that the wandering began somewhere on the field. • In
constructions where *on* is an adverb attached to a verb, it should not be
joined with *to* to form a single word *onto: The meeting moved on to* (not
onto) *the next subject; hold on to* (not *onto*) *the railing as you climb the
stairs.* • In their uses to indicate spatial relations, *on* and *upon* are often
interchangeable: *The container was resting on* (or *upon*) *the flatcar. The
welder took it on* (or *upon*) *himself to finish the job before nightfall. We
saw a robin light on* (or *upon*) *the lawn.* To indicate a relation between
two things, however, instead of between an action and an end pont, *upon*
cannot always be used: *Hand me the book on* (not *upon*) *the file cabinet.*
Similarly, *upon* cannot always be used in place of *on* when the relation is
not spatial: *We will be in Des Moines on* (not *upon*) *Tuesday. A good book
on* (not *upon*) *word processing has just come out.*

onetime

Onetime (single word) means "former." *One-time* (hyphenated) means
"only once." Thus *a onetime employee* is a former employee; *a one-time
mayor* was mayor only once.

only

When used as an adverb, *only* should be placed with care to avoid ambiguity. Generally this means having *only* adjoin the word or words that it
limits. Variation in the placement of *only* can change the meaning of the

sentence, as the following examples show: *Dictators respect only force; they are not moved by words. Dictators only respect force; they do not worship it. She picked up the receiver only when he entered, not before. She only picked up the receiver when he entered; she didn't dial the number.* Though strict grammarians insist that the rule for placement of *only* should always be followed, there are occasions when placement of *only* earlier in the sentence seems much more natural. In the following example, *only* is placed according to the rule: *The committee can make its decision by Friday of next week only if it receives a copy of the latest report.* Placement of *only* earlier in the sentence, immediately after *can*, would serve the rhetorical function of warning the reader that a condition on the statement follows. *Only* is often used as a conjunction equivalent to *but* in the sense of "were it not that": *they would have come, only they were snowed in.* Many experts consider this example unacceptable in writing.

ought

Ought to is sometimes used without a following verb if the meaning is clear: *Should we begin soon? Yes, we ought to.* The omission of *to*, however (as in *no, we ought not*) is not standard. • Usages like *one hadn't ought to come* and *one shouldn't ought to say that* are common in many varieties of American English. They should be avoided in written English, however, in favor of the more standard variant *ought not to.*

pair

Pair as a noun can be followed by a singular or plural verb. The singular is always used when *pair* denotes the set taken as a single entity: *This pair of shoes is a year old.* A plural verb is used when the members are considered as individuals: *The pair are working more harmoniously now.* After a numeral other than *one*, *pair* itself can be either singular or plural, but the plural is now more common: *Six pairs* (or *pair*) *of stockings are defective.*

parent

The use of *parent* as a verb is unacceptable to many people. Since there is no acceptable one-word substitute for it, paraphrases like "perform the duties of parenthood" are recommended.

partly

Partly and *partially* are not always interchangeable. *Partly* is the better choice when reference is made to a part as opposed to the whole, especially when speaking of physical objects: *The letterhead is partly red and partly green. Partially* is used to mean "to a degree" when referring to conditions or states: *Our marketing efforts have only partially penetrated into New England.*

party

A person may be called a *party* in the sense of "participant" (*a party to the industrial espionage ring*) or in a humorous sense (*a wise old party*). But except in legal usage, *party* should not be used as a general synonym for *person*, as in this example: *The party who stole $12,000 worth of inventory was taken into custody.*

pass

The past tense and past participle of *pass* is *passed: They passed* (or *have passed*) *right by the front gate. Time had passed slowly. Past* is the corresponding adjective (*in centuries past*), adverb (*drove past*), and preposition (*past midnight; past the crisis*).

peer

Peer is sometimes misused in the sense of "a superior": *That manager is the equal, if not the peer, of any executive on the committee. Peer* refers to an equal, not a superior. Its misuse may stem from the fact that members of the English nobility are called *peers;* but they are so called because they are equals of each other, not because they are the superiors of the commoners. *Peer* is properly used in the expressions *peer group* and *a jury of one's peers.*

people

People and *persons* are distinguished in usage. *People* is the proper term when referring to a large group of individuals, collectively and indefinitely: *People use a wide variety of our products at work and at home. Persons* is applicable to a specific and relatively small number: *Ten persons were fired.* In modern usage, however, *people* is also acceptable with any plural number: *I counted twenty people.*   The possessive form is *people's* (*the people's rights*) except when *people* is used in the plural to refer to two or more groups considered to be political or cultural entities: *the Slavic peoples' history.*

per

Per is used with reference to statistics and units of measurement (*per mile; per day; per person*). Its more general use (as in *per the terms of the contract*) is acceptable in business writing.

per cent

Per cent, which also may be written as one word (*percent*), is generally used with a specific figure. The number of a noun that follows it or is understood to follow it governs the number of the verb: *Twenty per cent of the stock is owned by a conglomerate. Forty-seven percent of our sales come from consumer appliances.*

percentage

Percentage, when preceded by *the*, takes a singular verb: *The percentage of unskilled workers is small.* When preceded by *a*, it takes either a singular or plural verb, depending on the number of the noun in the prepositional phrase that follows: *A small percentage of the workers are unskilled. A large percentage of the defective press run was never shipped.*

perfect

Perfect has traditionally been considered an absolute term, like *chief* and *prime*, and not subject to comparison with *more, less, almost,* and other modifiers of degree. The comparative form nonetheless has the sanction of the United States Constitution, in the phrase *a more perfect union,* and must be regarded as entirely correct, especially when *perfect* is used to mean "ideal for the purposes," as in *A more perfect spot for our broadcasting station could not be found.*

perfectly

In writing, *perfectly* is sometimes objected to when it is used as a mere intensive denoting "quite," "altogether," or "just," as in *perfectly good* and *perfectly dreadful.* But it is widely used by educated speakers in this sense.

permit

Permit of is sometimes used for the transitive verb *permit* (to allow, to admit) as in *permits of two interpretations.*

person

Person is increasingly used to create compounds that may refer to either a man or a woman: *chairperson; spokesperson; anchorperson; salesperson.* These forms can be used when reference is to the position itself, regardless of who might hold it: *The committee should elect a new chairperson at its meeting.* They are also appropriate when speaking of the specific individual holding the position: *She was the best anchorperson the local station had ever had. The group asked him to act as its spokesperson.* In such cases, the alternatives *anchorwoman* and *spokesman* also would be appropriate, and sometimes are preferred by the holder of the position.

personality

Personality, meaning "celebrity" or "notable," is widely used in speech and journalism. In more formal writing, however, it is considered unacceptable by many.

personnel

Personnel is a collective noun and never refers to an individual; therefore, it is unacceptable when used with a numeral. It is acceptable, however, to use another qualifying word: *A number of armed forces personnel* (not *six armed forces personnel*) *testified.*

plead

In strict legal usage, one is said to *plead guilty* or *plead not guilty*, but not to *plead innocent.* In nonlegal contexts, however, *plead innocent* is well established.

plus

Traditionally, *plus* as a preposition does not have the conjunctive force of *and.* Therefore, when *plus* is used after a singular subject, the verb remains singular: *Two* (the numeral considered as a single noun) *plus two equals four. Our production efficiency plus their excellent distribution system results in a new industry leader. Plus* is sometimes used loosely as a conjunction to connect two independent clauses: *We had terrible weather this year, plus the recession affected us adversely.* Such use in writing is considered unacceptable by many, and should be avoided.

poor

Poor is an adjective, not an adverb. In formal usage it should not be used to qualify a verb, as in *did poor* or *never worked poorer. Poorly* and *more poorly* are required in such examples.

practicable

Practicable describes that which can be put into effect. *Practical* describes that which is also sensible and worthwhile. It might be *practicable* to build a bullet train between New York and Omaha, but it would not be *practical.*

practically

Practically is used unexceptionally in its primary sense of "in a way that is practical." In other senses it has become almost interchangeable with *virtually.* Such use is acceptable when the meaning is "for all practical purposes." Thus, a man whose liabilities exceed his assets may be said to be *practically bankrupt,* even though he has not been legally declared insolvent. By a slight extension of this meaning, however, *practically* is often used to mean "nearly" or "all but": *They had practically closed the deal by the time I arrived.* Such use should be avoided in writing, because it is disapproved of by many experts.

precipitate

Precipitate (adjective) and *precipitately* apply primarily to rash, overhasty human actions. *Precipitant* (adjective) and *precipitantly* are also used in the foregoing sense, with stress on rushing forward or falling headlong (literally or figuratively). *Precipitous* and *precipitously* are used primarily of physical steepness, as in *a precipitous slope* or in the figurative extensions of such literal uses, as in *a precipitous drop in interest rates.*

première

Première as a verb is unacceptable to a great number of people, despite its wide usage in the world of entertainment.

presently

Presently is now used primarily in the sense of "soon." Confusingly, it is also used in the sense of "at the present time." Writers who use the word should take care that the meaning is clear from the context.

principal

Principal and *principle* are often confused but have no meanings in common. *Principle* is only a noun, and all its senses are abstract. *Principal* is both a noun and an adjective. As a noun (aside from its specialized meaning in law and finance), it generally denotes a person who holds a high position or plays an important role (*a meeting between all the principals in the transaction*). As an adjective it has the same sense of "chief" or "leading."

protagonist

Protagonist denotes the leading figure in a theatrical drama or, by extension, in any work or undertaking. Sometimes in modern usage the sense of singularity is lost: *There are three protagonists in the takeover fight.* This watered-down meaning, though well established, is unacceptable to a great many people. *Protagonist* is informally used to indicate a champion or advocate.

prove

The regular form *proved* is the preferred past participle: *You have proved your point. The theory has been proved by our physicists.* The alternative *proven* in such examples is unacceptable to many experts. *Proven* is a Scots variant made familiar through its legal use: *The charges were not proven.* But *proven* is more widely used as an adjective directly before a noun (*a proven talent; a proven point*).

quick

Both *quick* and *quickly* can be used as adverbs. *Quick* is more frequent in speech: *Come quick!* In writing, the slightly more formal *quickly* is preferred: *When the signal was relayed to our parts center, we responded quickly.* In the latter example, *quick* would be unacceptable to many experts.

quote

Quote (transitive verb) is appropriate when words are being given exactly as they were originally written or spoken. When the reference is less exact, *cite* is preferable. • *Quote* (noun) as a substitute for *quotation* is considered unacceptable by many traditionalists.

raise

Raise is properly used as a transitive verb: *Raise the loading bay doors.* For intransitive uses, *rise* is standard: *The platform rises.* However, *raise* is sometimes used as an intransitive verb: *The window raises easily.* • *Raise* (noun) rather than *rise*, is now standard in the United States for an increase in salary, though one still speaks of a *rise in prices.*

rare

Rare and *scarce* are sometimes interchangeable, but *scarce* carries an additional implication that the quantities involved are insufficient or inadequate. Thus we speak of *rare books* or of *the rare qualities* of someone we admire, but of *increasingly scarce oil reserves.*

rarely

The use of *ever* after *rarely* or *seldom* is considered redundant. Thus, the example *he rarely* (or *seldom*) *ever makes a mistake* is unacceptable in speech and writing to a majority of experts. The following constructions, using either *rarely* or *seldom*, are standard, however: *rarely if ever; rarely or never* (but not *rarely or ever*).

rather

Rather is usually preceded by *should* or *would* in expressing preference: *They would rather not diversify the company.* But *had* is equally acceptable: *I had rather be dead than be unemployed.* In a contraction such as *he'd,* either *would* or *had* can be understood.

regard

Regard is traditionally used as a singular in the phrase *in* (or *with*) *regard to* (not *in regards to*). *Regarding* and *as regards* are used in the same sense of "with reference to" but are not acceptable to a great number of people. In the same sense *with respect to* is acceptable, but *respecting* is not. • *Respects* is sometimes preferable to *regards* in the sense of "particulars": *In some respects (not regards) we are similar to our competition.*

relatively

Relatively is appropriate when a comparison is stated or implied: *The first question was relatively easy* (that is, in comparison to the others). In formal style *relatively* should not be used to mean simply "fairly," as *I am relatively sure of it.*

repel

The verbs *repel* and *repulse* both have the physical sense of driving back or off. *Repulse* also may apply to rebuffing or rejecting discourteously, but only *repel* is used in the sense of causing distaste or aversion: *Your arrogance repelled us. He repulsed with rudeness all of our attempts to help him.*

replete

Replete means "abundantly supplied": *a takeover battle replete with scandal, mudslinging, and threats.* It should not be used to mean simply "complete" or "equipped": *a club replete with pool, tennis courts, and golf courses* (better, *complete with*).

responsible

Some usage experts say that *responsible* should be used only with reference to persons, not things, since only persons can be held accountable. The word is commonly used, however, with reference to things: *Defective welds were responsible for the buckled axle.*

restive

Restive and *restless* are now commonly used as equivalent terms. *Restive,* however, implies more than simply "nervous" or "fidgety": it implies resistance to some sort of restraint. Thus, a patient who is sleeping poorly may be *restless;* but the same patient is *restive* only if kept in bed against his or her will.

sacrilegious

Sacrilegious, the adjective of *sacrilege,* is often misspelled through confusion with *religious.*

said

The adjective *said* is seldom appropriate to any but legal writing, where it is equivalent to *aforesaid: the said tenant* (named in a lease); *said property.* In similar contexts in general usage, *said* is usually unnecessary and *the tenant* or *the property* will suffice.

same

Only in legal writing is *the same* or just *same* used as a substitute for *it* or *them.* In general writing, one should avoid sentences like *The charge is $5.00; please remit same.*

scarcely

Scarcely has the force of a negative; therefore, it is not properly used with another negative: *I could scarcely believe it* (not *I couldn't scarcely believe it*). A clause following *scarcely* is introduced by *when* or, less often, by *before* but not by *than: The meeting had scarcely begun when* (or *before* but not *than*) *it was interrupted.*

seasonal

Seasonal and *seasonable,* though closely related, are differentiated in usage. *Seasonal* applies to what depends on or is controlled by the season of the year: *a seasonal rise in unemployment. Seasonable* applies to what is appropriate to the season (*seasonable clothing*) or timely (*a seasonable intervention in the dispute*). Rains are *seasonal* if they occur at a certain time of the year. They are *seasonable* at any time if they save the crops.

see

The phrase *see where* sometimes occurs in speech as an informal equivalent of *see that*, as in this sentence: *I see that everything is running smoothly at the grain elevator.* The same applies to *read where.* These informal usages, permissible in speech, should be avoided in formal writing.

set

Originally *set* meant "to cause (something) to sit," so that it is now in most cases a transitive verb: *The worker sets his shovel down. One sets the table. Sit* is generally an intransitive verb: *They sit at the microphone.* There are some exceptions: *The sun sets* (not *sits*). *A hen sets* (or *sits*) *on her eggs.*

shall

In formal writing, *shall* is employed in the first person to indicate futurity: *I shall leave tomorrow.* In the second and third persons, the same sense of futurity is expressed by *will: He* (or *she*) *will come this afternoon.* Use of the auxiliaries *shall* and *will* is reversed when the writer wants to indicate conditions such as determination, promise, obligation, command, compulsion, permission, or inevitability; *will* is then employed in the first person and *shall* in the second and third. Thus, *I will leave tomorrow* (meaning, I am determined, or obligated, or compelled, or fated to leave). *He* (or *she*) *shall come this afternoon* likewise can express any of the conditions enumerated, such as promise, permission, command, or compulsion. Such, at least, are the rules of traditional grammar. However, these distinctions are only rarely observed in American English, even in formal writing. In general usage, *will* is widely employed in all three persons to indicate futurity: *We will be in New York next week* (acceptable in writing on all levels). *Shall* is largely neglected, except in some interrogatives, such as *Shall we go? Where shall we have our sales conference this year?* and in a few set phrases: *We shall overcome. Will*, in all three persons, is employed more often than *shall* in expressing any of the forms of emphatic futurity. In speech, the degree of stress of the auxiliary verb is usually more indicative of the intended meaning than the choice of *shall* or *will.* In writing, a condition other than mere futurity is often expressed more clearly by an alternative to *shall* or *will*, such as *must* or *have to* (indicating determination, compulsion, or obligation) or by use of an intensifying word, such as *certainly* or *surely*, with *shall* or *will.* Informally, contractions such as *I'll, we'll,* and *you'll* are generally employed without distinction between the functions of *shall* and *will* as formally defined.

should
In traditional grammar the rules governing the use of *should* and *would* were based on the rules governing the use of *shall* and *will*. In modern times and especially in American usage, these rules have been greatly eroded, even more in the case of *should* and *would* than in the case of *shall* and *will*. Either *should* or *would* is now used in the first person to express conditional futurity: *If I had known that, I should* (or *would*) *have made a different reply*. In that example either *should* or *would* is acceptable. But in the second and third persons only *would* is acceptable: *If he had known that, he would have made a different reply*. *Would* cannot always be substituted for *should*, however. *Should* is used in all three persons in a conditional clause: *if I* (or *you* or *he* or *she*) *should decide to go*. *Should* is also used in all three persons to express duty or obligation (the equivalent of *ought to*): *I* (or *you* or *he* or *she*) *should go*. On the other hand, *would* is used to express volition or promise: *I agreed that I would do it*. Either *would* or *should* is possible as an auxiliary with *like, be inclined, be glad, prefer*, and related verbs: *I would* (or *should*) *like to call your attention to an oversight in the accountant's report*. Here *would* is acceptable on all levels and is more common in American usage than *should*. *Should have* is sometimes incorrectly written *should of* by writers who have mistaken the source of the spoken contraction *should've*.

slow
Slow sometimes may be used as a variant form of the adverb *slowly*, when it comes after the verb: *We drove the car slow*. In formal writing *slowly* is generally preferred. *Slow* is often used in speech and informal writing, especially when brevity and forcefulness are sought: *Drive slow! Slow* is also the established idiomatic form with certain senses of common verbs: *The watch runs slow. Take it slow.*

so
In formal writing the conjunction *so* is preferably followed by *that* when it introduces a clause stating the purpose of or reason for an action: *The supervisor stayed late so that she could catch up on her paperwork*. If *that* were omitted in the preceding example, the sentence would be unacceptable. • *So* generally stands alone, however, when it is used to introduce a clause that states the result or consequence of something: *The canning process kills much of the flavor of the food, so salt is added.*

sometime
Sometime as an adjective is properly employed to mean "former." It is also used colloquially with the meaning "occasional" (*the team's sometime pitcher*). This latter use, however, is unacceptable to a great many experts and should be avoided.

sooner

No sooner, as a comparative adverb, should be followed by *than,* not *when,* as in these typical examples: *No sooner had I arrived than I had to leave for an emergency meeting. I had no sooner made an offer than they said the property had been sold to another person.*

special

Special and *specially* have wider application than *especial* and *especially.* In the senses that it shares with *especial,* the adjective *special* is now much more commonly used. *Especial* is increasingly rare and is used chiefly to stress pre-eminence or an outstanding quality: *a work of especial ingenuity.* The adverb *especially,* on the other hand, has not been similarly displaced by *specially. Specially* is used with reference to a particular purpose (*specially trained; specially arranged*). *Especially* is used in the sense of "particularly" or "pre-eminently": *Their writers are especially talented. The first defendant especially is implicated in the fraud. Prudence is the best policy, especially now.*

stratum

The standard singular form is *stratum*: the standard plural is *strata* (or sometimes *stratums*) but not *stratas.*

tend

Tend is an informal variant of *attend* in the phrase *tend to,* meaning "to apply one's attention to": *A special session of the legislature has been called to tend to the question of a windfall profits tax.* This example is unacceptable in writing that is not expressly informal.

than

In comparisons, a pronoun following *than* or *as* may be taken as either the subject or the object of a "missing" verb whose sense is understood. Thus, in a sentence such as *John is older than I,* the nominative *I* is traditionally required on the grounds that the sentence is equivalent to *John is older than I am.* In *It does not surprise me as much as her,* the use of the objective *her* is justified by analogy to the sentence *It does not surprise me as much as it surprises her.* • On the other hand, pronouns introduced by *but* or *except* should properly be regarded as objective, demonstrated by the following sentence whose subject is a complex phrase of which a pronoun is a part: *Everybody but us* (not *we*) *has* (and not, of course, *have*) *left.* Since the verb in such a sentence always agrees in person and number with the element preceding *but,* logic similarly favors *No one except them* (not *they*) *has* (not *have*) *seen the report.* Some grammarians nonetheless illogically insist on the nominative in sentences like these and require *no one but they, everyone but he,* and so forth. When the phrase with *but* or *except* is moved to the end of the sentence, however, the objective form *except* is moved to the end of the sentence, however, the objective form of the pronoun is universally acceptable: *Everyone left but me. No one left except us.*

there

There (adverb) meaning "in that place" comes after the noun in constructions introduced by the demonstrative *that: That truck there should be moved away from the front gate.* Use of *there* before the noun, as in *that there truck*, is inappropriate in formal English.

this

This and *that* are both used as demonstrative pronouns to refer to a thought expressed earlier: *The door was unopened; that* (or *this*) *in itself casts doubt on the guard's theory. That* is sometimes prescribed as the better choice in referring to what has gone before (as in the preceding example). When the referent is yet to be mentioned, only *this* is used: *This* (not *that*) *is what bothers me. We have no time to consider late applications.* • *This* is often used in speech as an emphatic variant of the indefinite article *a: This friend of mine inquired about working here. I have this terrible headache.* This usage should be avoided in writing.

thusly

Thusly was formerly used and is now occasionally employed humorously for mock-stylish effects. Otherwise, as a variant of *thus* (itself an adverb), *thusly* is termed unacceptable by most experts.

tight

Tight as an adjective appears after the verb when it is used to qualify the process denoted by the verb (*hold on tight; close it tight*). In a few cases *tight* is the only form that may be used (*sit tight; sleep tight*). In most cases the adverb *tightly* also may be used in this position (*close it tightly*). Before a verb only the adverb is used: *The money supply will be tightly* (not *tight*) *controlled.*

together

Together with, like *in addition to*, is often employed following the subject of a sentence or clause to introduce an addition. The addition, however, does not alter the number of the verb, which is governed by the subject: *The chairman* (singular), *together with two aides, is expected in an hour.* The same is true of *along with, as well as, besides, in addition to*, and *like: Common sense as well as training is a requisite for a good job.*

too

Too preceded by *not* or another form of negative is frequently employed as a form of understatement to convey humor or sarcasm: *The workers were not too pleased with the amount of their raises. This applicant is not too bright.* When used for effect, it is employed on all levels. *Not too*, when used to mean approximately "not very," is generally considered informal: *Passage of the bill is not now considered too likely* (unacceptable in written usage to many). *Too* can often be eliminated from such sentences without loss, but if deletion gives undue stress to the negative sense, the writer may find *not very* or *none too* preferable choices. *Too* is often used in writing in place of *moreover* or *in addition* to introduce a sentence, as in *There has been a cutback in oil production. Too, rates have been increasing.* This usage is not so well established as to be entirely acceptable.

torn

Torn, never *tore*, is the standard past participle of the verb *tear. I have torn the book* (not *tore*).

tortuous

Although *tortuous* and *torturous* have a common root, their primary meanings are distinct. *Tortuous* means "twisting" (*a tortuous road*) or by extension "extremely strained or devious" (*tortuous reasoning*). *Torturous* refers primarily to the pain of torture. However, *torturous* also can be used in the sense of "twisted" or "strained," and *tortured* is an even stronger synonym (*tortured reasoning*).

transpire

Transpire has long been used in the sense of "to become known": *It soon transpired that they intended to gain a controlling interest in the corporation.* The meaning "to happen" or "to take place" has come into use more recently: *The board wondered what would transpire next.* This use, though widespread, is unacceptable to a majority of traditionalists and should be avoided so as not to incur criticism.

try

Try and is common in speech for *try to*, especially in established combinations such as *try and stop me* and *try and get some rest.* In most contexts, however, it is not interchangeable with *try to* unless the level is clearly informal. For instance in formal writing, the following would be unacceptable to many critics: *It is a mistake to try and force compliance with a regulation that is so unpopular* (preferably *try to force*).

type

Type is followed by *of* in constructions like that *type of leather.* The variant form omitting *of*, as in *that type leather*, is considered unacceptable, though it is common in many varieties of American English. *Type* is most appropriate when reference is being made to a well-defined or sharply distinct category, as in *that type of chassis, this type of aspirin.* When the categorization is vaguer or less well accepted, *kind* or *sort* is preferable: *That is not the sort of analysis one can trust. This is the kind of annual report that puts you to sleep after the first page.*

unexceptional

Unexceptional is often confused with *unexceptionable.* When the desired meaning is "not open to objection" or "above reproach," the term is *unexceptionable: unexceptionable arguments.*

various

Various, sometimes appearing as a collective noun followed by *of,* as in *He spoke to various of the members,* is an unacceptable usage.

verbal

In the sense "by word of mouth," *verbal* is synonymous with oral. In other senses *verbal* has to do with words, whether written or spoken: *verbal communication* (as opposed, say, to gestures). *Verbal,* when applied to terms such as *agreement, promise, commitment,* or *understanding,* is well established in the sense of *oral.* But anyone who fears misunderstanding may use *oral* instead.

wait

Wait on is correctly used in the sense of "to serve." Though some dialects use *wait on* as an equivalent of *wait for,* in general usage this variation has not yet become established: *We will wait for* (not *on*) *the purchaser's decision.*

want

When *want* is followed immediately by an infinitive construction, it does not take *for: I want you to go* (not *want for you*). When *want* and the infinitive are separated in the sentence, however, *for* is used: *What I want is for you to finish that one first. I want very much for you to take the other company's offer.*

–ward *or* **–wards**

Since the suffix *-ward* indicates direction, there is no need to use *to the* with it: *The containerized cargo ship is sailing westward* (or *to the west* but not *to the westward*).

way

Way, not *ways,* is the generally accepted form in writing when the term refers to distance: *a long way to go.* The phrase *under way* (meaning "in motion" or "in progress") is written thus in all contexts, including the nautical (not as *under weigh*). Confusion sometimes arises because an anchor is *weighed* and, when off the bottom, is *aweigh.*

well

As well as in the sense of "in addition to" does not have the conjunctive force of *and.* Consequently, in the following examples the singular subjects remain singular and govern singular verbs: *The parent company, as well as its affiliate, was named in the indictment. Harris, as well as Lewis, has bought a personal computer.* As well as is held to be redundant in combination with *both*. Therefore, the following example should be avoided: *Both in theory as well as in practice, the idea is unsound.* Acceptable alternatives are *both in theory and in practice; in theory, as well as in practice.*

what

When *what* is the subject of a clause, it may be construed either as singular or as plural, depending on the sense. It is singular when it is taken as equivalent to *that which* or *the thing which: What seems to be a mechanical problem in the stamping equipment is creating defective panels.* It may be plural when it is equivalent to *those which* or *the things which: What were at first minor incidents have now become major problems in the chemical disposal system.* But when a *what* clause is the subject of a sentence, it will not in general take a plural main verb unless it is the subject of a plural verb in its own clause. Thus we say *what most surprise me are the remarks at the end of the study*, where the main verb *are* is plural because the verb *surprise* is plural in the subordinate clause. But we say *what the man was holding in his lap was* (not *were*) *four letters*, because *what* is not the subject of a plural verb in its own clause. In the same way, we say *what were called predicates by traditional grammarians are called verb phrases by modern linguists*, but *what I am most interested in is* (not *are*) *the latest stock quotations.*

whatever

Whatever (pronoun) and *what ever* are used in questions and statements: *Whatever* (or *what ever*) *made them say that?* Both forms are used, although some meticulous writers prefer the two-word form. The same is true of *whoever, whenever, wherever,* and *however* when used in corresponding senses. For the adjective, only the one-word form is used: *Take whatever office supplies you need.* • When a clause beginning with *whatever* is the subject of its sentence, no comma should be used: *Whatever you do is right.* Otherwise, a comma may be used: *Whatever you do, don't forget to record your expenses.* • When the phrase preceding a restrictive clause is introduced by *whichever* or *whatever, that* should not be used in formal writing. It is held to be incorrect to write *whatever book that you want to look at;* one should write instead *whatever book you want to look at will be sent to your office* or *whichever book costs less* (not *that costs less*) *is fine with us.*

when

In informal style *when* is often used to mean "a situation or event in which," as in *A dilemma is when you don't know which way to turn.* This usage should be avoided in formal writing.

where

When *where* refers to "the place from which," it requires the preposition *from: Where did you come from?* When it refers to "the place to which," it requires no preposition: *Where did they go* (better than *where did they go to?*). When *where* refers to "the place at which," it also requires no preposition: *Where are they* (not *where are they at?*).

which

Which sometimes refers to an entire preceding statement rather than to a single word: *The drilling failed to turn up any new reserves, which disturbed the geologist.* In this acceptable example, the reference is clear. But when *which* follows a noun, the antecedent may be in doubt and ambiguity may result: *The inspector filed the complaint, which was a surprise.* If *which* is intended to refer to the entire first clause rather than to *complaint*, the desired sense would be expressed more clearly by this construction: *We learned that the inspector had filed the complaint, and that discovery came as a surprise to us.*

whose

Whose, as the possessive form of a relative pronoun, can refer to both persons and things. Thus, it functions as the possessive of both *who* and *which*. The following example, in which *whose* refers to an inanimate object, is acceptable on all levels: *The car, whose design is ultramodern, is typical of the new styles.* The alternative possessive form *of which* is also used in referring to things but is sometimes cumbersome in application.

why

Why is sometimes held to be redundant in *the reason why*. Although the expression is frequently used, it is found unacceptable by many in this example: *The reason why they opposed the new policy is not clear.* Alternative phrasings include: *Why they opposed the new policy is not clear. Their reasons for opposing the new policy are not clear.*

win

Win used as a noun in the sense of "victory" or "success" is frequently used in sports reporting and other informal contexts. Some object to its use in more formal writing, as in *An impressive win in the primary would strengthen his position greatly.*

–wise

The suffix *-wise* has a long history of use in the sense "in the manner or direction of" (*clockwise, likewise, otherwise,* and *slantwise*). In recent times, *-wise* has been in vogue as a suffix meaning "with relation to" and attachable to any noun: *saleswise, inflationwise.* But indiscriminate use of these coinages can lead to confusion, as the exact nature of the relation the writer intends is not always clear from the context. Most new or temporary coinages of this sort are thus unacceptable in writing and are considered by many to be inappropriate in speech. The following typical examples are unacceptable in general speech: *The report is not encouraging saleswise. Taxwise, it is an unattractive arrangement.*

with

With does not have the conjunctive force of *and*. Consequently, in the following example the verb is governed by the singular subject and remains singular: *The governor, with her aides, is expected at the trade show on Monday.*

wreak

Wreak is sometimes confused with *wreck*, perhaps because the wreaking of damage may leave a wreck: *The storm wreaked* (not *wrecked*) *havoc along the coast.* The past tense and past participle of *wreak* is *wreaked*, not *wrought*, which is an alternative past tense and past participle of *work*. Thus, the Bible says *God wreaked punishment on sinners*, but Samuel F. B. Morse properly asked, *"What hath God wrought?"*

CLICHÉS

Careful writers try to avoid trite or overused expressions in their prose. Here is a list of such expressions.

a little of that goes a long
  way
absence makes the heart
  grow fonder
add insult to injury
age before beauty
agonizing reappraisal
agree to disagree
albatross around one's
  neck
all in a day's work
all in all
all in the same boat
all over but the shouting
all things being equal
all things considered
all things to all men (or
  people)
all work and no play
apple of one's eye
apple-pie order
armed to the teeth
arms of Morpheus
as luck would have it
as the crow flies
at a loss for words (or
  never at a loss. . . .)
at first blush
at one fell swoop
(an) axe to grind

babe in the woods
backhanded compliment
bag and baggage
bark up the wrong tree
bated breath
bathed in tears
battle of the giants
battle royal
beard the lion in his den
beat a dead horse
beat a hasty retreat
beat around the bush
before hell freezes over
beg to disagree
beggar description
bend (or lean) over
  backward
best foot forward
best-laid plans
best of all possible worlds
best of both worlds
better late than never
between a rock and a hard
  place
between the devil and the
  deep blue sea
beyond the call of duty
beyond the pale
bigger than all outdoors
bigger than both of us

bigger (or larger) than life
bite off more than one can
  chew
bite the bullet
bite the hand that feeds
  one
bitter pill to swallow
black-and-white issue
bloody but unbowed
bloom is off the rose
bloom of youth
blue-sky thinking (or idea)
blush of shame
blushing bride
boggle the mind
bolt from the blue
bone of contention.
boom to bust
born with a silver spoon in
  one's mouth
bosom of the family
brave the elements
breathe a sigh of relief
bright and early
bright as a button
bright-eyed and
  bushy-tailed
bright future
bring home the bacon
brown as a berry

budding genius
bull in a china shop
burn the midnight oil
busy as a bee
butter wouldn't melt in
  one's mouth
by leaps and bounds
by the same token
calm before the storm
can't see the forest for the
  trees
carry (or have) a chip on
  one's shoulder
carry its share of the
  burden
(a) case in point
cash cow
caught on the horns of a
  dilemma
caught red-handed
chip off the old block
clear as a bell
clear as mud
coals to Newcastle
coin a phrase
cold as ice
(a) cold day in July (or
  Hell)
come (with) hat in hand
compare apples to oranges
conspicuous by one's
  absence
cool as a cucumber
cross the Rubicon
crying need
crying shame
cut a long story short
cut off one's nose to spite
  one's face
cynosure of all eyes
daily repast
David and Goliath
dead as a doornail
dead giveaway
dead in the water
deaf as a post
death warmed over
defend to the death one's
  right to. . . .
depths of despair
diamond in the rough
die in harness
die is cast

distaff side
do it up brown
do one's thing
dog in the manger
dog of a company
dollars to doughnuts
doom is sealed
doomed to disappointment
down in the dumps
down in the mouth
down one's alley
down-side risk
draw the line
drown one's sorrows
drunk as a lord (or skunk)
dull thud
dyed in the wool
ear to the ground
early bird gets the worm
early to bed, early to
  rise. . . .
easier said than done
eat one's hat (or words)
epoch-making
eternal reward
eyes of the world
face the music
fair sex
fall between the cracks
fall on deaf ears
far be it from me
(a) far cry
fast and loose
fate worse than death
fat's in the fire
feather in one's cap
feather one's nest
feel one's oats
festive board
few and far between
few well-chosen words
fiddle while Rome burns
fight like a tiger
fill the bill
filthy lucre
fine and dandy
first and foremost
fit as a fiddle
flash in the pan
flat as a flounder (or
  pancake)
flesh and blood
fly off the handle

fond farewell
food for thought
fool's gold
fool's paradise
fools rush in
foot in one's mouth
foot in the door
foot the bill
foregone conclusion
forewarned is forearmed
frame of reference
free as a bird (or the air)
fresh as a daisy
generous to a fault
gentle as a lamb
get a jump on the
  competition
get down to brass tacks
get one's back (or dander)
  up
get one's ducks in a row
get one's feet wet
gift of gab
gild the lily
go belly up
(a) good time was had by
  all
goose that laid the golden
  egg
grain of salt
grand and glorious
graphic account
green-eyed monster
grin like a Cheshire cat
grind to a halt
hail fellow well met
hale and hearty
hand that rocks the cradle
handsome is as handsome
  does
handwriting on the wall
hapless victim
happy as a lark
happy pair
hard row to hoe
haughty stare
haul (or rake) over the
  coals
have a foot in the door
have a leg up
head over heels
heart of gold
heave a sigh of relief

heir apparent
hew to the line
high and dry
high as a kite
high on the hog
hit the nail on the head
hit the spot
hitch one's star to
hook, line, and sinker
hook or crook
horse and pony show
hot as a firecracker (or
  pistol or six-shooter)
hue and cry
hungry as a bear (or lion)
if (the) truth be told
in full swing
in no uncertain terms
in on the ground floor
in seventh heaven
inspiring sight
in the final (or last)
  analysis
in the limelight
in the long run
in the nick of time
in this day and age
iron out a difficulty
irons in the fire
irony of fate
irreparable damage (or loss)
it goes without saying
it is interesting to note
it never rains but it pours
it's a small world
it's an ill wind
it's six of one and a half a
  dozen of the other
it stands to reason
it takes all kinds to make
  a world
it takes two to tango
(the) jig is up
just deserts
keep a low profile
keep a stiff upper lip
keep one's chin up
keep (or lose) one's cool
keep one's ear to the
  ground
knock into a cocked hat
knock on wood
labor of love

land of milk and honey
land of opportunity
land office business
land war in Asia
last but not least
last straw
law unto one's self
lead to the altar
lean and hungry look
lean over backward
leave holding the bag
leave in the lurch
leave no stone unturned
left-handed compliment
leg up on the competition
lend a helping hand
lest we forget
let one's hair down
let the cat out of the bag
let well enough alone
lick into shape
lick one's wounds
lid of secrecy
light at the end of the
  tunnel
like a house afire (or on
  fire)
like a newborn babe
limp as a dish rag
lock, stock, and barrel
long arm of the law
look a gift horse in the
  mouth
look for a needle in a
  haystack
(as) luck would have it
mad as a hatter (or March
  hare)
mad as a hornet (or wet
  hen)
mad dash
make a clean breast of
make a long story short
make a virtue of necessity
make bricks without straw
make ends meet
make hay while the sun
  shines
make no bones about
mantle of snow
matter of life and death
meaningful dialogue
meek as Moses

meet one's Waterloo
method in one's madness
milk of human kindness
mince words
mind one's p's and q's
miss the boat
moment of truth
monarch of all one surveys
month of Sundays
moot question (or point)
more easily said than done
more sinned against than
  sinning
more than meets the eye
(the) more the merrier
motley crew
naked truth
name is legion
necessary evil
needs no introduction
neither fish nor fowl
neither here nor there
neither hide nor hair
never a dull moment
never say die
nip in the bud
none the worse for wear
no holds barred
no sooner said than done
not to be sneezed (or
  sniffed) at
not wisely but too well
not worth its salt
not worth the paper it's
  printed on
nothing new under the sun
of a high order
old before one's time
on cloud nine
on one's uppers
on the ball (or stick)
on the best (or
  unimpeachable) authority
on the bum (or the fritz)
on the lam
on the other hand
on the QT
on the wagon
once in a blue moon
one man's meat is another
  man's poison
one's own worst enemy
open and shut case

open secret
opportunity knocks
other side of the coin
other things being equal
out of the frying pan and
  into the fire
over a barrel
overcome with emotion
paint the town red
pandemonium reigned
part and parcel
pay the piper
paying its own freight
penny for one's thoughts
pennywise, pound foolish
perfect gentleman
pet peeve
pillar of society
pillar to post
pinch pennies
plain and simple
plain as day
plain as the nose on one's
  face
play fast and loose
play hardball
play it by ear
play second fiddle
play the devil's advocate
(a) plum of a job (or
  position)
plumb the depths
(at this) point in time
point with pride
poor but honest
(the) powers that be
pretty as a picture
pretty kettle of fish
pretty penny
psychological moment
pull no punches
pull the wool over one's
  eyes
pure as the driven snow
put on the dog
put on the Ritz
quick and dirty
quick as lightning (or a
  flash)
quiet as a mouse
rack one's brains
rain cats and dogs
raise Cain

raise the roof
read the riot act
(the) real McCoy
red as a beet
red-letter day
reign supreme
render a decision
rest assured
ring true
ripe old age
rising star
roll up one's sleeves
rollercoaster earnings
rub one the wrong way
run it up the flagpole and
  see if anyone salutes it
sadder but wiser
sad to relate
save for a rainy day
seal one's fate (or doom)
second to none
seething mass
sell like hot cakes
separate the men from the
  boys
separate the sheep from
  the goats
shoot from the hip
(a) shot in the arm
shout from the rooftops
show one's hand
show one's true colors
show the white feather
sick and tired
sight to behold
silver lining
sing like a bird
skeleton in one's closet
small world
smell a rat
sow one's wild oats
spinning (or turning over)
  in one's grave
spinning straw into gold
stagger the imagination
stair-step earnings
start (or get) the ball
  rolling
steal one's thunder
stem to stern
stick in one's craw
stick out like a sore thumb

stick to one's guns
stick to one's knitting
stir up a hornet's nest
straight and narrow
straight from the shoulder
straw in the wind
straw that broke the
  camel's back
strictly speaking
strong as an ox
stubborn as a mule
sweat of one's brow
sweet sixteen
sweet smell of success
sweeten the pot (or kitty)
take a dim view of
take a raincheck
take it easy
take off one's hat to
take the bull by the horns
take up the cudgels
talk through one's hat
tell someone who cares
that is to say
that's for sure
throw caution to the wind
throw in the towel (or
  sponge)
throw one's hat in the ring
throw the book at
time hangs heavy
time immemorial
time of one's life
tip the scales
tired as a dog
tit for tat
to tell the truth
to the manner born
too funny for words
too little, too late
tried and true
trip the light fantastic
true blue
turn over a new leaf
ugly duckling
uncharted seas
up and comer
up the creek without a
  paddle
up to one's ears
up-side potential
usually reliable source(s)
vale of tears

viable option
view with alarm
walk on eggshells
wash one's hands of
wax poetic (or eloquent)
wear two hats
wee (small) hours
well worth one's while (or trouble)
wet behind the ears
wet to the skin

what makes the world go 'round
when all is said and done
when you come right down to it
whistle Dixie
whistle in the dark
wide-open spaces
wise as an owl
without a doubt

without further ado
wolf in sheep's clothing
work one's fingers to the bone
worst-case scenario
you can bank on that
you can bet your bottom dollar
you can take that to the bank

REDUNDANT EXPRESSIONS

Redundancy—needless repetition of ideas—is one of the principal obstacles to writing clear, precise prose. The list below gives some common redundant expressions. The elements repeated in the phrases and in the brief definitions are italicized. To eliminate redundancy, delete the italic elements in the phrases.

anthracite *coal*
(a hard *coal* having a high carbon content)

old **antique**
(an object having special value because of its *age*, especially a work of art or handicraft more than 100 years *old*)

ascend *upward*
(to go or move *upward*)

assemble *together*
(to bring or gather *together*)

pointed **barb**
(a sharp *point* projecting in reverse direction to the main point of a weapon or tool)

first **beginning**
(the *first* part)

big *in size*
(of considerable *size*)

bisect *in two*
(to cut *into two* equal parts)

blend *together*
(to combine, mix, or go well *together*)

capitol *building*
(a *building* in which a legislative body meets)

coalesce *together*
(to grow or come *together* so as to form a whole)

collaborate *together* or *jointly*
(to work *together*, especially in a *joint* effort)

fellow **colleague**
(a *fellow* member of a profession, staff, or academic faculty)

congregate *together*
(to bring or come *together* in a crowd)

connect *together*
(to join or fasten *together*)

consensus *of opinion*
(collective *opinion*)

courthouse *building*
(a *building* in which judicial courts or county government offices are housed)

habitual **custom**
(a *habitual* practice)

descend *downward*
(to move, slope, extend, or incline *downward*)

doctorate *degree*
(the *degree* or status of a doctor)

endorse a check *on the back*
(to write one's signature *on the back of*, e.g., a check)

erupt *violently*
(to emerge *violently* or to become *violently* active)

explode *violently*
(to burst *violently* from internal pressure)

real **fact**
(something with *real*, demonstrable existence)

passing **fad**
(a *transitory* fashion)

few *in number*
(amounting to or made up of a *small number*)

founder *and sink*
(to *sink* beneath the water)

basic **fundamental**
(a *basic* or essential part)

fuse *together*
(to mix *together* by or as if by melting)

opening **gambit**
(a remark intended to *open* a conversation)

gather *together*
(to come *together* or cause to come *together*)

free **gift**
(something bestowed voluntarily and *without compensation*)

past **history**
(a narrative of *past* events, something that took place *in the past*)

hoist *up*
(to raise or haul *up* with or as if with a mechanical device)

current or *present* **incumbent**
(one *currently* holding an office)

new **innovation**
(something *new* or unusual)

join *together*
(to bring or put *together* so as to make continuous or form a unit)

knots *per hour*
(a unit of speed, one nautical mile *per hour*, approximately 1.15 statute miles *per hour*)

large *in size*
(greater than average *in size*)

merge *together*
(to blend or cause to blend *together* gradually)

necessary **need**
(something *necessary* or wanted)

universal **panacea**
(a remedy for *all* diseases, evils, or difficulties)

continue to **persist**
(to *continue* in existence)

individual **person**
(an *individual* human being)

advance **planning**
(detailed methodology, programs, or schemes worked out *beforehand* for the accomplishment of an objective)

chief or *leading* or *main* **protagonist**
(the *leading* character in a Greek drama or other literary form; a *leading* or *principal* figure)

original **prototype**
(an *original* type, form, or instance that is a model on which later stages are based or judged)

protrude *out*
(to push or thrust *outward*)

recall *back*
(to summon *back* to awareness; to bring *back*)

recoil *back*
(to kick or spring *back*; to shrink *back* in fear or loathing; to fall *back*)

new **recruit**
(a *new* member of a body or organization, especially of a military force)

recur *again* or *repeatedly*
(to occur *again* or *repeatedly*)

temporary **reprieve**
(a *temporary* relief, as from danger or pain)

revert *back*
(to *return* to a *former* state)

short *in length* or *height*
(having very little *length* or *height*)

shuttle *back and forth*
(to move, go, or travel *back and forth*)

skirt *around*
(to move or pass *around* rather than across or through)

small *in size*
(characterized by relatively little *size* or slight dimensions)

tall *in height*

(having greater than average *height*)

two **twins**
(one of *two* offspring born at the same birth; one of *two* identical or similar persons, animals, or things)

completely **unanimous**
(being in *complete* harmony, accord, or agreement)

visible *to the eye*
(perceptible *to the eye*)

from **whence**
(*from* where; *from* what place; *from* what origin or source)

THE BUSINESS LETTER

The business letter represents you, your employer, and your entire company to its recipient; it is therefore essential that your letters convey a sense of competence, correctness, and organization.

Writing Effective Business Letters

The main stylistic features of business letters are explained and illustrated in detail in Chapter Three. This section discusses the actual techniques used in composing good letters for your employer. At times you will have to write letters for the employer or in the name of the company. When doing so, keep in mind that the reader will most likely be as busy as, or busier than you; hence, keep the message short and right to the point. W. Somerset Maugham is said to have described the process of good writing thus: "Cut, cut, cut. And when you've finished cutting, cut some more." This rule is especially appropriate to today's business correspondence: remember, somebody's meter is always running and the costs of writing time, keyboarding time, and reading time do mount up. Here are some specific points to keep in mind when composing letters:

1. Get right to the point; the reader may have a pile of mail to get through.
2. Keep your sentences short and crisp; break down overly long ones into separate sentences if you can do so without making the prose choppy.
3. Use the active voice (as *We are excited about your proposal*) instead of the passive voice (*Your proposal has been met with excitement on our part*); while the active voice conveys the idea straightforwardly and precisely, the passive voice often blunts the intended effect and requires more words.

4. Precede the bad news with the good news whenever possible; this makes the recipient feel better:

> Thank you, Bob, for your proposal with regard to the product marketing survey. I really think it's great that you want to use the FRT Research Corporation's sampling techniques: this shows that your research plan is state-of-the-art. However, we simply don't have that kind of money in the budget at this point. I will bring the matter up with Ms. Lee as soon as she returns; perhaps some fiscal adjustment can be made during the next Operating Committee meeting.

5. Avoid the use of bureaucratic jargon (*Operational lifecycle statistics re the configuration of this weapons system belie the system's estimated utility vis-à-vis strategic plans* et cetera) but at the same time try not to be folksy or cutesy (*Gosh, we'd love to talk to you guys about your proposal*). A straightforward businesslike approach is always acceptable.

6. Try to order your thoughts and the paragraphs containing them in a logcial, coherent manner. (See the material on paragaphing at the end of the section on business grammar earlier in this chapter.)

7. Use—but don't overuse—the recipient's name in the body of the letter (see the example in #4 above). Overuse of the recipient's name in direct address will make your message sound like a canned sweepstakes announcement.

Types of Business Letters

The letters that follow are intended to help you in the composition of some of the communications often written in offices. You can use them as guides in formulating messages in your own words.

A Sales Letter

Ms. Laura Fennimore
President
Monroe Publishing Company
111 Hamilton Street
Township, US 98765

Dear Ms. Fennimore:

Did you know that the right word processing equipment can
cut your workload by as much as 50%?   .

Our computer representative to Monroe Publishing informs
me that your company does not yet use word processing
equipment. I am taking the liberty of sending you copies
of the latest studies on word processing and its effect on
office productivity. You will find that word processing is
especially suited to operations such as yours. No other
piece of office equipment is able to improve your efficiency, timeliness, and organization the way a word
processor can.

I am also enclosing a brochure about ADP's own line of
word processors. Not only are we the third largest main-
frame computer manufacturer—we are also the leading word
processing company in the United States, whose equipment is
used by more Fortune 500 companies than any other.

If you would like more information about our products, or
about word processing in general, I would be glad to meet
with you. I encourage you to come to the ADP Demonstration
Center to see our models in action. I will call you in a
few days to ask if I may go ahead and schedule a visit.

Cordially,

William Warner
District Sales Director

A Letter of Inquiry

Ms. Diana Prince
Executive Director
Department of Labor
One Statehouse Plaza
City, US 12345

Dear Ms. Prince:

The fall issue of *Computing* magazine featured a very
interesting article about the effect of word processing
on office productivity. In the endnotes, the editor
mentions that the Department of Labor has published a
report on that same subject, titled "The Computerized
Work Station." Could you please send a copy of that study
to me at the address above?

Thank you for your prompt attention to this matter.

Sincerely,

Lewis Shepard

An Order Letter

Mr. Anthony DiDomenici
Manager
Legg & Greene Inc.
22 Hayes Boulevard
Suburbia, US 01234

Dear Mr. DiDomenici:

We would like to order the following for shipment to
Medical Associates, 12 State Street, Ourtown, US 98765:

Quantity	Item	Unit price	Total
2	"Reliable" electric typewriters X-3 Cat. # 133-6466-01	$250.00	$500.00

Please ship the order via UPS Second Day Delivery, as
we need to receive the typewriters in less than the
usual two-week delivery time mentioned in your catalogue.
Thank you.

Sincerely,

Melanie Nelson
Administrative Assistant

A Letter of Appreciation

Melanie Nelson
Administrative Assistant
Medical Associates
12 State Street
Ourtown, US 98765

Dear Ms. Nelson:

Thank you for your recent order, which we have shipped
out via our express service as you requested. It is always
a pleasure to welcome a new customer to Legg and Greene.

I'm enclosing a copy of our new spring/summer catalogue
for your convenience. You should be able to find all of the
business equipment your expanding medical practice needs.
If you have any questions feel free to call me.

Sincerely,

Anthony DiDomenici
Manager

A Letter of Adjustment

Ms. Julia Takahashi
Office Manager
MetroBank
Metropolis, US 33440

Dear Ms. Takahashi:

We were very sorry to learn that the electronic typewriters you ordered from us on September 1 arrived in
such terrible condition; as you stated in your complaint,
assembly should not be required. The damage was apparently
caused by the shipper, but I will personally make certain
that the problem is solved. New models are being sent to
you immediately, via Express Freight—free of charge, of
course. In that shipment, I am enclosing a small token of
our appreciation for your patience.

We deeply regret the inconvenience you have undergone
and we hope that you find the replacement typewriters
acceptable. Please let me know if we can do anything else
to correct this unfortunate situation. Customer satisfac-
tion means a great deal to us. Should you need additional
office equipment and supplies, we hope you will continue
to think of Meenan Office Supply.

Sincerely yours,

Richard Meenan, Jr.
Vice President, Sales

A Collection Letter

Mr. Howard Lewitt
Twinkle Gifts 'n' Gags
251 St. James Street
Ville, US 34567

Dear Mr. Lewitt:

While we understand that the recession has been hard on
many retailers during this past year, it is important that
each member of our buyers' cooperative lives up to the
terms of our credit agreement.

Your account is now 90 days past due, and we must request
that your bring it up to date. If special circumstances
surround this delinquency, please call me at (200) 200-2000
and explain the matter to me.

Sincerely,

Mike Hotchkiss
Credit Manager

A Cancellation Letter

Mr. Howard Lewitt
Twinkle Gifts 'n' Gags
251 St. James Street
Ville, US 34567

Dear Mr. Lewitt:

We regret to inform you that as of today your credit line
has been closed to further purchases. Mr. Lewitt, we have
approached you many times by mail and by telephone to
remind you of the importance of keeping your account
current. Unfortunately, you have failed to do so and your
account is now 120 days in arrears. This leaves us no
other choice but to take drastic action.

We will not be able to reopen your account until it is
brought back up to date. Please call me to discuss how
you intend to repay this debt.

Regretfully,

Mike Hotchkiss
Credit Manager

An Invitation Response

The Honorable Harriet Hay
Governor of State
Governor's Mansion
Metropolis, US 33440

Dear Governor Hay:

Congratulations on your recent election victory! We all
look forward to six more years of your sensible stewardship.

Of course, I will be honored to attend the dinner at
8:00 p.m. on December 1. It just so happens that I need to
be in Metropolis on business in early December. Now I can
plan my trip around one of your delightful social functions.
I am looking forward to seeing you, and I am eager to discuss the particulars of the legislature's bill to raise
corporate taxes.

Cordially,

Simon A. Kirby

A Reservation Letter

Mr. Thomas Sewell
Reservations Manager
Chatelet Hotel
P.O. Box 102435
Metropolis, US 33440

Dear Mr. Sewell:

This is to confirm our telephone conversation of November
3, 1990. Simon A. Kirby, President of Wasser Communications, will require an executive stateroom beginning the
afternoon of December 1, 1990. He will be departing on
December 5.

As discussed, Wasser Communications will also require two
one—bedroom suites for John Sullivan, Vice President of
Marketing, and Sarah Washington, Corporate Attorney, for
those same four nights (December 1—4). All billing should
be directed to Wasser Communications' Universe Credit
Card account, number 321—900—222. Please call me at
(123) 456—7890 if any questions or complications arise.

Sincerely,

Jack Schrager
Administrative Assistant

A Transmittal Letter

Mr. Frank Hart
Staff Writer
The City Daily Times
99 River Street
City, US 12345

Dear Mr. Hart:

Thank you for your interest in interviewing our Vice
President of Marketing, Mr. Sullivan. While Mr. Sullivan
would be delighted to meet with you to discuss Wasser
Communications, all press interviews are scheduled through
our Public Relations Department. I am therefore forwarding
your request to Jane LaRosa, Director of Corporate Communications. You should be hearing from her shortly. I can tell
you in advance, though, that Mr. Sullivan will be out of
town on business during the week of December 1.

Thank you again for your interest, and I look forward to
meeting you when an appointment has been arranged.

Sincerely,

Deloris Martin
Secretary to Mr. Sullivan

An Application Letter

Stanley Broughton, Esq.
Society of City Trial Attorneys
4790 Memorial Drive
City, US 12345

Dear Mr. Broughton:

It was a pleasure meeting with you and Sarah Washington
during lunch on Tuesday. It's always invigorating to find
other young and idealistic State University Law School
graduates in our city.

I was particularly impressed with all that you said about
the Society of City Trial Attorneys. I have decided that I
would like to apply for membership. Please consider this my
application.

Enclosed is a copy of my résumé, together with four
letters of recommendation. Thank you very much for your
guidance; I hope to hear from you soon.

Yours truly,

James Newton, Esq.

A Letter of Introduction

```
Stanley Broughton, Esq.
Society of City Trial Attorneys
4790 Memorial Drive
City, US 12345
```

Dear Mr. Brougnton:

This is a letter of introduction for James Newton, Esq., who has worked with the firm of Firenze, Ingraham, & Lee for the past two years. I understand he is interested in joining the Society of City Trial Attorneys, and I whole-heartedly endorse his application.

Mr. Newton is a bright, hard-working attorney. He has performed superbly and consistently in his work here, and has already handled several difficult cases for us. He clearly has a promising future in the legal profession.

As you probably know, Mr. Newton's credentials and law school records are outstanding. He is also well versed in your state law, since before joining our firm here in City he served as a judicial assistant to the highly respected criminal court Judge Brian M. Rothberg.

If you would like any further information about Mr. Newton, please feel free to call me at (123) 456-7000, x789.

Sincerely,

William Ingraham III
Senior Partner

FOOTNOTES AND BIBLIOGRAPHIES

Footnotes

Footnotes may be a major part of a study—especially an academic one. Although the members of our Advisory Board inform us that they do not have to typewrite footnotes and bibliographies, we have nevertheless included this section for the benefit of those of you who are employed in academic or research settings where such material is often used. Footnotes may be included at the bottom of the text page on which the quoted matter appears, or they may be grouped at the very end of the paper. Footnotes are numbered in the order of their appearance in the text. The first line of a footnote is indented by five spaces and runover lines are typed flush with the left margin. (For detailed typewriting guidelines see Chapter Three under the section on corporate report formats.)

The author's given name appears first, followed by the surname, a *comma*, and the title of the work cited. The publishing data (location of publisher, name of publisher, date of publication, etc.) appear next in the note, followed by the pages cited. Here are some sample footnotes ordered according to the kind of publication and nature of the authorship. Follow these examples when styling your employer's footnotes.

Books

one author

[1]Maria Montessori, <u>Education for a Better World</u> (Albuquerque, New Mexico: American Institute for Psychological Research, 1986), p. 78.

two or three authors

[2]Michael T. Skully and George G. Viksnins, <u>Financing Asia's Success: Comparative Financial Developments in Eight Asian Countries</u> (New York: St. Martin's Press, 1988), p. 50.

more than three authors

[3]Kiril Sokoloff, et al., <u>Investing in the Future: 10 New Industries and over 75 Key Growth Companies That Are Changing the Face of Corporate America</u> (Garden City, NY: Doubleday, 1982), p. 121.

translation

[4]Maya Turovskaya, <u>Tarkovsky: Cinema as Poetry</u>, trans. Nastasha Ward (London: Faber & Faber, 1990), p. 25.

later edition

[5]Manuel G. Velasquez, <u>Business Ethics: Concepts and Cases</u>, 2nd ed. (Englewood Cliffs, NJ: Prentice Hall, 1987), p. 164.

corporate author

[6]<u>Report of the Ad Hoc Committee on Insurance</u> (Washington, DC: National Association of Regulatory Utility Commissioners, 1987), p. 13.

anonymous

[7]<u>The American Heritage Dictionary, Second College Edition</u> (Boston: Houghton Mifflin Company, 1982), p. 1101.

Articles:

from a journal paged consecutively throughout its annual volume

[8]Gordon Young, "The Miracle Metal Platinum," <u>National Geographic</u>, Vol. 164, No. 5 (Nov. 1984), 686–706.

from a journal paged separately for each of its issues

[9]Roscoe L. Egger, Jr., "Maintaining the Viability of the U.S. Tax System," <u>Journal of Accountancy</u>, 156, No. 6 (Dec. 1983), 84–90.

from a monthly magazine

[10]Sue Hubbell, "Polly Pry, the Denver Dynamo," <u>Smithsonian</u>, Jan. 1991, pp. 48–56.

from a weekly magazine

[11]Joanne Tangorra, "Spring Computer Books," <u>Publishers Weekly</u>, 30 March 1990, pp. 17–32.

from a daily newspaper

[12]Michael Marriott, "Videodisks Coming to Class as Versatile High-Tech Tools for Teaching," <u>The New York Times</u>, 20 March 1991, p. B8, col. 1.

letter to the editor

[13]Martin Frost, Letter, <u>Forbes</u> (30 Jan. 1984), p. 14.

Bibliography

A bibliography is an alphabetically ordered list of publications appearing at the end of a study or other long paper. In the following examples you can see the proper format and style of a bibliography. The same titles used in the section on footnotes have been used here to emphasize the differences in styling.

Books:

one author

Montessori, Maria. <u>Education for a Better World</u>. Albuquerque, New Mexico: American Institute for Psychological Research, 1986.

two or three authors

Skully, Michael T., and George G. Viksnins. <u>Financing Asia's Success: Comparative Financial Developments in Eight Asian Countries</u>. New York: St. Martin's Press, 1988.

more than three authors

Sokoloff, Kiril, et al. <u>Investing in the Future: 10 New Industries and over 75 Key Growth Companies That Are Changing the Face of Corporate America</u>. Garden City, NY: Doubleday, 1982.

translation

Turovskaya, Maya. <u>Tarkovsky: Cinema as Poetry</u>. Trans. Natasha Ward. London: Faber & Faber, 1990.

later edition

Velasquez, Manuel G. <u>Business Ethics: Concepts and Cases</u>. 2nd ed. Englewood Cliffs, NJ: Prentice Hall, 1987.

corporate author

<u>Report of the Ad Hoc Committee on Insurance</u>. Washington, DC: National Association of Regulatory Utility Commissioners, 1987.

anonymous

<u>The American Heritage Dictionary, Second College Edition</u>. Boston: Houghton Mifflin Company, 1982.

Articles:

from a journal paged consecutively throughout its annual volume

Young, Gordon. "The Miracle Metal Platinum." <u>National Geographic</u> Vol. 164, No. 5 (Nov. 1984), 686–706.

from a journal paged separately for each of its issues

Egger, Roscoe L., Jr. "Maintaining the Viability of the U.S. Tax System." <u>Journal of Accountancy</u>, 156, No. 6 (Dec. 1983), 84–90.

from a monthly magazine

Hubbell, Sue. "Polly Pry, the Denver Dynamo." <u>Smithsonian</u>, Jan. 1991, pp. 48–56.

from a weekly magazine

Tangorra, Joanne. "Spring Computer Books." <u>Publishers Weekly</u>, 30 March 1990, pp. 17–32.

from a daily newspaper

Marriott, Michael. "Videodisks Coming to Class as Versatile High-Tech Tools for Teaching." <u>The New York Times</u>, 20 March 1991, p. B8, col. 1.

letter to the editor

Frost, Martin. Letter, <u>Forbes</u> (30 Jan. 1984), p. 14.

2

Creating Business Documents: Dictation and Transcription

INTRODUCTION

Generation of documents is obviously an important and highly visible means of communication in the business world. Here are some notes and guidelines to help you perfect the ability to transform the spoken word into the written word, the first step toward producing a clear, effective document.

THE WORKSTATION

Your workstation is an extension of yourself, inasmuch as it is part of your total, on-the-job appearance. Humorous colloquialisms extolling the virtues of a cluttered or messy desk as being a sign of genius (or a clean or bare desk as signifying the antithesis) are just that—humorous, and have no basis in fact. In reality, managing the workstation efficiently and sensibly will help you work effectively with your coworkers, assist your supervisor(s) competently, and make your duties proceed more swiftly— if not more easily. In short, keeping your workstation organized will yield subtle benefits day after day.

Supplies. The best way to attack the workload a hectic business day entails is to be prepared for whatever may happen at any given time. All possibilities are succinctly stated in Murphy's laws:

Nothing is as easy as it looks.
Everything takes longer than you think.
If anything can go wrong, it will.

Once you accept this probability, you can concentrate on being prepared for anything. There are basic supplies every office worker needs, and they are listed here to avoid an act of omission: stapler and staple remover, paper clips of several sizes, pens, pencils, markers, erasers, tape, small notepaper, water bottle, correction tape or fluid, ink pad, and date stamp.

115

The most important tool, however, is your desk itself. It should be functional, compact, versatile, and, it is hoped, attractive. You have probably noticed that most executive desks have a very large desktop area and two or three small drawers. Usually a matching credenza stores the executive's files and other documents.

At the secretary's desk, space is a valuable commodity, so virtually everything needed during the course of the day should be no more than three to five feet away from the focal point of the workstation. One necessity of a functional desk is that from a seated position on a swivel chair, you should be able to swing around from point A, past point B, and end at point C without any barriers or additional maneuvering other than a 90° arc (see the next illustration). The main portion of the desk ideally houses three drawers, but sometimes has only two. The center drawer should be reserved for writing implements, scissors, confidential papers, work in process, manuals, and the like. To the right will be a small, regular-size drawer useful for storing other supplies, such as boxes of paper clips, glue, packages of labels, typewriter cleaning brushes, a typewriter cover, masking tape, cassettes, equipment maintenance supplies, and so forth. The bottom drawer is for files. Here you should keep the files you or your boss refer to most often or which are current, confidential, or high-priority. It is up to you to devise the most useful and effective filing system for your office.

To the left and extending at a 90° angle from the main part of the desk is a typing table designed so that your typewriter or word processor fits conveniently on the right half. The height of the table is a few inches lower than the main desk, therefore placing the keyboard in such a position that you are comfortable while using it. There is enough surface area

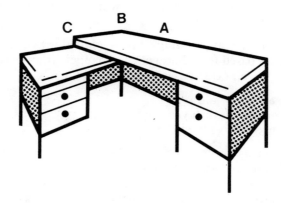

A secretary's desk should be functional, compact, and versatile.

to the left of the machine to place at your fingertips a copyholder (if the left is a more comfortable direction for you than the right), sufficient stationery or paper to complete the job, or any additional documentation related to the project at hand. In some desks, the typing table area houses three drawers with dividers for keeping the various office forms and stationery separated—letterhead, second sheets, envelopes, memo paper, scrap paper, special mailing labels and forms, and so on. Other desks have one large drawer that slides out or opens up to several slots serving the same purpose as the three separate drawers. You should remember that this drawer (or drawers) usually cannot be locked as the drawers in the main part of the desk can, so never store any valuables or confidential materials in this section.

The top of your desk ought to be organized for maximum efficiency. Place the phone on the side that is most convenient. For example, if you are right-handed, place the phone to the left of your body so that you can quickly pick up the receiver with your left hand and begin writing with your right. This plan avoids wasteful switching of hands for taking messages. Always keep a message pad and pen next to the phone.

You will also need some desk organizers to keep your various documents in order and to provide points of reference for your coworkers and your boss(es), who deliver and retrieve materials to or from your workstation. The preferred organizer is a set of stacked trays or grouped vertical racks. Whichever one you choose, the uses can be quite versatile. One tray or rack should be for outgoing mail. Another can be for materials your boss drops at your desk on the way by, and another can be a temporary holding space for documents to be filed later on. However you decide to systematize the flow of work across your desk, the main idea is to make it as suitable as possible for everyone who comes in contact with the system. Label the trays or racks clearly. You would not want your boss to deposit an edited report in the outgoing mail rack or in the filing tray when you were not around to rescue the document from its ill fate. Though you will quickly memorize the proper places for your things, others may not.

Last but not least in the way of essential supplies are reference materials. You should have easily accessible a current edition of a collegiate-level dictionary or a dictionary specifically designed for the office. Office automation, technology, and business science are changing and expanding rapidly. Our language reflects these changes. An outdated dictionary will not tell you how to spell any of these new words, let alone what they mean or in what contexts they are used. Of course, a secretarial handbook is also a valuable asset to your reference library. As with the dictionary, it should cover the conventional rules of thumb and reflect the state of the art. Other useful reference materials include an employee's manual, supply catalogues, and telephone books.

Management.   Once you have all the necessary materials, you must be able to pool these resources and make them work effectively for you. With everything in its place and kept in proper working order, you must create a system. (A *system* is a group of related elements that work together toward a common goal.)

Your system of generating documents should be managed in such a way that you are able to receive the information—or data—at a moment's notice, produce a perfect document, and follow through with swift, intact delivery of the document to its correct destination. It is a very simple process: input → output → implementation. The system breaks down when you cannot find your steno book; when the typewriter or word processor is unusable because you forgot to call the repair service at the time the machine stopped working properly; or when a document has been misdirected. But when you manage things well, paying attention to details, your office will run smoothly. Remaining organized, knowing what corners not to cut, and managing your time well will help you to achieve your—and your boss's—objectives whatever the situation, whatever the crisis, whatever the document.

Productivity.   High productivity is the natural course of events when you have established a functional workstation (adequately supplied and efficiently managed). When generating a document, establish your guidelines prior to beginning your work. Be aware of any special problems or sensitivities surrounding the material that you are generating and take any necessary precautions. Keep your equipment in good working order. With all these components of your system working together, combined with your skills and experience, you will increase your productivity and, furthermore, your worth to your supervisor and your company.

DICTATION

Transcribing the spoken words of the dictator to written words is not as easy as it sounds. For example, accents, inflections, individual speech patterns or impediments, and specialized vocabularies all affect what the transcriber hears. As a result, the hard copy generated may or may not accurately reflect the information that the dictator was trying to relay.

It is imperative to know how to use the designated equipment correctly, not only for the purposes of dictation and transcription but also in terms of day-to-day maintenance and reliable, expedient repair services. You may be called out of your department to assist in another department that uses a different kind of machine. Look at such an assignment as an opportunity to learn a new skill and thereby add to your repertoire of capabilities instead of as an infringement upon the sanctity of your job description.

Equipment

From the corporate standpoint, one of the most endearing qualities of dictation/transcription equipment is economy. Business letters are expensive to produce, but technologically advanced input and output equipment helps defray the cost of letters and other documents by reducing the amount of time spent generating copy.

Ease of operation and interchangeability are also important considerations. Our time is too precious to be squandered trying to discern what functions are performed by an array of twenty-five multicolored buttons. A machine does not serve our needs if its recording medium is unique to the machine system. Ideally, it should be adaptable to many different machines. Additionally, the pace of today's business does not always afford executives the convenience of calling secretaries into the office for lengthy dictation sessions. Therefore, alternatives must suit the needs of the employees and allow them more time for equally important tasks.

Portable machines.   A significant portion of machine dictation is given into lightweight (eight to twenty-five ounces), portable units that can be carried safely and unobtrusively in the pocket or attaché case. These portable machines are versatile units usable on planes, at home, or in cars. They are the next best thing to a telephone or to office personnel; for example, portable units are particularly useful at conferences and in fieldwork.

Many portable units are designed so that the functions of record, playback, fast forward, and rewind can be controlled with one finger. Such simplicity encourages the busy executive to use and rely on the portable model. The recording time offered ranges from fifteen to ninety minutes, depending on whether the medium is a cassette, minicassette, mag belt, or visible belt.

For the executive, portable machines offer several other useful features. First, a pause button allows the dictator to deliver correspondence at his or her desired pace. Second, a digital counter identifies the amount of tape available on the medium in use. This feature is also useful in locating correspondence quickly. Index strips are important tools for both the dictator and the transcriber. These strips identify the number and lengths of dictation segments. Furthermore, they allow you to keep track of your place within a segment of dictation and flag priority transcription or instructions, and they can identify what the dictation is. The notation of confidentiality also can be indicated.

Indexing may be executed in several ways: by using an audible tone on the recording medium; by putting a visible mark on the index strip; or by electronically cuing the tape so that instructions or the ends of documents may be seen on the display panel of the transcribing machine. When the tape is played at high speed, audible signals, or cue tones, can be heard to alert the transcriptionist to instructions and/or priorities.

When the practice is to use an actual index strip, the procedure is as follows. The strip is inserted into the appropriate slot on the machine. As the dictator's voice is recorded, a needle moves across the strip. Should an instruction be inserted or an end-of-letter signal be required, the dictator depresses the applicable button and subsequently a mark is made on the strip. When the executive concludes the dictation, he or she simply removes the strip and sends or delivers the tape and index strip to the transcriptionist. As an additional aid to the indexing feature, some transcribing machines will automatically stop at points cued on the system. See the section on transcription for further explanation.

For the transcriptionist, the portable unit can double as a transcribing machine. A headset jack may be inserted directly into the unit. Volume and speed controls allow adjustment of the recorded speaking voice to a comfortable, comprehensible playback speed. The fast forward and reverse functions afford the transcriber the freedom to back up or to fast forward the tape when desired.

Finally, a transcribe module adapter can be used to transfer the recorded information into a centralized endless-loop system. Recorder couplers take pre-recorded dictation and immediately transmit it to the office simply by the dictator's dialing the number of the office. The dictation is re-recorded from the original tape onto a tape in the office, at which point it is ready for transcription. Each of the aforementioned features is available on all, but is not specific to, portable machines. Desktop units are also equipped to handle the demands of complicated dictation and transcription.

Desktop units.   The portable machine does not always meet the needs of offices experiencing heavy loads of dictation. The desktop transcription unit can be a useful, practical companion to the portable machine or it can be used alone for both dictation and transcription. When used as a dictation machine, a microphone must be attached. As a transcription machine, the microphone is replaced with a headset, and a foot pedal is also attached. However, the desktop machine can perform only one of these functions at a time. Therefore, it is important to anticipate times of heavy dictation and to arrange for the availability of compatible units in order to prevent a backlog of work.

As with portable units, the market is moving toward designing compact, attractive units that are easy to use. Many models offer instant-on and automatic-off features, as well as one-button control of major functions (record, rewind, fast forward, etc.). The microphones that accompany desktop models are sometimes shaped like telephone receivers. They are designed to help the user feel less uncomfortable while using the device. All controls are located on the microphone for ease of operation, regardless of whether the medium in use is a standard, mini- or microcassette, or cartridge-loaded magnetic disk.

Desktop models also have the ability to record conferences and telephone conversations. Models with speakers allow groups to listen to recordings at a single time and place. The executive and assistant may use the machine as a means of interoffice communication when unable to confer with each other. The secretary may record telephone calls and messages that occur during the executive's absence. In turn, the executive may record messages, instructions, or assignments for the assistant. On some machines, a feature is included whereby the unit may serve as an intercom between the executive and secretary.

Though desktop units may provide all the features an office with a high level of dictation may require, they are also compatible with portable machines. The secretary and executive may skillfully and expediently utilize these dictation systems to generate documents swiftly through their offices. There is, however, a more advanced technology that carries the conveniences of the aforementioned models one step further; this is the centralized dictation system.

Centralized dictation systems.   Today, many firms are utilizing word processing centers for dictated matter. These centers are designed as work group configurations. The staffing and location of the work group(s) are determined by the size of the company and the dictation demands of its executives. Large firms may employ hundreds of transcriptionists in one configuration in a single, central station. Conversely, small groups can be stationed in satellite, or remote, centers in various places throughout the company.

Within the configuration, a supervisor is responsible for delegating assignments and reviewing the finished products. The supervisor also keeps records of the quality and amount of output from each transcriptionist. Some centralized dictation systems are helpful to supervisors in that they can monitor the amount of work each transcriptionist completes and how much dictation is yet to be transcribed; some models can even calculate the transcriptionists' typing speeds.

The means used to transmit dictation from a remote location—depending on whether the dictator is within the grounds of the firm—is via either a telephone or a specially wired microphone. If an executive uses the system infrequently, provisions can be made for him or her to use a standard telephone. If the dictation is frequent and extensive, it is advisable for the executive to have in the office a phone used exclusively for dictation. This phone, or private wire, is accessed to a cassette recorder. Most centralized systems record data through the use of endless loops (or tanks) or multiple-cassette systems. Endless loops (found in Private Branch Exchanges—PBXs) provide many hours of continuous recording capabilities. The multiple-cassette system uses several cassettes loaded into the system in sequence. When the tape runs out on one cassette, the used tape drops out of the machine and a new, blank cassette is dropped into its place. Or, when one cassette is filled, the system automatically begins recording on the next available cassette.

The most attractive qualities of the centralized system, from either the executive's or the company's point of view, are that they not only can provide many hours of continuous recording but also can receive input 24 hours a day, 7 days a week, 365 days a year. Additionally, the centralized system can be standardized to allow for growth and modification according to the needs of the corporation.

Guidelines for Equipment Purchase

Many factors should be considered when choosing dictation equipment. The decision should not be made in haste and should cover a realm of equipment vendors. You can find a listing of appropriate manufacturers in the Yellow Pages or in the Business-to-Business Book. Your inquiries will be answered with brochures and/or visits from a salesperson. Once you have made your decision and have purchased a dictation system, a representative from the company will come to your office and instruct you in the use of the machine and the scope of its capabilities, should you request this service. Following is a list of factors to consider when looking at equipment. Remember to consider the unique environment of your office as you evaluate them:

1. Amount/frequency of dictation

2. Place of dictation (i.e., does the dictator dictate while traveling or in the office exclusively?)

3. Number of people using the dictation system

4. Amount and complexity of functions

5. Price

6. Standardization capabilities

7. Compatibility with other machines and/or media

8. Size of equipment

9. Space available at the workstation(s)

10. Quality of manufacturing

11. Warranty

12. Guarantees

13. Serviceability (ease and speed of repairs)

14. Quality of voice rendition

15. Ability to provide other communications needs within your office, department, or company

Location

One of the considerations when choosing an appropriate dictation system is its location; that is, the office environment and space and the equipment in use. The desktop transcription unit should be close enough to the typewriter or word processor so that both the manual buttons and foot pedal are operable from your seat. The unit should be far enough away from the edge of the desk so that it will not be accidentally knocked off the desk. If your work area is noisy or if there are frequent passers-by, you will want to have headphones readily accessible. Always be careful not to place food or beverages on or near the equipment.

The dictation media should be stored in a clean, little- trafficked place. Normally, magnetic media are almost indestructible and indefinitely reusable, but should the media become dust-covered, wipe them with a clean, dry cloth. Should you get or find fingerprints on the media, again, wipe with a clean, dry cloth. (Fingerprints may cause malfunctioning in the record or playback functions of some media.)

The location of your workstation may not be under your control; however, the organization of it is. Arrange your area so that it is efficient, well supplied, and neat. Your workstation should also be functional for your boss(es), so that the executive and assistant function as a team and paperwork is produced swiftly, smoothly, and accurately.

Shorthand

Shorthand is a beneficial skill to have even at a time when offices are increasingly automated. Many executives still dictate to stenographers, and the finished product is just as polished and accurate as any accomplished with a machine. The techniques you use to generate a document go far beyond the words-per-minute rate at which you are able to receive dictation. Actually, the techniques involved are developed through education, observation, experience, and, unfortunately, trial and error. The techniques you learn can be universal or specific to your own office situation.

Education.   Here are helpful suggestions for making the dictation session as unstressful as possible for you (see the following illustration):

1. Start each day's dictation on a clean notebook page.

2. Bind off the used portion of your notebook with a rubber band; this way, you can turn directly to the next available sheet without delay.

3. If daily dictation is light to moderate, write the date above the column you will use when dictation first begins; number the pages consecutively (1, 2, 3, 4, etc.) at the top and circle this number on each page. When you begin taking dictation the next session, start with ①again.

Shorthand techniques: (A) courtesy copy notation, insertion, and underscore; (B) insertion continued, end of letter, and discrepancy; (C) discrepancy continued and end-of-session notation; and (D) next session notation, longhand, and rush indication.

4. At the end of a letter or memo—but not the end of the session—draw a single, bold line after the last line of dictation. When the session has ended, draw bold double lines after the last line of the final letter or memo.

5. If dictation is heavy, you should indicate the date on every page to ensure that all material for the session or day remains intact. Follow instruction 4 for marking the end of dictated matter.

6. Use a pen that allows your hand the greatest writing fluency. Usually, a fine-point ink pen is the best, but the choice is personal. Leave the cap of the pen on your desk instead of storing it on the end of the pen while you are taking dictation. This will afford you even greater fluency when every second counts.

7. Use circled letters to mark significant changes (more than a few words) in the notes; i.e., write Ⓐ at the point where the first change occurs. Key the new material with an Ⓐ also. The next change will be marked with a Ⓑ, and so forth. ALTERNATIVE: If the dictator customarily makes many significant changes during the course of a dictation session, you may find it wiser to take notes in only one column, leaving the other blank for corrigenda.

8. Write in longhand any name, address, or technical term the dictator spells out.

9. Leave a few lines of space between dictation items to insert processing or mailing instructions, courtesy copies, or other notations. Be careful not to overlook instructions.

10. Flag rush items with a clip or by folding back the corner of the page so that it extends outside the trim of the notebook.

11. Draw one line under words to be underscored; two lines under words to be typed all in capitals.

12. Should you notice discrepancies within the dictated material, mark the area with an X. After the dictator has finished speaking, you may question him or her and verify the data.

13. Turn notebook pages efficiently and noiselessly. You can gradually move up the page with the thumb from your free hand as you write and quickly flip the page over when you run out of room. Or, you can begin to grasp the corner of the page when you near the end of the last column. Regardless of the method used, be careful not to snap or rustle the paper loudly so that it distracts the dictator or causes you to miss a word or two.

14. If you are behind and are losing the meaning of the dictation, it is then permissible to interrupt the dictator at an appropriate pause in the dictation. Read back the sentence immediately preceding the place where you lost the flow of the dictation.

15. Transcribe material as soon after the dictation session as possible. This way, much of the information is still fresh in your mind.

Experience.   Though it is usually not a good practice to categorize people, in your work experience you may come across dictators whose styles fall into one or more of the following modes: maundering, roaming, speeding, assuming, and last-minute dictating. Any one of these idiosyncracies can cause the secretary problems either in recording or transcribing the dictation accurately or in delivering perfect final copy. Oftentimes, the dictator may not realize how difficult he or she is making the stenographer's job by subscribing to one of the aforementioned speaking or behavior patterns. Following are some suggestions on how you may deal with any of these situations:

1. For whatever reason, some dictators do not enunciate clearly and thus make it very difficult for the secretary to distinguish many words during the course of a session. If you cannot determine the missing word from the context of the sentence (often even a phrase is slurred), you should interrupt the dictator either at a pause happening soon after the poorly enunciated material or at the end of the letter or memo. Do not wait too long or after too many missed words (three or four) to ask the dictator for clarification.

2. Some dictators find it helpful to roam around the room while dictating. Under any circumstances, it is difficult to hear what someone is saying when his or her back is turned to you. In the dictating session, this is an annoying situation. Follow the same instructions mentioned in #1. If roaming is a considerable problem and severely impedes the progress of the session, you and your supervisor will have to review the situation and find an agreeable compromise.

3. Some executives are extremely well organized in their correspondence, and, as a result, dictate extremely fast; so fast, in fact, that even the best of stenographers would have trouble catching every word. As long as your shorthand is up to par, it is permissible and advisable to inform the dictator that you are not getting all that is said.

4. Another hazard you may encounter in the course of your working relationship with your supervisor is his or her assuming that you have certain information, when, in fact, you do not. They may think they have told you what course of action they are planning to follow or in what form they wish the dictated document to be presented. Their

neglecting to impart this information is not out of inconsideration; more likely, it is simply an oversight due to an overload of work or an eagerness to begin or complete a project. It is best to clarify any doubtful areas at the conclusion of the session and/or before you present the executive with the final document. You will save yourself and the executive valuable time by doing so.

5. Last-minute dictating creates a problem in that it is usually necessary to transcribe and generate a presentable document in a severely restricted amount of time. In this situation, inquire which documents must go out that business day and determine the levels of urgency of the remaining letters and memos. Learning to set priorities is a vital skill. Meanwhile, at a time other than during the dictation session, tactfully discuss the alternatives to the predicament of last-minute dictation.

The Dictation: A Paradigm

As with any other office procedure, a dictation session should not be entered into without sufficient preparation. You either know now or will learn from experience that when dictation is off the top of the head, the result is usually unsatisfactory and incomplete, meaning that both the dictator and the transcriber must go through the letter at least one more time to get it into its proper form.

Preparing to give dictation.   If you think the dictator's job is an easy one, think again. It is not easy to compose memos, letters, or reports by dictating your thoughts into a machine or to a stenographer. In fact, several studies conducted by the International Information/Word Processing Association (IWP) reveal that longhand is the preferred method of input (75%). Machine dictation follows at 12%, shorthand at 8%. The remaining 5% of input is composed of miscellaneous methods of dictation. Though longhand may be the preferred way, it certainly is not the most efficient. And since our goal is to achieve maximum efficiency and quality, you should take the necessary amount of preparatory time to achieve this end:

1. Delivering dictation earlier in the day usually means a faster turnaround time.

2. Gather your thoughts and materials prior to the session. Collect any data you may require during the course of your dictation.

3. Outline in your mind or on paper the logical sequence of the presentation of the material. Review the correspondence or documentation being answered to be sure that your dictation will cover all aspects.

4. If you are dictating into a word processing center, identify yourself, your department or location number, and your telephone extension.

5. State that your material will be a letter, memo, or report.

6. State how many copies of the final document you wish to receive.

7. Indicate how you wish your name to be typed, your title, the closing you prefer, and what kind of envelopes (if any) must be submitted with the final document.

8. Indicate the need for confidentiality when applicable. Give instructions for erasing this material from tape or for destroying or storing the written version of the dictation.

9. Give addresses and spell out unfamiliar words or unusual spellings.

10. Speak at a slow, intelligible rate. Be extra careful about dates, names, and figures. Dictate numbers one at a time, e.g., one eight nine five.

11. If you wish to have certain forms of punctuation inserted, you must indicate these as they occur.

Dictation Simulation

Following is a step-by-step simulation of dictation. Though the instructions begin with directions for using a machine for recording, the instructions to the transcriptionist and the actual dictation are conducted in the same manner.

1. Make sure the tone, speed, and volume controls are set appropriately.

2. Insert the minicassette and close the holder. When you have done this, the tape will automatically rewind.

3. Place a fresh index strip into its compartment.

4. Take the microphone from its holder—this causes the machine to be activated. Hold the microphone three to four inches away from your mouth. Speak across the face of the instrument rather than directly into it.

5. Depress the dictate switch and the light will come on. Slide the start/stop switch downward when you begin dictating.

6. To give instructions to the transcriber, slide the designated switch up, and the index strip or electronic cuing system will be marked.

Instructions

This is Amanda Billings, Director of the Elementary Education Division. I will dictate a memo to Robert Desmond. I would like a copy to go to Carl Edwards and two copies to my office. Use single spacing with two lines between paragraphs. Do not indent each new paragraph—I would like everything flush left on the margin.

Dictation

Subject (all capitals) staff requirements for one nine nine one (triple space) (capital A) at our (capital O) october one six weekly meeting (comma) the question was raised as to when management would be interviewing candidates for the editor's position that was vacated (correction, left empty) when (capital T) tom (capital W) westman relocated (period) (capital T) the position has been vacant since (capital A) august (period) I know that you have been busy with several other projects (correction, time hyphen consuming projects) during the last few months (comma) but I do feel that we should address the situation at this time (period) (new paragraph) (capital P) please submit by (capital T) thursday morning a brief job description to be used on the internal job postings (period) (capital A) as you know (comma) I must have the copy to the (capital P) personnel (capital D) department by 2 pm (capital T) thursday in order for the job to be listed on next (capital M) monday's (that's apostrophe s) postings (period) (new paragraph) (capital Y) your description should include requirements such as previous experience (comma) educational background (comma) and specific skills (comma) duties (comma) and responsibilities (period) (correction: transpose educational background to precede previous experience) (capital Y) you may want to retrieve a copy of (capital T) tom's job description to help you with this task (period) (end memo)

If you are dictating to a stenographer, be aware of who your stenographer is. For example, if you know the secretary is not especially adept at comma rules, paragraph breaks, or discerning the ends of some sentences, by all means put these instructions into your dictation. However, if the secretary has a firm command of grammar, there is no need for you to do this.

TRANSCRIPTION

A flawless document is the just reward of transcribing dictation well. To aim toward perfection, you must develop the techniques that work for you—the ones that help you get the job done accurately and swiftly.

Transcribing from a Machine

If you were to transcribe the dictation given in the previous dictation simulation, you would first need to prepare your workstation and equipment for the job.

1. Put the recorded medium into your machine.

2. Connect the headset or earpiece.

3. Adjust the foot pedal or the thumb control panel.

4. Check the start button, tone, volume, and speed control levers for correct positions.

5. Insert the index strip.

6. Move the scanner to the first priority item.

7. Determine the length of the item by reading the index strip.

8. Set your margins and tabs and insert the paper to the correct depth for the length of the item.

9. Activate the machine.

10. Listen to any instructions before beginning to type.

11. Reposition the scanner at the beginning of the item you are about to transcribe.

12. Depress the foot pedal or thumb control and listen to the first thought unit.

13. Type the first thought unit.

14. Listen to the second thought unit as you are finishing typing the first.

15. Establish a rhythm of listening and typing as described in items 13 and 14.

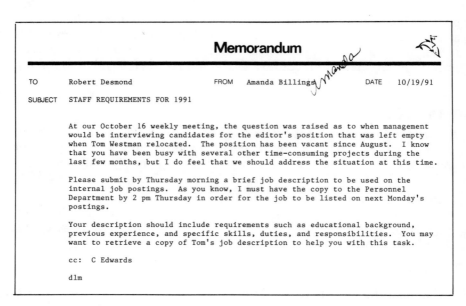

Memorandum

TO   Robert Desmond   FROM   Amanda Billings   DATE   10/19/91

SUBJECT   STAFF REQUIREMENTS FOR 1991

At our October 16 weekly meeting, the question was raised as to when management would be interviewing candidates for the editor's position that was left empty when Tom Westman relocated. The position has been vacant since August. I know that you have been busy with several other time-consuming projects during the last few months, but I do feel that we should address the situation at this time.

Please submit by Thursday morning a brief job description to be used on the internal job postings. As you know, I must have the copy to the Personnel Department by 2 pm Thursday in order for the job to be listed on next Monday's postings.

Your description should include requirements such as educational background, previous experience, and specific skills, duties, and responsibilities. You may want to retrieve a copy of Tom's job description to help you with this task.

cc: C Edwards

dlm

Transcription

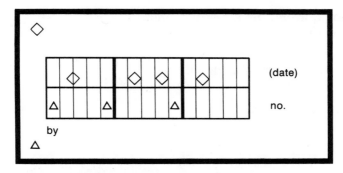

The index strip provides the transcriber with useful information.

Index strips.   The index trip illustrated here has fifteen calibrations. Each calibration represents one minute of recorded dictation. The diamond symbol is used to indicate the end of a letter and the triangle symbolizes the location of an instruction or correction. The index strip shown here gives the transcriber the following information: the first item is 25 lines long; the second, 45; the third, 20; and the fourth, 30. There are instructions for items one, two, and four.

Transcribing from Shorthand

Transcribing from shorthand comes with its own set of procedures. The main thrust of your concentration switches from using your ears to using your eyes. However, you still need to establish a routine, or rhythm that gives you the best working conditions and the desired finished document.

1. Place your notebook on a copyholder positioned at the most comfortable angle for you.

2. Review any priority items that may be flagged.

3. Look over your notes for insertions or other notations so that you are aware of their places in the document.

4. Estimate the length of the letter and set your margins and tabs accordingly.

5. Insert the paper to the appropriate depth.

6. Aim to establish a rhythm between reading and typing.

7. Double-check your typewritten document against your notes to verify that all the material has been incorporated correctly.

8. Draw a single vertical line through the document in your notes to show that you have transcribed the material.

Transcribing from a Shorthand Machine

Transcribing from a shorthand machine involves its own processes. The following list gives a breakdown of the basic steps.

1. Remove the notes from the platen.

2. Insert the tape into a transcription box. Make sure that two lengths of the tape are visible at any given time.

3. Check for priority or rush items.

4. With a colored pencil, edit the notes for corrections, insertions, or deletions. Flag changes in copy with three asterisks, stacked vertically before and after the change. Begin the new copy with the number 2 and record the new material.

5. Estimate the length of the document. This can be done by estimating the number of words in one fold of the tape. Multiply this figure by the number of folded sections of tape for the complete document. The result is an estimated word count.

6. Set margins and tabs accordingly on your typewriter.

7. Establish a rhythm between reading and typing phrases.

8. Remove the finished tape from the transcription box and store it properly.

Table 1. **Letter Placement**

Stationery	Top Margin	Side Margins	Bottom Margin
Standard	Begin date on line 15	20 and 85 (elite) 25 and 80 (pica)	If it's the end of a letter, leave at least 6 lines; if the letter is continued, you may leave up to 12 lines.
Monarch	Begin date on line 14	20 and 85 (elite) 25 and 80 (pica)	Same as above.
Baronial	Begin date on line 12	25 and 80 (elite) 30 and 75 (pica)	Same as above.

*If you need to lengthen or shorten a letter, you can adjust the date line to fall higher or lower; also you may add or decrease line spaces around the inside address, salutation, closing, reference initials, or the indicators for any courtesy copies or enclosures.

MINUTES OF MEETINGS

Many executives spend a significant amount of their time in meetings. Therefore, it is very important that the structure of these meetings be well planned from all aspects. No one likes to spend hours belaboring one or two subjects when they could be settled in a much briefer period, had only one of several things happened prior to the meeting:

1. Ample notice of the meeting given

2. Agendas distributed prior to the day of the meeting

3. Meeting room reserved and prepared properly for the duration of the meeting

The secretary's role in planning and participating in any meeting that involves his or her supervisor(s) is instrumental to ensuring a successful meeting insofar as each of the aforementioned items is concerned.

Preparing for the Meeting.   Once your supervisor has instructed you to set up a meeting, you should determine the date and time the meeting is to be held. Often these criteria will depend on the availability of a meeting room, in which case you will be required to shop around for a room, present alternatives to the executive, and proceed with plans derived from his or her decision. Next, you need to know who is to attend the meeting and if any of the attendees is required to bring specific documents or to present a report. You will also need to know what your recourse should be in the event that one or more of the people on the attendance list is unable to attend. Can the meeting take place without that person? Should the meeting be postponed to a time more convenient to that person? Can a substitute sit in for the one unable to attend? Finally, you need to know what, if any, audiovisual equipment will be needed during the course of the meeting.

Once you have done the preliminary work for the meeting, you are ready to inform the participants. Seven to ten business days are considered appropriate notification of a meeting. Depending on the level of formality in your company or the nature of the meeting, you may phone the participants' offices and then confirm the verbal notification in writing by sending a brief letter stating the date, time, location, nature of the meeting along with the agenda, and any special requests of the individual. Phoning first is often a better way to arrange a meeting because you can coordinate the participants' responses and iron out any problems before transmitting written material. Preplanning goes a long way toward saving time for everyone involved. It may not always be possible to transmit a final agenda with the meeting notification. As soon as possible, distribute the agenda so that all participants will have ample time to prepare themselves for the topics of discussion. The agenda will also give them clues as to what documentation they should bring to the meeting. (See the next illustration.)

Taking the Minutes.   Arrive first at the meeting to ensure that everything is ready. To take the minutes, you should have plenty of materials — whatever the medium — to get you through a lengthy dictation session. When the meeting is called to order, the hard work begins. Make sure you have a copy of the agenda for yourself. Even if it is not followed in exact order, you will need it to key your notes, a process addressed later in this section.

The most difficult part of taking minutes is deciding what information has to be written down verbatim, what can be paraphrased, and what is unessential for the official record. Minutes are meant to be concise, factual, and objective recordings of what has happened during the course of a meeting. You cannot inject personal preferences into your notes. You cannot give more weight to what certain people say and not record the pertinent remarks of others. You must be able to interpret statements for what is truly being said, not what you hear by way of the deliverer's voice inflections, intonations, or mannerisms. It can be very difficult to discriminate from among all the opinions and facts just what should be recorded in the minutes. For example, if the implementation of a new procedure is being discussed and it appears that the motion for its institution will be passed, it is equally important to write down why the Publisher feels the procedure will not work, as it is to record why the editors feel that it will.

You must listen carefully *and* take down information even when more than one person is talking at the same time. You will have to do some quick sorting in your mind in order to record facts accurately without distortion, while at the same time making sure you attribute all statements to their correct sources. In corporate or organizational meetings, it is necessary to record motions and resolutions verbatim as well as the names of those who made them.

Knowing what you are to be aware of during the progress of the meeting, you are ready to record. Here's how you should do it:

1. Write down the date, location, and time the meeting begins.

2. Record the names of those present and absent (if the number is less than twenty). A quorum check is necessary for larger meetings.

3. Label the meeting (regular, weekly, annual, special, or executive).

4. Name the presiding officer.

5. Record the action. When the meeting begins, key your notes to match the activity. That is, if the discussion is "works in progress" and this

AGENDA

Editorial Meeting

April 16, 19--

1. Call to order

2. Roll call

3. Minutes of previous meeting (corrections, omissions)

4. Director's report

5. Publisher's report

6. Production Manager's report

7. Unfinished business

   a. works in progress

   b. proposals before the board

   c. staff

8. New business

   a. budget

   b. new proposals

9. Announcements (including date of next meeting)

10. Adjournment

Always type the agenda with at least three line spaces between each item.

subject is item "a" under "7. Unfinished Business," then key your notes "7a" and record the discussion. This relieves you of writing "7. Unfinished Business: a, works in progress." When you type your notes, you simply refer to your agenda to transcribe the key "7a."

6. Record the time of adjournment.

See the section on shorthand for suggestions on coding your stenographic notebook for changes, deletions, and additions while taking minutes.

Transcribing the Minutes

Always keep in mind that minutes serve as official records of meetings. Therefore, it is imperative that you objectively record the minutes and conscientiously transcribe them into the final, formal document anticipated by the attendees.

Drafts.   Drafts are like dress rehearsals. Everything is in place, except the audience. If you make a mistake, you can correct it before the audience sees it—and they will never be the wiser. When you sit down at your typewriter, you should have the following materials accessible:

1. the agenda

2. your notes (do not rely on memory)

3. *Robert's Rules of Order* or similar reference books on parliamentary procedure

4. any reports or other documents distributed at the meeting

5. verbatim copies of motions and resolutions

6. the constitution or bylaws of the group (if applicable)

Prepare the draft in the following manner:

1. The draft should be double-spaced so that handwritten corrections may be easily and clearly inserted.

2. Pages should be numbered consecutively.

3. A heading or subheading should not be separated from the first two lines of the summary that follows it when falling at the bottom of a page.

4. Include all materials that will be attached when final, formal minutes are distributed.

It is good practice (and usually required) to present the presiding officer with a typewritten draft of the minutes. If this is not feasible, then you should present the draft to your supervisor before typing the final copy.

<pre>
                    Editorial Scheduling Meeting

                         October 16, 19--

The weekly editorial scheduling meeting of Friday, October 16,
convened at 10 a.m. in the conference room. The presiding officer
was Amanda Billings. Members of the staff present included Robert
Desmond, Carl Edwards, Denise Jameson, Martha Nichols, and Philip
Thompson. Roger Lochman was unable to attend.

The minutes of the previous meeting, held on Friday, October 9,
were read and accepted. There were no corrections or omissions.

Mrs. Billings reported that the Corporation is looking to the office
products line to balance the shortfall in sales expected in the
Secondary Education Division. She asked that everyone keep this
goal in mind when ambitious schedules are established for new
projects.

Robert Desmond informed the staff that he is preparing an analysis of
the titles in progress in relation to their marketability, production
costs, production schedules, and longevity. He requested that each
editor submit a summary of costs to date for freelance services.

Carl Edwards reemphasized the need for constant, even workflow so
that both editorial and production functions will proceed efficiently.
He will be free to meet with any editors who wish to discuss flow
of manuscript to composition.

Amanda Billings reminded everyone that they must submit their ap-
propriate sections of the formal publishing plans for the office
products line to her by October 23.

The staff voted to reject a manuscript entitled DICTIONARIES: FRIENDS
OR FOES? that was circulated among them during September. The vote
was unanimous.

Denise Jameson raised the question again as to when a new editor
will be hired to replace Tom Westman. Due to the ambitious schedules
and shorthanded staff, this situation should be addressed as soon as
possible.

Mrs. Billings requested that Mr. Desmond and Mr. Edwards submit a
preliminary budget for 1984 to her by December 1.

Mr. Desmond gave Amanda Billings a new manuscript he received this
week from a retired linguistics professor. His preliminary reaction
to the proposal is that it would be better suited for the College
Division. The manuscript will be routed in the normal fashion, and
a decision will be made at the December 2 meeting.

The next meeting of the editorial staff will be held on Friday,
October 23.

The meeting was adjourned at 11:30 a.m.
</pre>

Minutes

Either person will be able to weed out any misinterpretations or extremely sensitive material that should not be published.

Final copy.   The final copy may be single- or double-spaced. Check copies of previous minutes for your organization's preferred style. The paper used also depends on precedent. Some groups have specially printed stationery for official minutes, while others use white bond paper of second-sheet quality.

When designing your minutes, refrain from using distracting symbols or excessive, heavy lines to mark different topics of discussion or to separate portions of the meeting. Make sure that significant points are easily identifiable in the typewritten minutes, but do not overdo it. Simple, straightforward documents will be much more attractive than pages marred with repetitive asterisks, ellipses, and underscores. Most minutes today are written in a narrative style, compared with the perfunctory style once used. Because of this significant change, it is especially important that your summaries of the discussions succinctly express the scope of the conversations. If you have not conveyed what went on during the meeting, your efforts have been for naught. See the preceding illustration for an example of acceptable official minutes.

The importance of developing the proper dictation and transcription techniques cannot be stressed enough. Once you have mastered these skills at maximum speed and efficiency you must produce a final document that is attractively presented, free of errors, and styled in acceptable business form. The next chapter provides written and visual guidance toward that end.

3

Styling Business Documents

INTRODUCTION TO THE FORMATTING
OF BUSINESS DOCUMENTS

In the Introduction to their book *In Search of Excellence: Lessons from America's Best-Run Companies*, Thomas J. Peters and Robert H. Waterman, Jr. inform us that "one of the main clues to corporate excellence has come to be. . .incidents of unusual effort on the part of apparently ordinary employees. When we found not one but a host of such incidents, we were pretty certain that we were on the track of an exceptional situation. What's more, we were fairly sure we would find sustained financial performance that was as exceptional as the employees' performance." (New York: Harper & Row, 1982, p. xvii.)

Product quality and reliability, service to the consumer, and in Peters and Waterman's words, "productivity through people" are the linchpins of corporate success and of individual success within the corporate entity. Since the secretary and the executive work in close cooperation to achieve corporate and individual goals in business, the remarks made by Peters and Waterman are clearly pertinent to your overall function. But what does all of this have to do with a routine daily activity such as the preparation of executive-generated documents? First of all, it is a well-known fact that paperwork and meetings consume the greater part of an executive's day. As a result of the first activity, you are called on to spend much of your own time typewriting or keyboarding the executive's letters, memorandums, and reports. This expenditure of time costs the company money: it has been estimated that the cost of one business letter is now about $10.00, including managerial and secretarial time, supplies, and postage fees. And costs are expected to climb every year. (For example, in 1979 the cost of a single letter was a little over $5.00, while in 1974 it was only about $3.00.) Multiply the current cost of $10.00 by the total number of letters generated in your office alone in one year and you're into Big Money.

Secondly, the appearance of your outgoing documents has a direct impact on the recipients' perception of your company's product quality and reliability, not to mention the caliber of its personnel. How can one presume that a company's products are excellent and its employees competent if its routine business communications are improperly formatted, full of errors, or sloppily corrected? In short, an unacceptable written communication reflects adversely on you, the executive for whom you work, and the corporation. Keeping these things in mind, you have a daily opportunity to exhibit in your typewritten documents exceptional concern for quality, neatness, and accuracy—tangible indicators of your company's style and substance. With every outgoing letter, memorandum, press release, or report you should show the recipients that yours is a top-of-the-line corporation. The forthcoming sections of this chapter are intended to assist you in translating dictated or handwritten material into a keyboarded format that will convey a visual, as well as a written message to the reader. The visual message—indicated by correct format, total neatness, absence of errors, and irreproachable grammar—is this: our company and all of its employees from the chief executive officer to the lowest-ranking worker are quality-conscious, and our concern for quality ranges from our most sophisticated product to our most routine piece of outgoing business mail.

BUSINESS LETTERS

The following styles are most often used in modern corporate correspondence: the Block Letter, the separate elements of which are positioned flush with the left margin; the Simplified Letter, also flush left in format but lacking a salutation and a complimentary close; the Modified Block Letter and the Modified Semi-block Letter, some elements of which are indented or are placed near or to the right; and the Executive Letter, the inside address of which appears flush left after the complimentary close and the signature space. The Hanging-indented Letter, also discussed herein, is most often used in direct-mail sales, advertising, and product promotion. The half-sheet is used for very brief notes. All of these are illustrated in full-page facsimile form on pages 159–166.

Major Parts of Business Letters

The major parts of most business letters are the date line, the inside address, the salutation, the message, the complimentary close, and the signature block. Ancillary elements included when needed or according to corporate policy include a reference line, special mailing instructions, special handling instructions, an attention line, a subject line, writer/typist initials, an enclosure notation, a copy notation, and a postscript. These elements are discussed in a separate subsection following this one.

Date line.   The date line includes the month written out in full (i.e., it is neither abbreviated nor styled in Arabic numerals), the day in Arabic numerals, a comma, and the full year also in numerals: January 15, 1992. You may position the date two to six lines beneath the last line of the printed corporate letterhead, depending on the estimated length of the letter or on the guidelines in your company's correspondence manual. Three-line spacing is the most flexible choice, with extra space added between the date and the first line of the inside address if the letter is rather short. The date is positioned flush to the left in the Block and Simplified Letters; about five spaces to the right of center, in the exact center, or flush right in the Modified Block and the Modified Semi-block Letters; and flush right in the Executive and Hanging-indented Letters.

Inside address.   The inside address, the second essential letter element, includes the recipient's courtesy title (such as *Ms., Dr.,* or *Mr.*) or honorific (such as *Esq.,* with which one never uses *Mr., Ms., Miss,* or *Mrs.*), and his or her full name on line one; the recipient's corporate title (such as *Vice President, Marketing*), if required, on the next line; the recipient's official corporate affiliation (such as *National Broadcasting Corporation*) on the next line; the street address on another line; and the city, state, and Zip Code on the last line. Include suite, apartment, or room numbers on the street address line if necessary. If the address includes an intracompany mail stop number such as MS 2B 31A, do not include that number on the address line; instead, put it after the company name with at least two spaces intervening. If the letter is addressed to a corporation rather than to an individual, the full corporate name appears on line one followed by a departmental designation (if required) on the next line, and the full address on subsequent lines. In all letter styles, the inside address is positioned flush left in blocked, single-spaced format. In all letter styles except the Executive, the inside address is the second element after the date line. (In the Executive Letter, the inside address appears at the bottom left after the complimentary close and signature space.) You may position the inside address from eight to twelve lines beneath the line on which the date appears, except in the Simplified Letter in which you must place the inside address exactly three lines below the date. Examples of the wording of typical inside addresses are:

Ms. Joan Goodwin
Vice President, Sales
CCC Corporation   MS 2A 341C
1234 Matthews Street   Suite 34
City, US 98765

Joan Goodwin, MD
Chief, Emergency Department
City Hospital
44 Hospital Drive
City, US 98765

Joan Goodwin, Esq.
Goodwin, Talbot & Kendall
One Court Street
City, US 98765

Ms. Joan Goodwin
Vice President, Research and
  Development
CCC Chemicals
One Industrial Drive
City, US 98765

Common Questions about Inside Addresses

1. How do I style the addressee's name and business title?

Check the letterhead or the signature block of previous correspondence for correct spelling, or check with the writer. If all else fails, call the recipient's secretary for spelling verification. An incorrect title or a misspelled name creates a very negative impression on the recipient of a letter.

2. When may I use abbreviations in an inside address?

You may use abbreviated courtesy titles and honorifics such as *Mr., Ms., Mrs., Dr., MD,* and *Esq.* Do not abbreviate company names, departmental designations, or corporate titles. You may, however, use abbreviations such as *Co., Inc.,* or *Ltd.* if they have been so used on the printed letterhead and form part of the official company name. Words such as *Street* may be abbreviated to *St.* If you are addressing large numbers of letters for automated sorting, use the capitalized, unpunctuated abbreviations recommended by the U.S. Postal Service. See the section on addressing envelopes for automated mail sorting in this chapter. In all cases, however, you should use the capitalized, unpunctuated two-letter state abbreviations recommended by the Postal Service.

3. How do I handle overly long lines in an inside address?

When an addressee's title (such as *Vice-president, Research and Development*) overruns the center of the page, carry over part of the title to another line and indent it by two spaces, as:

Vice-president,
  Research and Development

4. How many lines should an inside address have?

The inside address should not exceed 5 full lines (runovers excepted).

5. How do I style addresses involving street numbers under *three?*

Write out in full numbers up to *three:* One Washington Street; Two Park Street; except in the case of fractional numbers: 2¹/₂ Elm Street. Use Arabic numerals for *three* and above: 3 Marlborough Street; 8 Carson Terrace.

6. How do I style numbered streets such as *42nd Street?*

You may use ordinals or you may write out the number in full: 500 42nd Street *or* 500 Forty-second Street; 200 5th Ave. *or* 200 Fifth Avenue; 1234 19th St., NW *or* 1234 Nineteenth Street, NW.

7. Where do I position suite numbers, mail stops, and so forth?

Put suite, room, and apartment numbers on the street address line, two spaces after the last word on the line, as:

500 Fifth Avenue   Suite 44V

Mail stop indicators, however, appear two spaces after the last word on the corporate name line:

CCC Corporation   MS 12Z 451

8. How do I style an inside address involving two or more recipients having different addresses?

Type two (or more) complete sets of names and addresses, one after the other in alphabetical order or in order of importance, with double spacing separating the units one from another. Single-space each unit internally. If you are using a word processor, command the machine to print out two originals, one for each addressee. If you are using a conventional typewriter, make a photocopy of the original for each recipient and keep the original as a file copy. Ensure that the photocopies are clear and sharp. Use separate envelopes for the letters, of course, and include only one name and address thereon.

Salutation.   The salutation, used with all letter styles except the Simplified, appears two lines below the last line of the inside address, flush with the left margin. In the Executive Letter the salutation appears from two to six lines below the line on which the date has been typed, depending on the length of the message. The first word of the salutation as well as the first word of a proper name or title is capitalized:

Dear Dr. Lee:

My dear Dr. Lee:

Dear Joan:

Ladies and Gentlemen:

Your Excellency:

Gentlepeople:

Most Reverend Sir:

Dear Engineering Department:

A colon typically punctuates the salutation. However, if you are using a minimal punctuation system (the so-called "open punctuation system") in order to reduce keystrokes, you may leave the salutation unpunctuated. Remember, though, that when you leave the salutation unpunctuated you also must leave the complimentary close and any enclosure or copy notations unpunctuated.

Common Questions about Salutations

1. What's the current usage status of *Dear Sir* and *Dear Madam?*

Dear Sir is considered passé in general business correspondence: it is now used only in form letters and in letters to important personages such as a President-elect of the United States. The same goes for *Dear Madam* (in addition, some women find its use offensive). See the forms of address section in this chapter for detailed guidelines regarding the use of these two salutations.

2. What do I do when I can't determine the gender of the recipient from the written or typed signature on previous correspondence?

You can simply omit the courtesy title *Mr., Ms., Mrs.,* or *Miss* and say: Dear Lee Lawson. Or you can use the neuter abbreviation *M.* before the person's surname: Dear M. Lawson.

3. How do I address a mixed-gender group?

Style the salutation collectively, as: Dear S&S Engineers, Dear Engineering Managers, Dear Management, Dear Chemists, Ladies and Gentlemen, and so on.

4. Are people really using the gender-neutral alternatives to *Gentlemen?*

Yes, and some of them (aside from the patterns shown above) are: Gentlepeople, Dear People, Dear Roth Corporation (or whatever the company name is), Dear Salespeople, and so on.

Message.   The message begins two lines below the salutation in all letter styles except the Simplified, in which it begins three lines below the subject line. (See the subsection on subject lines and the full-page Simplified Letter facsimile for details.) Paragraphs in conventional business letters are usually single-spaced themselves, with double spacing separating them one from another. Only in very short letters on half-sheet stationery is double spacing used today. If the message of a very short letter is double-spaced, you must indent the first line of each paragraph by six spaces. Paragraphs in the Block, Simplified, and Modified Block Letters are typed flush with the left margin. The first line of each paragraph in the Executive Letter may be blocked flush left or indented, depending on the preference of the writer or the typist. In the Modified Semi-block Letter, the first line of a paragraph is indented about five or six spaces. In the Hanging-indented Letter the first line of each paragraph is positioned flush left with subsequent lines block indented by five or six spaces, thus creating a stylish visual effect.

If the message contains an enumerated list you should block and center the listed matter by five or six more spaces, right and left. Single-space the individual units in the list but allow two spaces between each unit. Tables also should be centered on the page. Long quoted matter (i.e., a quotation exceeding six typed lines) must be centered on the page and single-spaced internally. No quotation marks are used unless there is a quotation within a quotation (see the rules for the use of quotation marks in Chapter One herein). Use double spacing above and below lists, tables, and long quotations to set the material off from the rest of the message.

If the message exceeds one page, use a blank continuation sheet matching the letterhead sheet in size, color, texture, and weight. At least three lines of the message must be carried over to the continuation sheet: at no time should the complimentary close and signature block stand alone there. The margin settings used on subsequent sheets should match those chosen for the letterhead sheet. Allow at least six blank lines from the top edge of the sheet before typing the heading, which includes the name of the recipient (courtesy title + first name and surname or courtesy title + surname only), page number, and date. The continuation sheet heading may be single-spaced and blocked flush with the left margin:

Page 2
Ms. Jean McGhee
June 24, 19—

or, it may be spread across the top of the page, beginning flush left, and ending flush right:

Ms. Jean McGhee   -2-   June 24, 19—

The flush left block style is required with the Block and Simplified Letters. The spread is used with the Modified Block, Modified Semi-block,

Executive, and Hanging-indented Letters. With the spread, the page number is centered and enclosed with two hyphens, either set tight with the numeral as shown above or spaced: – 2 –. Never abbreviate the date on a continuation sheet.

Complimentary close.　The complimentary close is used in all letters except the Simplified. The complimentary close is typewritten two lines beneath the last message line. The first word of the complimentary close is capitalized:

Very truly yours,	Sincerely yours,	Regards,
Yours very truly,	Yours sincerely,	Best regards,

A comma typically punctuates a complimentary close. If, however, you are using a minimal punctuation system, you may omit the comma. Remember, though, that when the comma is omitted here, the colon also must be dropped in the salutation, and ancillary notations such as enclosure notations and copy notations must go unpunctuated. Placement of the complimentary close varies with the style of letter chosen. Table 1 lists choices of letter styles and provides indicators of complimentary close page placement for each style.

You should use the complimentary close indicated by the writer because the chosen wording often reflects the nature of the relationship between writer and recipient. For instance, "Very truly yours" is rather neutral though somewhat formal in tone, while "Respectfully yours" indicates the high degree of formality often required in letters to heads of state or high-ranking clerics. "Sincerely" is much more informal, and wording such as "Best ever" or "Cheers" indicates particularly friendly, close relations between the writer and the recipient. Table 2 lists and discusses a number of frequently used complimentary closes.

Sometimes the relationship between the writer and the recipient may change from close to distant, or from friendly to hostile. The tone of the

Table 1.　Complimentary Close

Letter Style	Complimentary Close Position
Block	flush left
Simplified	none
Modified Block	center page aligned with date *or* 5
Modified Semi-block	spaces to right of center page;
Hanging-indented	aligned with date *or* flush right aligned with date; position of date dictates placement of complimentary close
Executive	flush right aligned with date

Table 2. **Complimentary Close Wording**

Tone	Example
most informal: indicates close personal relationship between writer and recipient	Cheers Regards Best Regards Best ever As ever Kindest regards Kindest wishes
informal and friendly: indicates personal relationship between writer and recipient who may or may not be on a first-name basis	Yours Cordially Most cordially Cordially yours
friendly but rather neutral: appropriate to all but the most formal letters	Sincerely Sincerely yours Very sincerely Most sincerely Very sincerely yours Most sincerely yours Yours sincerely
polite, neutral, and somewhat formal: often used in law office correspondence as well as in general business correspondence	Very truly yours Yours very truly Yours truly
highly formal: indicates that the recipient outranks the writer; often used in high-level diplomatic, governmental, or ecclesiastical correspondence	Respectfully Respectfully yours Yours respectfully Most respectfully Very respectfully

message may indicate such a change, but you cannot always be sure. This is yet another reason for you always to use the closing designated by the writer.

Signature block.   The signature block indicates the writer's name and possibly his or her corporate title, if the title does not already appear in the printed letterhead. With the Block, Modified Block, and Modified Semi-block Letters, this matter is aligned vertically with at least four or five blank spaces intervening between the complimentary close and the first line of the typed signature block to allow for the written signature. Leave even more space here if your executive's signature tends toward the flamboyant. With the Hanging-indented and Executive Letters, the type-written signature block is often omitted, with space left for a written signature. The Simplified Letter features a typed signature block positioned flush with the left margin, at least five lines below the last line of the message. The writer signs in the space allotted. The executive's name

Table 3. **Signature Block**

Letter Style	Vertical Spacing from Last Message Line	Page Placement	Placement of Writer's Name and Corporate Title within Typed Signature Block
Block	2 lines	flush left	writer's name (line 1) writer's title (line 2)
Simplified	at least 5 lines	flush left	writer's name and title all on line 1
Modified Block, Modified Semi-block	2 lines	aligned with date and complimentary close: center, right of center, or flush right	writer's name (line 1) writer's title (line 2)
Executive, Hanging-indented	2 lines	flush right	written signature only if writer's name forms part of the printed letterhead

and corporate title are typed in capital letters with a spaced hyphen separating them.

A rather infrequently used signature block is the one in which the company name appears after the complimentary close, with the writer's name and title appearing after the written signature. This style is used primarily with small business direct-mail advertising and in some contracts. Skip two lines between the complimentary close and the company name. Type the company name in capital letters. Skip five lines for the written signature and then type the writer's name in capital and lower-case letters followed on the last line by the writer's title:

Very truly yours,

HOWARD PLUMBING CONTRACTORS, INC.

John R. Howard
President

Table 3 explains the page placement of typed signature blocks with respect to the chosen letter style. The full-page letter facsimiles on pages 159–166 illustrate various letter styles and the placement of the complimentary close and signature block in them.

Houghton Mifflin Company

One Beacon Street, Boston, Massachusetts 02108
(617) 725-5000   Cable HOUGHTON

September 20, 1991
Reference 12A 90C 17D

Ms. Linda Martinez
Production Manager
E-Z Typesetters Inc.
1200 Simpson Street
City, US 98765

Dear Ms. Martinez:

Reference Line: Modified Block or Modified Semi-block Letter

Ancillary Elements in Business Letters

The following elements are optional in a business letter, with inclusion or omission dependent upon the nature of the letter or the writer's wishes: a reference line, special mailing instructions, special handling instructions, an attention line, a subject line, writer/typist initials, a copy indicator, an enclosure notation, and a postscript. Forthcoming subsections discuss and illustrate the page placement and styling of these elements.

Reference line.   This notation, including data such as a file, policy, invoice, or order number, may be included if the recipient has requested it or if the writer knows that its inclusion will facilitate the filing of correspondence. The reference line may be centered on the page between one and four lines under the date line. However, with the Block and Simplified Letters the reference line is always aligned flush left, one line below the date. (See the facsimile.) If you include a reference line on the letterhead sheet you also must insert it on every continuation sheet. When using the Block style, place the reference line on line four of the continuation sheet heading:

Page 2
Ms. Laura LaValle
March 15, 19—
Z–123–456–7

When using the Modified Block or the Modified Semi-block Letters, include the reference line one space below the date:

Ms. Laura LaValle   -2-   March 15, 19–
                                                           Z–123–456–7

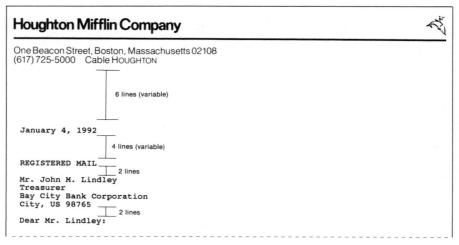

Houghton Mifflin Company

One Beacon Street, Boston, Massachusetts 02108
(617) 725-5000   Cable HOUGHTON

6 lines (variable)

January 4, 1992

4 lines (variable)

REGISTERED MAIL

2 lines

Mr. John M. Lindley
Treasurer
Bay City Bank Corporation
City, US 98765

2 lines

Dear Mr. Lindley:

Special Mailing Instructions

Avoid using the Simplified, Executive, or Hanging-indented Letters with material requiring the inclusion of reference lines.

Special mailing instructions.   Indicate on the letter itself as well as on the envelope any special mailing instructions designated by the writer. These include certification, registration, special delivery, or overseas air mail. Such instructions are typed in capital letters, flush left, about four line spaces below the line on which the date appears and about two lines above the first line of the inside address. Vertical line spacing between the date and the special mailing instructions may vary slightly, depending on the length of the message and page space available.

Special handling instructions.   Sometimes a writer generates a letter requiring either a PERSONAL or a CONFIDENTIAL indicator. These instructions are typewritten in capital letters on the envelope and on the letter itself. The designation PERSONAL means that the letter is an eyes-only communications for the recipient. CONFIDENTIAL means that the recipient and any other persons so authorized may open and read the letter. Special handling notations are placed about four lines below the date and from two to four lines above the first line of the inside address. If the message is quite brief, you may place the notation as many as six lines below the date. PERSONAL and CONFIDENTIAL notations are always positioned flush with the left margin. If a special mailing instruction such as CERTIFIED MAIL has been included too, put the special handling instruction below it and block both of them flush with the left margin as shown in the next facsimile.

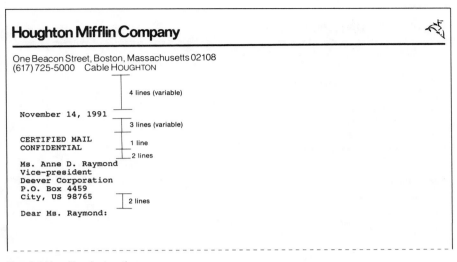

Special Handling Instructions

Attention line.   Letters addressed to a corporation, a department, or an organization collectively but at the same time routed to the attention of a specific person within the group require insertion of an attention line. Block this line flush left in all letter styles except in the Modified Semiblock Letter where the line is centered. Position the attention line two lines below the inside address and two lines above the salutation. Never

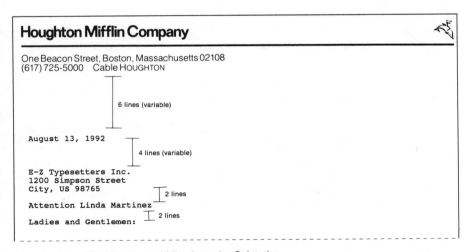

Attention Line: Block Letter and Mixed-gender Salutation

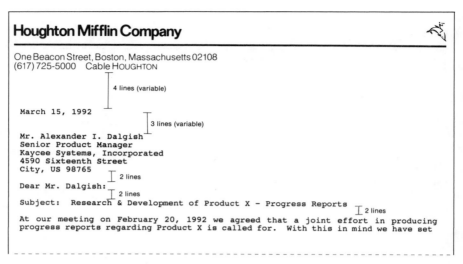

Houghton Mifflin Company

One Beacon Street, Boston, Massachusetts 02108
(617) 725-5000   Cable HOUGHTON

4 lines (variable)

March 15, 1992

3 lines (variable)

Mr. Alexander I. Dalgish
Senior Product Manager
Kaycee Systems, Incorporated
4590 Sixteenth Street
City, US 98765

2 lines

Dear Mr. Dalgish:

2 lines

Subject: Research & Development of Product X - Progress Reports

2 lines

At our meeting on February 20, 1992 we agreed that a joint effort in producing
progress reports regarding Product X is called for. With this in mind we have set

Subject Line: Block Letter

underscore an attention line. Use capital letters for the *A* in *Attention* and
for the first letters of the proper name that follows. Never abbreviate
Attention. Use a colon after *Attention,* or if you are using a minimal
punctuation system, drop the colon. Examples:

Attention: John Hodges

or with minimal punctuation:

Attention John Hodges

Never insert a period after an attention line. The salutation that follows
must be a collective one, for the letter is directed to a collective readership. Use a salutation such as *Gentlemen, Ladies and Gentlemen,* or *Dear
CCC Company.*

Subject line.   The subject line, an ancillary element in all letter stylings
except the Simplified in which it is required, presents the main thrust of
the message in as few words as possible. Typewritten in capital letters, it
appears three lines below the last line of the inside address and three lines
above the first line of the message in the Simplified Letter. In all other
letter styles the subject line appears two lines below the salutation and
two lines above the first line of the message. The subject line in all styles
except the Simplified may be introduced by the word *Subject* styled in
any one of the following ways, or the word may be omitted:

Subject: Pretrial Conference with Judge Baxter
SUBJECT: Pretrial Conference with Judge Baxter
SUBJECT: PRETRIAL CONFERENCE WITH JUDGE BAXTER

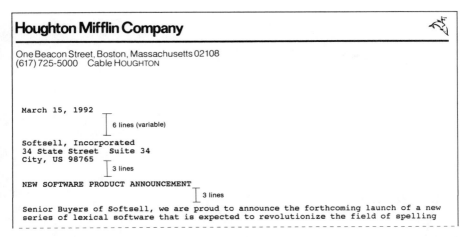

Houghton Mifflin Company

One Beacon Street, Boston, Massachusetts 02108
(617) 725-5000   Cable HOUGHTON

```
March 15, 1992
                  ⌐
                  | 6 lines (variable)
                  ⌐
Softsell, Incorporated
34 State Street   Suite 34
City, US 98765
                  | 3 lines
                  ⌐
NEW SOFTWARE PRODUCT ANNOUNCEMENT
                  | 3 lines
Senior Buyers of Softsell, we are proud to announce the forthcoming launch of a new
series of lexical software that is expected to revolutionize the field of spelling
```

Subject Line: Simplified Letter

In the Simplified Letter, you may not use the word *Subject.* Simply state the subject in capital letters:

PRETRIAL CONFERENCE WITH JUDGE BAXTER

In some law office correspondence, subject lines are introduced by the terms *In re:* or *Re:* but these terms are not used in modern general correspondence. Avoid insertion of a period after a subject line, and avoid using the Executive or Hanging-indented Letters in correspondence requiring this line.

Writer/typist initials.   The initials of the writer and/or typist are positioned flush left with the left margin two lines below the last line of the signature block in all letter styles. Most companies use two or three capitalized letters for the writer's name and two or three lowercase letters for the typist's name. Modern trends indicate omission of these initials unless someone other than the writer signs the letter or unless their inclusion is necessary for filing or output control purposes. In the Simplified Letter only the typist's initials appear. Examples:

MAR:ahs	MAR/as	MAR:AS	Michael A. Roberts: AS
MAR:as	MAR/ahs	MAR:AHS	Michael A. Roberts
mar:ahs	MR/as	MR:AS	AS

A letter to be signed by one person (such as a chief executive) but written or dictated by another (such as an executive assistant) and typed by the secretary bears three sets of initials styled as follows:

HTM:PTK:lc

Here, HTM stands for the chief executive, PTK stands for the executive assistant, and lc stands for the typist/secretary.

```
┌ ─ ─ ─ ─ ─ ─ ─ ─ ─ ─ ─ ─ ─ ─ ─ ─ ─ ─ ─ ─ ─ ─ ─ ─ ─ ─ ─ ─ ─ ─ ─ ─ ─ ─
│
│ and so we will expect to receive the final page proofs on January 19,
│ 19--. Many thanks for your adherence to our schedules.
│                                               2 lines ⊤
│                                                       ⊥ Sincerely yours,
│
│                                               4 lines ⊤
│
│                                                       ⊥
│                                               1 line ⊤ Christopher I. Kendall
│                                                         Production Manager
│                              ⊤ 2 lines
│ CIK: ahs                     ⊥
│                              ⊤ 2 lines
│ enclosures:   4              ⊥
│                                  ⊤ 2 lines
│ cc: Janet T. Booker              ⊥
│     Mary Y. Miller     ⊤ 1 line
│                        ⊥
```

Signature Block, Typists Initials, and Enclosure and Copy Indicators: Modified
Semi-block letter

Enclosure notation.   If a letter contains an enclosure or enclosures, type
a notation to this effect flush with the left margin two lines below the
writer/typist initials or two lines below the signature block if no such
initials have been included. Use any one of these styles:

conventional punctuation	minimal punctuation
Enclosures: 3	3 Enclosures
Enclosures (3)	Enclosure
3 encs.	3 encs
Enc. 3	encl
encl.	enc
enc.	encs
encs.	

Particularly important enclosures ought to be listed numerically and
described. Block and single-space such material:

    encs: 1. Proxy Statement
          2. P & L Statement, 1983–1984

If the enclosures themselves have not been clearly labeled as to subject
and content, affix to the material a self-adhesive sticker identifying each
one. To avoid confusion, use on the stickers the same descriptors used in
the typed enclosure notation. If materials referred to in the letter are to be
mailed under separate cover, indicate this fact:

    Separate Mailing: Press Kit
                       Media Reception Schedule

Copy notation.   Since photocopiers have all but replaced carbons, the abbreviation *cc* is now referred to as a *copy notation* or a *courtesy copy.* If included in a letter, this notation should be typed flush with the left margin, two lines below the signature block or two lines below any other notation preceding it. If used with writer/typist initials or enclosure notations, the copy notation usually appears last. Use any one of these styles:

conventional punctuation	**minimal punctuation**
cc: Harold T. Martin	cc Harold T. Martin
CC: Harold T. Martin	CC Harold T. Martin
cc: Mr. Martin	cc Mr. Martin
Mr. Peters	Mr. Peters
Mr. Smith	Mr. Smith
CC: Ms. Taylor	CC Ms. Taylor
Ms. Uhlander	Ms. Uhlander
Ms. Vest	Ms. Vest
cc: HTM	cc HTM
RWY	RWY
MCZ	MCZ

Multiple recipients are listed in alphabetical order according to full name or initials as shown above. If the writer so desires, give the copy recipient's full name and address:

single copy recipient
cc: Gene D. Dawson, Esq. (1 copy, Medical Claim)

several copy recipients
cc: Gene D. Dawson, Esq. (1 copy, Medical Claim)
    One Court Street   Suite 14
    City, US 98765
    Albert T. Goldberg, MD (1 copy, Discovery)
    Two Hospital Drive
    City, US 98765

Notice that double spacing separates each unit from the other, although the units are themselves single-spaced. If the writer wishes to send enclosures to the copy recipients, the enclosures are listed next to the names of the recipients.

A writer may wish that copies of a letter be distributed to others without that fact being revealed on the original. In this case, use *bcc* or *bcc:* before the names or initials of the recipients. The notation stands for *blind copy* or *blind courtesy copy* and appears only on the copies, either in the same position as the regular copy notation or in the top left corner of the letterhead sheet.

Postscript.   If a postscript must be appended to a letter, it is typed from two to four lines below the last notation. In the Block and Modified Block

Letters the postscript is set flush left. In other letter styles involving indented paragraphs, the postscript is indented exactly as the body paragraphs are. All postscripts are single-spaced, with margins matching those in the rest of the letter. In modern practice, it is now customary to omit the heading *P.S.* Have the writer initial all postscripts.

The Look of the Letter

Having discussed in detail all of the elements making up business letters, let us now turn to the matter of total visual impact. As soon as one opens a letter, one is immediately struck by its overall appearance on the page. Are the margins equal? Are the margins sufficient on right and left and at the top and bottom? One also notices and responds to the color and texture of the paper when holding the letter. Has the stationery been neatly folded and inserted into the envelope, or has it been untidily creased? Is the paper smudged or torn? Is the paper heavy enough to have withstood the impact of keystrokes, the ink of the printed letterhead, and the often rough handling of the mail system? Then, when one reads the letter, one immediately notices spelling and typographical errors, unsightly corrections, and ugly strikeovers, should they be present. As we have said before, the total letter is a product of your company. It is also a product of your skills as a secretary, and its look and feel should project a positive corporate image. This section discusses various ways by which you can enhance both product and image.

Margins and letter symmetry.   To achieve maximum balance and symmetry on the page, follow these rules:

1. Try to estimate the length of the letter before touching the keyboard. Read through the executive's handwritten notes, reread your shorthand notes, or listen to the electronically stored dictation to get a ballpark estimate of the word count.

2. Consider the inclusion of any long quotations, tables, or lists to be displayed within the running text. Inclusion of such material will affect your total format and will add to the amount of tabbing you must do.

3. Determine if any special characters such as Greek letters or scientific symbols and mathematical/chemical formulas are to be included.

4. Set your margins after you have completed steps 1 through 3. Use these guidelines: 1″ margins for lengthy letters of over 300 words or over 2 pages; $1\frac{1}{2}$″ margins for medium-length letters of about 100–250 words; and 2″ margins for short letters of 100 words or less. Note that the $1\frac{1}{2}$″ margin is the most commonly used setting.

5. Be sure to take into account the fact that the closing section of a letter usually encompasses 2″ of vertical page space or 10–12 lines plus the

bottom margin. Thus, you ought to reserve at least 1" (or 6 vertical line spaces) for the bottom margin, especially if printed matter has been included there as part of the letterhead. Letters overrunning the bottom margin indicate amateurish work.

6. If you are using a word processing system follow the guidelines specific to that system in order to format correct bottom margins and continuation pages.

Be sure that the marginal settings on the continuation sheet match those on the letterhead. Avoid setting the stops to the inflexible six-inch typed line: every letter differs in content, length, and purpose so you must be flexible enough in your own formatting to accomodate these differences. A rigid line length setting is useful only in printing out multiple form letters, the content and length of which will remain relatively constant once the prototype has been input into memory.

Paper.   Top quality stationery is an indicator of the company's concern about its public image. Factors to consider when purchasing business papers include weight, texture, and color. The paper ought to be heavy enough to withstand corrections without tearing, buckling, or disintegrating. Likewise, it should withstand the pressure of keystrokes without pitting. At the same time it should be readily foldable without cracking. The ink from the printed letterhead must not bleed through onto the obverse side. The texture should be such that the typed characters are clear and undistorted and the written signatures and any handwritten symbols or signs appear smooth and even without blotching. If colored

Table 4. Business Papers

Business Paper	Application	Weight
standard	correspondence	24 or 20
executive (Monarch)	CEO and other top management correspondence	24 or 20
half-sheets	very short letters	20 or 24
professional	short letters	24 or 20
bill	invoices, billings	24 or 20
manifold or onionskin	overseas air or carbon copies	13 or 9
memorandum	interoffice communications	20 or 16
continuation sheets	communications exceeding one page	weight must match that of the first sheet

stationery is selected, its dye should be fast so that the paper will remain in good condition over time without fading.

The letterhead is printed on the felt side of the paper—i.e., the side from which you can read the watermark. In this connection, remember that you should type on the felt side of the continuation sheet. As we have said before, all continuation sheets and envelopes should match the letterhead in color, texture, and weight. Paper weight equals the weight in pounds of one ream cut to standard size. The heaviest paper weight is 24 for business correspondence, and the lightest is 9. Weights differ according to application in the office as shown in Table 4.

Prices of paper vary according to weight and composition. Prices also fluctuate widely from time to time. The one constant is that paper prices seem to rise from year to year. Hence, you should protect your supplies for the sake of cost-effectiveness. Store your stationery in the original boxes with the tops on. Store only a small supply in your desk stationery drawer; otherwise, you can expect deterioration and soiling over time.

Letter Facsimiles

The following illustrations are full-page facsimiles of the traditionally used business letters. The illustrations are shown in this sequence: the Simplified Letter, the Block Letter, the Modified Block Letter, the Modified Semi-block Letter, the Executive Letter, the Hanging-indented Letter, and the Half-sheet Letter. Within each illustration you will find detailed guidelines regarding the proper margin settings, the type of spacing used within and between paragraphs, and the positioning of the essential and ancillary elements of the letters.

Following is a detailed discussion of envelope addressing procedures, envelope sizes according to business application, computerized mail handling as it affects envelope addressing techniques, and abbreviations recommended for use by heavy commercial mailers to facilitate fast sorts and delivery.

Envelopes

Envelopes must match the letterhead and continuation sheets in color, texture, and weight. The standard $8\frac{1}{2}'' \times 11''$ stationery will fit the Numbers $6\frac{3}{4}$, 9, and 10 commercial, window, or overseas air envelopes. Executive stationery fits the Monarch envelope. Half-sheet paper fits the Baronial, or $3\frac{5}{8}'' \times 6\frac{1}{2}''$ envelope. Table 5 provides standard envelope configurations and sizes.

Envelope addresses must include these data:

addressee	**sender**
full name	full name
street address	street address
city, state, Zip Code	city, state, Zip Code

Houghton Mifflin Company

One Beacon Street, Boston, Massachusetts 02108
(617) 725-5000   Cable HOUGHTON

Trade & Reference Division

January 4, 1992

Ms. Barbara C. Mackie
HCI Corporation   MS 34A 78N
One State Street
City, US 98765

ADMINISTRATIVE MANAGEMENT SOCIETY'S SIMPLIFIED LETTER

Ms. Mackie, this is a facsimile of the Simplified Letter recommended for many
years by the Administrative Management Society. It is a lean, clean format that
saves you time through fewer keystrokes and less keyboard movement, saves money,
boosts productivity, and enhances the look of the outgoing product.

The date is flush with the left margin from three to six lines beneath the
letterhead. The inside address, also flush left, is typed three lines below the
date to facilitate the use of window envelopes. There is no salutation; this
solves the gender question in letters to correspondents who have signed previous
letters with their initials and a surname only. (In the inside address of a
letter to such a correspondent, you too can omit the courtesy title and type the
person's initials plus the surname.)

Type a capitalized subject line three vertical line spaces below the last line
of the inside address. Position the subject line flush with the left margin and
omit the words <u>Subject</u> or <u>Re</u>. The subject line encapsulates the main topic of
the message and should be brief and to the point. It is also a convenient filing
tool.

The message begins three lines below the subject line. All paragraphs are set
flush left. Paragraphs are single-spaced internally. Double spacing separates
one paragraph from another.   The first paragraph opens with use of the
recipient's name in direct address as shown here--a polite way of engaging the
recipient's interest at the outset.

Enumerated lists and tabular data, if included, are set flush left with double
spacing separating one item from another. Items are single-spaced internally.
Long quotations are block indented by six character spaces. Such quoted matter
is single-spaced internally, with double spacing separating it top and bottom
from the rest of the message.

If the letter exceeds one page, use a continuation sheet matching the letterhead
in size, color, texture, and weight. Begin the heading at least six vertical

Atlanta / Dallas / Geneva, Illinois / Lawrenceville, New Jersey / Palo Alto / London

The Simplified Letter

Ms. Mackie
Page 2
January 4, 1992

lines below the top left edge of the page. The flush-left heading includes the recipient's name on line one, the page number on line two, and the full date on line three. Maintain continuation sheet margins and paragraph style as described for the first sheet. At least three message lines must be carried over to the continuation sheet: at no time should the signature block stand alone there.

The Simplified Letter has no complimentary close. This feature saves keystrokes. Type the writer's name and corporate title in capital letters at least five or six lines below the last line of the message, and flush with the left margin. A spaced hyphen separates the writer's name and title. The writer then signs the letter in the space allowed.

Skip two spaces and typewrite your own initials flush with the left margin. There is no need to include the writer's initials in this notation. If a courtesy copy or enclosure notation is required, enter the material two lines beneath your initials.

The Administrative Management Society tells us that "the Simplified Letter stresses real economy of motion for secretaries. Its use results in better looking letters with less effort. It will give them the pride of producing more effective letters, and will result in increased productivity of a company's secretarial force--which ultimately saves money."

We recommend the Simplified Letter to all of our readers, and especially to those who produce high volumes of correspondence.

Jane M. Doe

JANE M. DOE - SENIOR EDITOR

lpc

cc   Marietta K. Lowe
      Roberta Y. Peterson
      Candice S. Taylor

enclosures (7)

Houghton Mifflin Company

One Beacon Street, Boston, Massachusetts 02108   Trade & Reference Division
(617) 725-5000   Cable HOUGHTON

January 4, 1992

Mr. Peter C. Cunningham
Vice-president, Operations
CCC Chemicals, Ltd.
321 Park Avenue
City, US 98765

Dear Mr. Cunningham:

Subject: Block Letter Style

This is the Block Letter--a format featuring elements aligned with the left margin.
The date is typed from two to six (or more) lines below the letterhead, depending on
the length of the message. The inside address may be typed from two to four lines
below the date line, also depending on message length. Double spacing is used between
the inside address and the salutation. A subject line, if used, appears two lines
below the salutation and two lines above the first message line. Had an attention line
been used here, it would have been positioned two lines below the last line of the
inside address and two lines above the salutation.

The paragraphs are single-spaced internally with double spacing separating them from
each other. Displayed matter such as enumerations and long quotations are indented by
six character spaces. Units within enumerations and any quoted matter are single-
spaced internally with double spacing setting them off from the rest of the text.

The heading for a continuation sheet begins six lines from the top edge of the page.
The heading is blocked flush with the left margin:

Page 2
Mr. Peter C. Cunningham
January 4, 1992

Skip two lines from the last line of the message to the complimentary close. Allow at
least four blank lines for the written signature. Block the typed signature and
corporate title under the complimentary close. Insert ancillary notations such as the
typist's initials two spaces below the last line of the signature block.

Sincerely yours,

John M. Swanson
Executive Vice-president

JMS:lpc

Enclosures: 4

Atlanta / Dallas / Geneva, Illinois / Lawrenceville, New Jersey / Palo Alto / London

The Block Letter

Houghton Mifflin Company

One Beacon Street, Boston, Massachusetts 02108   Trade & Reference Division
(617) 725-5000   Cable HOUGHTON

                                                        January 14, 1992

CERTIFIED MAIL
CONFIDENTIAL

Sarah H. O'Day, Esq.
O'Day, Ryan & Sweeney
One Court Street
City, US 98765

Dear Ms. O'Day:

SUBJECT: MODIFIED BLOCK LETTER

This is the Modified Block Letter, the features of which are similar to those of the
Block Letter with the exception of the positioning of the date line, the complimentary
close, and the typewritten signature block.   The positioning of the date line
determines the placement of the complimentary close and the signature block, both of
which must be vertically aligned with the date. The date itself may be centered on the
page, placed about five spaces to the right of center as shown here, or set flush with
the right margin. Any one of these positions is acceptable.

The subject line, typed here in capital letters, is set flush left. Had an attention
line been used, it too would have been positioned flush with the left margin. Note
that the special mailing and handling notations appear flush left, two lines above the
first line of the inside address.

The continuation sheet heading, unlike that of the Simplified and Block Letters, is
spread across the top of the page, at least six vertical lines beneath the top edge:

Ms. O'Day   - 2 -   January 14, 1992

Notice the centered page number enclosed by spaced hyphens. Another way of styling the
page number is to enclose it with hyphens set tight to the number. Either style is
entirely acceptable.

The complimentary close--aligned with the date--appears two lines below the last
message line. At least four blank lines have been allowed for the written signature.
The typed signature block is then aligned with the complimentary close.

Ancillary notations such as typist's initials, enclosure notations, and lists of copy
recipients are placed two lines below the signature block, flush with the left margin.

                                        Very truly yours,

                                        Kathleen N. Lear

                                        Kathleen N. Lear
                                        Permissions Editor

KNL:lpc

                Atlanta / Dallas / Geneva, Illinois / Lawrenceville, New Jersey / Palo Alto / London

The Modified Block Letter

Houghton Mifflin Company

One Beacon Street, Boston, Massachusetts 02108
(617) 725-5000   Cable HOUGHTON

Trade & Reference Division

```
                                        February 14, 1992
                                        Policy Number 34E 123W 9U

PERSONAL

Dr. David J. Peters
State Insurance Corporation
4556 Hightower Boulevard
City, US 98765

Dear Dr. Peters:
```

              SUBJECT: MODIFIED SEMI-BLOCK LETTER

   This is the Modified Semi-block Letter, many elements of which are positioned near or to the right or are indented. The date line determines the placement of the complimentary close and signature block which must be vertically aligned under it. Here, the date appears about five spaces to the right of center; it could have been centered or aligned so as to end flush with the right margin.

   A policy number (i.e., a reference line) has been used herein: notice that it is aligned one space below the date line. The subject line is centered on the page--a required placement in this letter style. It could have been typed in capital and lowercase letters, though.

   Notice that the first line of each new paragraph is indented by six spaces. Susequent lines are set flush left. Displayed data and long quotations are block indented by six more spaces:

    1. A continuation sheet heading is spaced across the top of the page six lines below the edge, as shown in the Modified Block Letter.

    2. The complimentary close appears two lines below the last message line, aligned with the date. At least four blank lines are allowed for the signature. The typed signature block, aligned with the complimentary close, includes the writer's name and title on separate lines.

    3. Ancillary notations appear two lines below the last line of the signature block, positioned flush left.

   If a postcard is included it is indented just like the message paragraphs are. There is no need to introduce it with the heading "P.S."

```
                                        Sincerely yours,

                                        Donna W. Reardon
                                        Personnel Manager

lpc
```

Atlanta / Dallas / Geneva, Illinois / Lawrenceville, New Jersey / Palo Alto / London

The Modified Semi-block Letter

Houghton Mifflin Company

One Beacon Street, Boston, Massachusetts 02108
(617) 725-5000   Cable HOUGHTON

October 14, 1991

Dear Mr. Fitzpatrick:

This is the Executive Letter. In this styling, the inside address appears from two to five lines below the last line of the signature space, depending on the length of the message. It is aligned tight with the left margin.

The Executive Letter is commonly used by secretaries to chief executive officers, especially in correspondence with their personal friends and corporate associates. The letterhead usually contains the writer's name and corporate title; hence this information need not be included in the typewritten signature block.

The date appears flush with the right margin. The paragraphs are indented from five to ten spaces. Carried-over lines are typed flush left. Paragraphs are single-spaced internally. Double spacing separates the paragraphs one from another.

The complimentary close is vertically aligned under the date line, i.e., flush with the right margin. Here, the typewritten signature block is included four lines below the complimentary close because the writer's name and title do not appear on the printed letterhead.

If the typist's initials or another notation is included, it appears two lines beneath the last line of the inside address, also blocked flush with the left margin.

Sincerely yours,

Michael A. Robinson
Vice President

John R. Fitzpatrick, Esq.
Fitzpatrick, Sweeney & Connon
Two Court Street
City, US 98765

MAR:lpc

Enclosure

The Executive Letter

Houghton Mifflin Company

One Beacon Street, Boston, Massachusetts 02108
(617) 725-5000   Cable HOUGHTON

June 24, 1992

Senior Buyers, Office Products
WiltonBooks Limited
1234 Clearwater Expressway
City, US 98765

Dear Senior Buyers

                    The Hanging-indented Letter Style

This is a facsimile of the Hanging-indented Letter, a letter style having a very
    elegant look. The Hanging-indented Letter is most often used in direct-mail
    advertising, sales, and product promotion. Since it requires much tabbing it is
    not a time-saving style appropriate to general correspondence.

Notice that we have used minimal (i.e., open) punctuation pattern in this letter: the
    salutation, complimentary close, and ancillary notations are unpunctuated. We
    also have inserted a capitalized and lowercased subject line to draw attention
    to the topic at hand. We centered it on the page for a more balanced look.

The chief feature of the Hanging-indented Letter is its unusual paragraph alignment.
    The first line of each paragraph is set flush left with subsequent lines block
    indented by at least five or six spaces. We have used the six-space setting in
    this facsimile.

The date line appears flush with the right margin in the Hanging-indented Letter, and
    the complimentary close and typed signature block are aligned under the date.
    Ancillary notations are set flush with the left margin, two lines below the last
    line of the signature block.

Continuation sheet headings, like those in the Modified Block and Modified Semi-block
    Letters, must be spaced across the top of the page about six vertical line spaces
    from the edge. At least three lines must be carried over to the continuation
    sheet: at no time should the complimentary close and the signature block stand
    alone there.

                                        Cordially

                                        Jan Smith
                                        Publicity

lpc

6 enclosures

The Hanging-indented Letter

Houghton Mifflin Company

Two Park Street, Boston, Massachusetts 02108
Tel: (617) 725-5921   FAX: (617) 573-4916

Joseph A. Kanon
Executive Vice President
Trade and Reference Publishing

January 15, 19--

Mr. Lee Martin
123 Salem Turnpike
City, US 98765

Dear Lee:

This is an example of a very short note typed on half-sheet stationery. The half-sheet is often used for one- or two-paragraph communications such as informal corporate invitations, letters of appreciation, or letters of congratulation.

Notice the narrow margins set to align with the right and left edges of the printed letterhead. We have chosen the Modified Semi-block Letter style here, but you may use the Block, Modified Block, or Executive Letters also.

Since the writer's name and title have been included in the printed letterhead there is no need to include it in the signature block.

Sincerely yours,

Executive Signature

ahs

enclosure: check

The Half-sheet

Optional data, included as required by the circumstances, are suite/room/apartment numbers, special mailing instructions (such as certification, registration, special delivery, or overseas air mail), special handling instructions (such as CONFIDENTIAL or PERSONAL), and attention indicators (such as Attention: Joseph Stone).

Guidelines for addressing envelopes.   Follow these suggestions based on the latest United States Postal Service regulations when addressing envelopes:

Envelope Size and Color

1. Use rectangular envelopes measuring no smaller than $3\frac{1}{2}'' \times 5''$ and no larger than $6\frac{1}{8}'' \times 11\frac{1}{2}''$.

2. Ensure that color contrast between paper and typescript is sharp.

Table 5. **Envelopes**

Type of Envelope	Number	Measurements
Commercial		
	$6\frac{1}{4}$	$3\frac{1}{2}''$ x $6''$
	$6\frac{3}{4}$	$3\frac{5}{8}''$ x $6\frac{1}{2}''$
	7	$3\frac{3}{4}''$ x $6\frac{3}{4}''$
	$7\frac{3}{4}$	$3\frac{7}{8}''$ x $7\frac{1}{2}''$
	Monarch	$3\frac{7}{8}''$ x $7\frac{1}{2}''$
	Check $8\frac{5}{8}$	$3\frac{5}{8}''$ x $8\frac{5}{8}''$
	9	$3\frac{7}{8}''$ x $8\frac{7}{8}''$
	10	$4\frac{1}{8}''$ x $9\frac{1}{2}''$
	11	$4\frac{1}{2}$ x $10\frac{3}{8}''$
	12	$4\frac{3}{4}''$ x $11''$
	14	$5''$ x $11\frac{1}{2}''$

Window
Standard window size and position
is $1\frac{1}{8}''$ x $4\frac{1}{2}''$, $\frac{7}{8}''$ left, $\frac{1}{2}''$ bottom.

	Number	Measurements
	$6\frac{1}{4}$*	$3\frac{1}{2}''$ x $6''$
	$6\frac{3}{4}$	$3\frac{5}{8}''$ x $6\frac{1}{2}''$
	7	$3\frac{3}{4}''$ x $6\frac{3}{4}''$
	$7\frac{3}{4}$	$3\frac{7}{8}''$ x $7\frac{1}{2}''$
	Monarch	$3\frac{7}{8}''$ x $8\frac{5}{8}''$
	Check $8\frac{5}{8}$**	$3\frac{5}{8}''$ x $8\frac{7}{8}''$
	9	$3\frac{7}{8}''$ x $8\frac{7}{8}''$
	10	$4\frac{1}{8}''$ x $9\frac{1}{2}''$
	11	$4\frac{1}{2}''$ x $10\frac{3}{8}''$
	12	$4\frac{3}{4}''$ x $11''$
	14	$5''$ x $11\frac{1}{2}''$

*Window position is $\frac{3}{4}''$ left, $\frac{1}{2}''$ bottom.
**Window size is $1\frac{1}{4}''$ x $3\frac{3}{4}''$; three positions, including $\frac{3}{4}''$ left, $\frac{13}{16}''$ bottom.

Styling of the Address Block

1. Single-space the address block; do not use double or triple spacing and never use a slanted format.

2. Type the address block about 5 spaces to the left of center.

3. The address block should fill no more than $1\frac{1}{2}''$ × $3\frac{3}{4}''$ of line space. At least $\frac{5}{8}''$ of blank space should be allowed from the last line of the address to the bottom of the envelope.

4. With window envelopes, ensure that the inside address on the letterhead has been positioned so that all elements are clearly visible through the window (this includes checking to see that the letter has been properly folded). You should have maintained margins of at

Table 5. (continued)

Type of Envelope	Number	Measurements
Monarch Window		
	Monarch	$3\frac{7}{8}''$ x $7\frac{1}{2}''$

Standard with Special Window
Positions

	$6\frac{1}{4}$	$3\frac{1}{2}''$ x $6''$
	$6\frac{3}{4}$	$3\frac{5}{8}''$ x $6\frac{1}{2}''$
	7	$3\frac{3}{4}''$ x $6\frac{3}{4}''$
	$7\frac{3}{4}''$	$3\frac{7}{8}''$ x $7\frac{1}{2}''$
	Monarch	$3\frac{7}{8}''$ x $7\frac{1}{2}''$
	Check $8\frac{5}{8}$	$3\frac{5}{8}''$ x $8\frac{5}{8}''$
	9	$3\frac{7}{8}''$ x $8\frac{7}{8}''$
	10	$4\frac{1}{8}''$ x $9\frac{1}{2}''$
	11	$4\frac{1}{2}''$ x $10\frac{3}{8}''$
	12	$4\frac{3}{4}''$ x $11''$
	14	$5''$ x $11\frac{1}{2}''$

Continuous

Mounted on computer carrier strip. Available in many styles and sizes. Plain or printed.

Courtesy of Boston Envelope, 150 Royall St., Canton, MA 02021 least $\frac{1}{4}''$ between the top, bottom, left, and right edges of the inside address block and the corresponding edges of the window space.

5. Nothing should be printed or typed in the space extending from the right and left bottom edges of the address block to the right and left bottom edges of the envelope. Likewise, the space extending below the center of the address block to the bottom center edge of the envelope should be blank.

Conventional address block styles.   If addressing a letter to an individual, follow the patterns shown earlier in this chapter. If addressing a letter to a corporation, follow this pattern:

CCC Corporation
987 Industrial Drive
P.O. Box 444
Keystone, US 12345

Remember, though, that if both a street and a box number are used, the location on the line just above the line on which the city, state, and Zip Code appear is the destination of the letter. Therefore, if you wish the letter to go to the street address and not to the post office box (which may involve another Zip Code), put the street address last before the city, state, and Zip Code. If using an attention line, follow this pattern:

CCC CORPORATION
Attention John Hodges
987 Industrial Drive
Keystone, US 12345

Special mailing instructions are typed in capital letters below the space for the postage (i.e., approximately nine vertical line spaces from the right top edge of the envelope and not overrunning a $\frac{1}{2}''$ margin). Special handling instructions are also typed in capital letters and are positioned to the upper left of the address block about nine vertical line spaces below the left top edge of the envelope. Any other such notations should be styled in underscored capital and lowercase letters, as <u>Please Forward</u> or <u>Please Hold for Arrival</u>, and should be typed about nine vertical line spaces from the left top edge of the envelope.

Addressing Envelopes for Computerized Sorting

Large-volume mailers are urged to address their envelopes in such a way as to expedite and not obstruct the Postal Service's electronic mail sorting system. (This topic is also discussed in Chapter Four.) The Postal Service recommends that you use any of seven basic address formats, all employing capital letters, abbreviations, and minimal punctuation. These formats—designed to facilitate automated mail handling—also save you

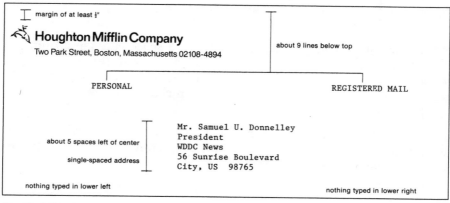

Standard Envelope

unnecessary keystrokes and thereby increase your own output. The seven formats are: (1) Post Office Box, (2) Rural Route, (3) Building/Business/Personal Name, (4) Standard Street Address/Numeric, (5) Standard Street Address/Alphabetic, (6) Community Identity, and (7) Dual Address. Examples:

Post Office Box
MS SARAH SMITH
PO BOX 123
CITY, US 98765

Rural Route
MR JG LOUGHRY
RR 5 BOX 94–C
RURAL LOCALE, US 12345

Standard Street Address/ Numeric
MS JANE DOE
123 E 53RD ST APT 221
CITY, US 98765

Standard Stret Address/ Alphabetic
MS JANE DOE
603 FIRST ST APT 80
CITY, US 98765

Community Identity
MR JOHN T WATSON
HILLENDALE
13 FRANKLIN ST
CITY, US 98765

Dual Address
RRR CORP
123 E PARK AVE
PO BOX 100
CITY, US 98765

or

RRR CORP
PO BOX 100
123 E PARK AVE
CITY, US 98765

Building/Business/ Personal Name
EZ CREDIT CORP
ATTN JAY MORTMAIN
123 E INDUSTRIAL PK
CITY, US 98765

Remember that the address to which you want delivery to be made must appear on the last line above the city, state, and Zip Code. In the first

Table 6.   **Abbreviations for U.S. States**

State	Abbreviation	State	Abbreviation
Alabama	AL	Missouri	MO
Alaska	AK	Montana	MT
American Samoa	AS	Nebraska	NE
Arizona	AZ	Nevada	NV
Arkansas	AR	New Hampshire	NH
California	CA	New Jersey	NJ
Colorado	CO	New Mexico	NM
Connecticut	CT	New York	NY
Delaware	DE	North Carolina	NC
District of Columbia	DC	North Dakota	ND
Federated States of Micronesia	FM	Northern Mariana Islands	MP
Florida	FL	Ohio	OH
Georgia	GA	Oklahoma	OK
Guam	GU	Oregon	OR
Hawaii	HI	Palau	PW
Idaho	ID	Pennsylvania	PA
Illinois	IL	Puerto Rico	PR
Indiana	IN	Rhode Island	RI
Iowa	IA	South Carolina	SC
Kansas	KS	South Dakota	SD
Kentucky	KY	Tennessee	TN
Louisiana	LA	Texas	TX
Maine	ME	Utah	UT
Marshall Islands	MH	Vermont	VT
Maryland	MD	Virginia	VA
Massachusetts	MA	Virgin Islands	VI
Michigan	MI	Washington	WA
Minnesota	MN	West Virginia	WV
Mississippi	MS	Wisconsin	WI
		Wyoming	WY

example under Dual Address, delivery will be made to the post office box, but in the second example, delivery will be made to the street address.

Zip + 4.   The Postal Service currently offers a voluntary Zip + 4 coding program for extra high-speed automated sorts. This program is particularly useful to high-volume business mailers. Rate incentives have been proposed to make the program even more attractive to commercial mailers. With Zip + 4, optical character readers (OCRs) in the originating post office can read the city, state, and Zip Code. Special printers apply a bar code on letter-size mail. The bar code—a series of vertical bars and half-bars—corresponds to Zip + 4 and allows all subsequent sorts to be done on low-cost, high-speed bar code readers (BCRs). The equipment reads Zip + 4 and then sorts the mail according to sector or segment. This process, in effect, separates the mail and routes it to a box number, a firm, a building, or the carrier assigned to a particular locale. Zip + 4 looks like this: 01075–1234 where the traditional five-digit Zip Code 01075 is followed by a hyphen and four more figures: 1234, in this hypothetical example. The digits 01075 represent the major geographic location (in this case, a town in Massachusetts). The numbers 1 and 2 in 1234 represent a sector within the major geographic location. The sector might include several selected blocks, a group of streets, a large building, or another smaller geographic location within the major one. The numbers 3 and 4 represent a segment within the "12" sector. The segment might be one side of a block, two sides of a street, one floor in a large building, a cluster of mailboxes, or one post office box in a cluster. Eventually, Zip + 4 will eliminate all hand sorting.

Address formats for military mail.   The Postal Service recommends that you use the format shown in this section for mail addressed to United States military personnel using Air Force, Army, and Fleet Post Offices. For Army and Air Force addressees, enter the addressee's name on line one, followed on line two by the addressee's unit and PSC number, followed on line three by the organization to which the addressee is assigned, followed on the last line by the APO:

PVT GG DOE
COMPANY F, PSC 3250
167TH INFANTRY REGT
APO, NY 09801

With mail addressed to members of the United States Navy and Marine Corps, type the addressee's name on line one, followed on line two by the name of the addressee's shore-based organization, mobile unit, or the name of the addressee's ship. On the last line type the Fleet Post Office and its number:

JOHN M DOE QMSN USN
USS SEA SQUIRT (DD 729)
FPO SAN FRANCISCO 96601

Table 7. Abbreviations for Streets and Words Often Appearing in Place Names

Street/Place Name	Abbreviation	Street/Place Name	Abbreviation
Academy	ACAD	Corner	COR
Agency	AGNCY	Corners	CORS
Air Force Base	AFB	Course	CRSE
Airport	ARPRT	Court	CT
Alley	ALY	Courts	CTS
Annex	ANX	Cove	CV
Arcade	ARC	Creek	CRK
Arsenal	ARSL	Crescent	CRES
Avenue	AVE	Crossing	XING
Bayou	BYU	Dale	DL
Beach	BCH	Dam	DM
Bend	BND	Depot	DPO
Big	BG	Divide	DV
Black	BLK	Drive	DR
Bluff	BLF	East	E
Bottom	BTM	Estates	EST
Boulevard	BLVD	Expressway	EXPY
Branch	BR	Extended	EXT
Bridge	BRG	Extension	EXT
Brook	BRK	Fall	FL
Burg	BG	Falls	FLS
Bypass	BYP	Farms	FRMS
Camp	CP	Ferry	FRY
Canyon	CYN	Field	FLD
Cape	CPE	Fields	FLDS
Causeway	CSWY	Flats	FLT
Center	CTR	Ford	FRD
Central	CTL	Forest	FRST
Church	CHR	Forge	FRG
Churches	CHRS	Fork	FRK
Circle	CIR	Forks	FRKS
City	CY	Fort	FT
Clear	CLR	Fountain	FTN
Cliffs	CLFS	Freeway	FWY
Club	CLB	Furnace	FURN
College	CLG	Gardens	GDNS
Common	CMM	Gateway	GTWY

Table 7.   (continued)

Street/Place Name	Abbreviation	Street/Place Name	Abbreviation
Glen	GLN	Manor	MNR
Grand	GRND	Meadows	MDWS
Great	GR	Meeting	MTG
Green	GRN	Memorial	MEM
Ground	GRD	Middle	MDL
Grove	GRV	Mile	MLE
Harbor	HBR	Mill	ML
Haven	HVN	Mills	MLS
Heights	HTS	Mines	MNS
High	HI	Mission	MSN
Highlands	HGLDS	Mound	MND
Highway	HWY	Mount	MT
Hill	HL	Mountain	MTN
Hills	HLS	National	NAT
Hollow	HOLW	Naval Air Station	NAS
Hospital	HOSP	Neck	NCK
Hot	H	New	NW
House	HSE	North	N
Inlet	INLT	Orchard	ORCH
Institute	INST	Oval	OVAL
Island	IS	Palms	PLMS
Islands	IS	Park	PARK
Isle	IS	Parkway	PKY
Junction	JCT	Pass	PASS
Key	KY	Path	PATH
Knolls	KNLS	Pike	PIKE
Lake	LK	Pillar	PLR
Lakes	LKS	Pines	PNES
Landing	LNDG	Place	PL
Lane	LN	Plain	PLN
Light	LGT	Plains	PLNS
Little	LTL	Plaza	PLZ
Loaf	LF	Point	PT
Locks	LCKS	Port	PRT
Lodge	LDG	Prairie	PR
Loop	LOOP	Radial	RADL
Lower	LWR	Ranch	RNCH
Mall	MALL	Ranches	RNCHS

Table 7.   *(continued)*

Street/Place Name	Abbreviation	Street/Place Name	Abbreviation
Rapids	RPDS	Street	ST
Resort	RESRT	Sulphur	SLPHR
Rest	RST	Summit	SMT
Ridge	RDG	Switch	SWCH
River	RIV	Tannery	TNRY
Road	RD	Tavern	TVRN
Rock	RK	Terminal	TERM
Row	ROW	Terrace	TER
Run	RUN	Ton	TN
Rural	R	Tower	TWR
Saint	ST	Town	TWN
Sainte	ST	Trace	TRCE
San	SN	Track	TRAK
Santa	SN	Trail	TRL
Santo	SN	Trailer	TRLR
School	SCH	Tunnel	TUNL
Seminary	SMNRY	Turnpike	TPKE
Shoal	SHL	Union	UN
Shoals	SHLS	University	UNIV
Shode	SHD	Valley	VLY
Shore	SHR	Viaduct	VIA
Shores	SHRS	View	VW
Siding	SDG	Village	VLG
South	S	Ville	VL
Space Flight Center	SFC	Vista	VIS
Speedway	SPDWY	Walk	WALK
Spring	SPG	Water	WTR
Springs	SPGS	Way	WAY
Spur	SPUR	Wells	WLS
Square	SQ	West	W
State	ST	White	WHT
Station	STA	Works	WKS
Stream	STRM	Yards	YDS

Addressing mail to Canada.   Follow the format recommended by Canada Post to expedite automated handling: use capital and lowercase letters with the addressee's name (line one), the firm name if included (line two),

Table 8.   Abbreviations for Canadian Provinces

Province	Abbreviation
Alberta	AB
British Columbia	BC
Labrador	LB
Manitoba	MB
New Brunswick	NB
Newfoundland	NF
Northwest Territories	NT
Nova Scotia	NS
Ontario	ON
Prince Edward Island	PE
Quebec	PQ
Saskatchewan	SK
Yukon	YT

and the street address (lines two or three). On a subsequent line, enter the city name in capital letters followed on the same line by the name of the province styled either in written-out or abbreviated form as shown in Table 8. The six-character Canadian Postal Code is typed on another line. Remember that one character space separates the first three numbers and letters from the last three in the Postal Code. Conclude the address block with the capitalized word CANADA if you are mailing the letter from outside Canada. Example:

Ms. Ann Fitzgerald
Fitzgerald and McHenry
123 Queen Street
OTTAWA ON
K1A 0B3
CANADA

Forms of Address

Business etiquette requires the proper use of forms of address in correspondence. Use of the right form of address applies to the inside address, the salutation, and the envelope address block. Forms of address include courtesy titles such as *Ms.* or *Dr.*, honorifics such as *Esq.* or *The Honorable*, military rank designations such as *Lt.* or *GySgt*, and titles such as *His Holiness, Senator,* or *The Right Reverend* for high-ranking personages. The next few subsections discuss particularly problematic usages of honorifics and courtesy titles. A complete forms of address table giving the proper forms of address for various academic, clerical, consular, diplomatic, governmental, military, and professional title holders concludes this section.

Esq.   This abbreviation stands for *Esquire*, which often follows the surnames of men and women in the American bar and in the consular corps. It is used in the inside address, on the envelope, and in the typed signature block but it is never used in the salutation. It is never used in conjunction with courtesy or professional titles such as *Ms.* or *Dr.* preceding a name. Likewise, it is never used in conjunction with another honorific such as *The Honorable*. Its plural form is *Esqs.*, used when referring to multiple addressees holding the title. In highly formal diplomatic correspondence, *Esquire* may be written out in full, but most recent evidence indicates that the United States Department of State is discouraging use of the term altogether. In Great Britain, *Esq.* is routinely used with the names of chief executive officers, prominent professionals in law and medicine, and high-ranking diplomats. Examples of the proper use of *Esq.* in American business correspondence are:

Janet L. Wills, Esq. Attorney-at-Law	Dear Ms. Wills:
John L. Wills, Esq. American Consul	Dear Mr. Wills:
Norton L. Levin, Esq. Samuel I. Gould, Esq. Attorneys-at-Law	Dear Mr. Levin and Mr. Gold: Dear Messrs. Levin and Gold:
Levin & Gold, Esqs. Attorneys-at-Law	Dear Mr. Levin and Mr. Gold: Dear Messrs. Levin and Gold:

Honorable.   *The Honorable* or its abbreviated form *The Hon.* is used in the United States with the names of certain high-ranking appointed or elected officials, as judges, clerks of courts, representatives, senators, governors, and the President and Vice President. It may be used in the inside address and on the envelope of a letter destined for the holder of the title, but it is never used by the holder in written or typed signatures, on letterhead or business cards, or in invitations.

Never use *The Honorable* with a surname only (i.e., "The Honorable Smith" is incorrect); a first name, an initial or initials, or a courtesy title must intervene (as in *The Honorable John Sweeney; The Honorable J.M. Sweeney; The Honorable Mr. Sweeney*).

The Honorable Lee Whalen
The Honorable L.B. Whalen
The Honorable L. Brantley Whalen
The Honorable Mr./Ms. Whalen
The Honorable Dr. Whalen

In addressing correspondence to a married couple, one of whom is the title holder, follow these patterns:

if husband holds the title

The Honorable John M. Sweeney
and Mrs. Sweeney
The Honorable and Mrs. John M.
Sweeney
The Hon. and Mrs. J.M. Sweeney

Dear Mr./Judge, etc., and
Mrs. Sweeney:

if wife holds the title/business correspondence

The Honorable Elizabeth Lee
and Mr. Lee
The Hon. Elizabeth Lee and Mr. Lee

Dear Judge, Senator, etc.,
Lee and Mr. Lee:

if wife holds the title/social correspondence

Mr. and Mrs. Albert A. Lee

Dear Mr. and Mrs. Lee:

if wife holds the title and has retained her own name/business correspondence

The Honorable Ann Stone and
Mr. Allen Wheeler
The Hon. Ann Stone and Mr. Allen
Wheeler

Dear Judge, Senator, etc.,
Stone and Mr. Wheeler:

if wife holds the title and has retained her own name/social correspondence

Ms. Ann Stone and Mr. Allen
Wheeler

Dear Ms. Stone and Mr. Wheeler:

In limited address space *The Honorable* may appear by itself on line one with the addressee's name on line two.

Madam/Madame.   Use Madam only in letters to women who are high-level diplomats or government officials, such as the United States Ambassador to the United Nations or a justice of the Supreme Court. The term is used only in salutations:

Dear Madam:
Dear Madam Justice:

Madame, on the other hand, is used in salutations of letters destined for foreign heads of state and diplomats:

if woman holds the office

Dear Madame Ambassador:
Dear Madame Prime Minister:

Madame is also used with the names of the wives of high-ranking foreign diplomats and with the names of the wives of foreign heads of state:

if husband holds the title
Excellency and Madame Cortez:

Mesdames.   This word is the plural of *Mrs.*, *Madam*, and *Madame*. It is the equivalent to *Messrs.* in business usage and may appear before the names of two or more women associated together in a firm. It is used in the inside address, on the envelope, and in the salutation:

Mesdames Sarah Walker and Laura Phelps	Dear Mesdames Walker and Phelps:
Mesdames Walker and Phelps	Mesdames:

If the two women share the same surname, follow these patterns:

Mesdames A.L. and L.T. Phelps	Dear Mesdames Phelps:
The Mesdames Phelps	Mesdames:

Never pluralize the surname in instances like this.

Messrs.   This term is the plural abbreviated form of *Mr.*, and, like *Mesdames*, it is used with the names of two or more men associated together in a firm. *Messrs.* is used in the inside address, on the envelope, and in the salutation:

Messrs. Dabney, Langhorne, and Lee	Dear Messrs. Dabney, Langhorne, and Lee:

If two men share the same surname, follow these patterns:

Messrs. C.D. and R.R. Langhorne	Dear Messrs. Langhorne:
	Gentlemen:

Never pluralize the surname in an instance like this.

Misses.   This is the plural of *Miss* and its use parallels that of *Messrs.* :

Misses Carleton and East	Dear Misses Carleton and East:
	Ladies:
Misses A.Y. Carleton and D.C. East	Dear Miss Carleton and Miss East:
Misses Maureen and Mary O'Day	Dear Misses O'Day:
The Misses O'Day	Ladies:

Ms.   *Ms.* may be used in the inside address, on the envelope, in the salutation, and in the typed signature block of a letter. Never use *Ms.* with a woman's married name (i.e., "Ms. Robert A. Keith" is incorrect). The plural form is either *Mses.* or *Mss.* Examples:

Mses. (*or* Mss.) Grey and Holt:	Dear Mses. (*or* Mss.) Grey and Holt
Mses. (*or* Mss.) C.C. Grey and D.D. Holt	Dear Ms. Grey and Ms. Holt:
Mses. (*or* Mss.) Nan and Pam Lee	Dear Mses. (*or* Mss.) Lee:
The Mses. (*or* Mss.) Lee	Dear Nan and Pam Lee:

Professor.   Avoid abbreviating *Professor* to *Prof.* in instances where it appears only with a surname (i.e., "Dear Prof. Webber" is incorrect). Avoid wording salutations to professors as just "Dear Professor" and never say "Dear Prof. Smith." Correct patterns are given below:

Professor (*or* Prof.) Lee O'Brien	Dear Professor O'Brien:
	Dear Dr. O'Brien:
	Dear Ms./Mr./Miss/Mrs. O'Brien:

In addressing correspondence to a married couple, one spouse of which is a professor and the other is not, follow these patterns:

if husband is a professor

Professor and Mrs. Lee O'Brien	Dear Professor and Mrs. O'Brien:
	Dear Dr. and Mrs. O'Brien:
	Dear Mr. and Mrs. O'Brien:

if wife is a professor/business correspondence

Professor Diana O'Brien and Mr. O'Brien	Dear Professor O'Brien and Mr. O'Brien:
	Dear Dr. O'Brien and Mr. O'Brien:

if wife is a professor/social correspondence

Mr. and Mrs. Lee O'Brien	Dear Mr. and Mrs. O'Brien:

If the woman has retained her own name, follow these patterns in social and business correspondence:

Professor Diana Quirk Mr. Lee O'Brien	Dear Professor Quirk and Mr. O'Brien:
	Dear Dr. Quirk and Mr. O'Brien:
	Dear Ms. Quirk and Mr. O'Brien:

Letters addressed to multiple recipients, all of whom are professors, are styled as follows:

Professors B.B. Doe and C.C. Roe	Dear Professors Doe and Roe:
	Dear Drs. Doe and Roe:
	Dear Mr. Doe and Mr. Roe:
	Dear Messrs. Doe and Roe:
	Gentlemen:
Professors C.L. Jones and D.C. Lawton:	Dear Professors Jones and Lawton:
	Dear Ms. Jones and Mr. Lawton:
	Dear Drs. Jones and Lawton:

Professors T.A. and A.Y. Lee	Dear Professors Lee:
The Professors Lee	Dear Drs. Lee:
	or if men
	Gentlemen:
	or if women
	Mesdames:
	or if married
	Dear Professors Lee:
	Dear Drs. Lee:
	Dear Mr. and Ms. (*or* Mrs.) Lee:

Reverend.   This title is the one most misused in business correspondence: few people seem able to remember that it ought to be preceded by *The*. Never use *The Reverend* or its abbreviated form *The Rev.* with a surname only (i.e., "The Reverend Smith" is incorrect). *The Reverend* or *The Rev.* is used on the envelope, in the inside address, and in the signature block but never in the salutation (i.e., "Dear Reverend Smith" is incorrect). Follow these patterns:

The Reverend John M. Mills
The Rev. John M. Mills
The Reverend Dr. John M. Mills
The Rev. Dr. John M. Mills

The Reverend, like *The Honorable,* may be used with a surname only if a courtesy title such as *Mr., Dr.,* or *Ms.* intervenes:

The Reverend Ms. Kendall
The Rev. Dr. King
The Reverend Professor O'Neill

When addressing a letter to a minister and the minister's spouse, follow these patterns:

if husband is a minister

The Reverend and Mrs. A.A. Lee	Dear Mr./Dr. and Mrs. Lee:
The Rev. and Mrs. A.A. Lee	*or depending on denomination*
	Dear Father Lee and Mrs. Lee:
	Dear Father Andrew and Mrs. Lee:

if wife is a minister

The Reverend Ann T. Lee and	Dear Mrs./Dr. Lee and Mr. Lee:
Mr. Lee	
The Rev. Ann T. Lee and Mr. Lee	

Two or more ministers may be addressed as *The Reverends, The Revs., The Reverend* (or *The Rev.*) *Messrs.* (if men), and *The Reverend* (or *The*

Rev.) *Drs.* plus their names. You also might wish to repeat *The Reverend* or *The Rev.* before each name instead of pluralizing the title:

The Reverends P.X. and F.I. Connon	Gentlemen:
The Revs. P.X. and F.I. Connon	*or, depending on denomination*
The Rev. Messrs. P.X. and F.I. Connon	Dear Father Patrick and Father Francis:
The Rev. Messrs. Connon	Dear Fathers:
The Reverend Messrs. Connon	
The Rev. P.X. Connon and The Rev. F.I. Connon	

If the clerics have different surnames, these patterns are appropriate:

The Rev. Messrs. P.X. Connon and F.I. O'Brien	Gentlemen:
	Dear Mr./Dr. Connon and O'Brien:
The Reverend P.X. Connon	*or, depending on denomination*
The Reverend F.I. O'Brien	Dear Father Patrick and Father Francis:
The Revs. Connon and O'Brien	Dear Fathers:

Table 9.   Forms of Address

Academics	Form of Address	Salutation
assistant professor	Professor Joseph/Jane Stone Mr./Ms./Dr. Joseph/Jane Stone	Dear Professor Stone: Dear Mr./Ms. Stone: Dear Dr. Stone:
associate professor	Professor Joseph/Jane Stone Mr./Ms./Dr. Joseph/Jane Stone	Dear Professor Stone: Dear Mr./Ms. Stone: Dear Dr. Stone:
chancellor, university	Dr./Mr./Ms. Joseph/Jane Stone	Dear Chancellor Stone:
chaplain	The Reverend Joseph/Jane Stone	Dear Chaplain Stone: Dear/Mr./Ms. Stone: Dear Father Stone:
dean, college or university	Dear Joseph/Jane Stone or Dr./Mr./Ms. Joseph/Jane Stone Dean, School of _____	Dear Dean Stone: Dear Dr./Mr./Ms. Stone:
instructor	Mr./Ms./Dr. Joseph/Jane Stone	Dear Mr./Ms./Dr. Stone:
president	President Joseph/Jane Stone or Dr./Mr./Ms. Joseph/Jane Stone	Dear President Stone: or Dear Dr./Mr./Ms. Stone:
president/priest	The Reverend Joseph Stone, S.J. President of _____	Sir: Dear Father Stone:

Table 9. *(continued)*

Academics	Form of Address	Salutation
professor, college or university	Professor Joseph/Jane Stone *or* Dr./Mr./Ms. Jane/Joseph Stone	Dear Professor Stone: *or* Dear Dr./Mr./Ms. Stone:

Clerical and Religious Orders

abbot, Roman Catholic	The Right Reverend Joseph Stone, O.S.B. Abbot of _____	Right Reverend Abbot: Dear Father Abbot:
apostolic delegate	His Excellency The Most Reverend Joseph Stone Archbishop of _____ The Apostolic Delegate	Your Excellency: My dear Archbishop:
archbishop, Armenian Church	His Eminence the Archbishop of _____	Your Eminence: Your Excellency:
archbishop, Greek Orthodox	The Most Reverend Joseph Archbishop of _____	Your Eminence:
archbishop, Roman Catholic	The Most Reverend Joseph Stone Archbishop of _____	Your Excellency:
archbishop, Russian Orthodox	The Most Reverend Joseph Archbishop of _____	Your Eminence:
archdeacon, Episcopal	The Venerable Joseph Stone Archdeacon of _____	Venerable Sir: Dear Archdeacon Stone:
archimandrite, Greek Orthodox	The Very Reverend Joseph Stone	Reverend Sir: Dear Father Joseph:
archimandrite, Russian Orthodox	The Right Reverend Joseph Stone	Reverend Sir: Dear Father Joseph:
archpriest, Greek Orthodox	The Reverend Joseph Stone	Dear Father Joseph:
archpriest, Russian Orthodox	The Very Reverend Joseph Stone	Dear Father Joseph:
bishop, Episcopal	The Right Reverend Joseph Stone Bishop of _____	Right Reverend Sir: Dear Bishop Stone:
bishop, Greek Orthodox	The Right Reverend Joseph Bishop of _____	Your Grace:
bishop, Methodist	The Reverend Joseph Stone Methodist Bishop	Dear Bishop Stone:
bishop, Roman Catholic	The Most Reverend Joseph Stone Bishop of _____	Your Excellency: Dear Bishop Stone:
bishop, Russian Orthodox	The Most Reverend Joseph Bishop of _____	Your Grace:

Table 9. *(continued)*

Clerical and Religious Orders	Form of Address	Salutation
brotherhood, Roman Catholic, member of	Brother Joseph Stone, C.F.C.	Dear Brother: Dear Brother Joseph:
brotherhood, Roman Catholic, superior of	Brother Joseph, C.F.C. Superior	Dear Brother Joseph:
canon, Episcopal	The Reverend Canon Joseph Stone	Dear Canon Stone:
cantor	Cantor Joseph/Jane Stone	Dear Cantor Stone:
cardinal	His Eminence Joseph Cardinal Stone	Your Eminence:
cleric, Protestant	The Reverend Joseph/Jane Stone *or* The Reverend Joseph/Jane Stone, D.D.	Dear Mr./Ms. Stone: *or* Dear Dr. Stone:
elder, Presbyterian	Elder Joseph/Jane Stone	Dear Elder Stone:
dean of a cathedral, Episcopal	The Very Reverend Joseph Stone Dean of _____	Dear Dean Stone:
metropolitan, Russian Orthodox	His Beatitude Joseph Metropolitan of _____	Your Beatitude:
moderator, Presbyterian	The Moderator of _____ *or* The Reverend Joseph Stone *or* Dr. Joseph Stone	Reverend Sir: My dear Sir: Dear Mr. Moderator: *or* My dear Dr. Stone:
monsignor, Roman Catholic (domestic prelate)	The Right Reverend Monsignor Joseph Stone	Right Reverend Monsignor: Dear Monsignor: Dear Monsignor Stone:
papal chamberlain	The Very Reverend Monsignor Joseph Stone	Very Reverend and Dear Monsignor Stone: Dear Monsignor Stone:
patriarch, Armenian Church	His Beatitude Patriarch of _____	Your Beatitude:
patriarch, Greek Orthodox	His All Holiness Patriarch Joseph	Your All Holiness:
patriarch, Russian Orthodox	His Holiness the Patriarch of _____	Your Holiness:
pope	His Holiness The Pope	Your Holiness: Most Holy Father:
president, Morman Church	President Joseph Stone Church of Jesus Christ of Latter-Day Saints	Dear President Stone:

Table 9.   *(continued)*

Clerical and Religious Orders	Form of Address	Salutation
priest, Episcopal	The Reverend Joseph/Jane Stone The Rev. Dr. Joseph/Jane Stone	Dear Mr./Ms. Stone: Dear Dr. Stone:
priest, Greek Orthodox	The Reverend Joseph Stone	Dear Father Joseph:
priest, Roman Catholic	The Reverend Joseph Stone	Dear Reverend Father: Dear Father: Dear Father Stone:
priest, Russian Orthodox	The Reverend Joseph Stone	Dear Father Joseph:
rabbi	Rabbi Joseph/Jane Stone *or* Joseph/Jane Stone, D.D.	Dear Rabbi Stone: *or* Dear Dr. Stone:
sisterhood, Roman Catholic, member of	Sister Mary Viventia, C.S.J.	Dear Sister: Dear Sister Viventia: Dear Sister Mary:
sisterhood, Roman Catholic, superior of	The Reverend Mother Superior, S.C.	Reverend Mother: Dear Reverend Mother:
supreme patriarch, Armenian Church	His Holiness the Supreme Patriarch and Catholicos of All Armenians	Your Holiness:

Diplomats

ambassador, U.S.	The Honorable Joseph/Jane Stone The Ambassador of the United States	Sir/Madam: Dear Mr./Madam Ambassador:
ambassador to the U.S.	His/Her Excellency Joseph/Jane Stone The Ambassador of _____	Excellency: Dear Mr./Madame ambassador:
chargé d'affaires, U.S.	The Honorable Joseph/Jane Stone United States Chargé d'Affaires	Dear Mr./Ms. Stone:
chargé d'affaires to the U.S.	Joseph/Jane Stone, Esq. Chargé d'Affaires of _____	Dear Sir/Madame:
consul, U.S.	Joseph/Jane Stone, Esq. United States Consul	Dear Mr./Ms. Stone:
consul, to the U.S.	The Honorable Joseph/Jane Stone Consul of _____	Dear Mr./Ms. Stone:
minister, U.S.	The Honorable Joseph/Jane Stone The Minister of the United States	Sir/Madam: Dear Mr./Madam Minister:

Table 9. *(continued)*

Diplomats	Form of Address	Salutation
minister to the U.S.	The Honorable Joseph/Jane Stone The Minister of ____	Sir/Madame: Dear Mr./Madame Minister:
representative (foreign), to the United Nations (with rank of ambassador)	His/Her Excellency Joseph/Jane Stone Representative of ____ to the United Nations	Excellency: My dear Mr./Madame Stone: Dear Mr./Madame Ambassador:
secretary general, United Nations	His/Her Excellency Joseph/Jane Stone Secretary General of the United Nations	Dear Mr./Madam/ Madame Secretary General:
undersecretary to the United Nations	The Honorable Joseph/Jane Stone Undersecretary of the United Nations	Sir:/Madam: (if American) Sir:/Madame: (if foreign) My dear Mr./Ms. Stone: Dear Mr./Ms. Stone:
U.S. representative to the United Nations	The Honorable Joseph/Jane Stone United States Representative to the United Nations	Sir/Madam: Dear Mr./Ms. Stone:

**Federal, State, and
Local Government
Officials**

alderman	The Honorable Joseph/Jane Stone	Dear Mr./Ms. Stone:
assistant to the President	Mr./Ms. Joseph/Jane Stone	Dear Mr./Ms. Stone:
attorney general, U.S.	The Honorable Joseph/Jane Stone Attorney General of the United States	Dear Mr./Madam Attorney General:
attorney general, state	The Honorable Joseph/Jane Stone Attorney General State of ____	Dear Mr./Madam Attorney General:
assemblyman, state	The Honorable Joseph/Jane Stone	Dear Mr./Ms. Stone:
cabinet member	The Honorable Joseph/Jane Stone Secretary of ____	Sir/Madam: Dear Mr./Madam Secretary:
cabinet member, former	The Honorable Joseph/Jane Stone	Dear Mr./Ms. Stone:
chairman, congres- sional committee	The Honorable Joseph/Jane Stone Chairman, Committee on ____	Dear Mr./Madam Chairman:
chief justice, U.S. Supreme Court	The Chief Justice of the United States	Dear Mr. Chief Justice: Sir:

Table 9. *(continued)*

Federal, State, and Local Government Officials	Form of Address	Salutation
associate justice, U.S. Supreme Court	Mr./Madam Justice Stone	Dear Mr./Madam Justice: Sir/Madam:
associate/chief justice, Supreme Court, former	The Honorable Joseph/Jane Stone	Dear Mr./Ms. Stone: Dear Mr./Madam Justice Stone:
clerk, county	The Honorable Joseph/Jane Stone	Dear Mr./Ms. Stone:
clerk, of a court	Joseph/Jane Stone, Esq. Clerk of the Court of _____	Dear Mr./Ms. Stone:
commissioner (federal, state, local)	The Honorable Joseph/Jane Stone	Dear Mr./Ms. Stone:
delegate, state	**—See assemblyman, state**	
director, federal agency	The Honorable Joseph/Jane Stone Director _____ Agency	Dear Mr./Ms. Stone:
district attorney	The Honorable Joseph/Jane Stone District Attorney	Dear Mr./Ms. Stone:
governor	The Honorable Joseph/Jane Stone Governor of _____	Dear Governor Stone:
governor-elect	The Honorable Joseph/Jane Stone Governor-elect of _____	Dear Mr./Ms. Stone:
governor, former	The Honorable Joseph/Jane Stone	Dear Governor Stone:
judge, federal	The Honorable Joseph/Jane Stone Judge of the United States District Court for the _____ District of _____	Sir/Madam: Dear Judge Stone:
judge, state or local	The Honorable Joseph/Jane Stone Judge of the Court of _____	Dear Judge Stone:
justice, Supreme Court, associate chief, and former	**—See chief justice, supreme court** and subentries thereto	
librarian of congress	The Honorable Joseph/Jane Stone The Librarian of Congress	Sir/Madam: Dear Mr./Ms./Dr. Stone:
lieutenant governor	The Honorable Joseph/Jane Stone Lieutenant Governor of _____	Dear Mr./Ms. Stone:
mayor	The Honorable Joseph/Jane Stone Mayor of _____	Dear Mayor Stone:
postmaster general	The Honorable Joseph/Jane Stone Postmaster General United States Postal Service	Dear Mr./Madam Postmaster General:

Table 9.   *(continued)*

Federal, State, and Local Government Officials	Form of Address	Salutation
president, U.S.	The President The White House	Dear Mr. President:
president-elect, U.S.	The Honorable Joseph Stone The President-elect of the United States	Dear Sir: Dear Mr. Stone:
president, U.S., former	The Honorable Joseph Stone	Dear Mr. Stone: Dear Mr. President: Dear President Stone:
press secretary, to the President	Mr./Ms. Joseph/Jane Stone Press Secretary to the President	Dear Mr./Ms. Stone:
representative, state	**—See assemblyman, state**	
representative, U.S.	The Honorable Joseph/Jane Stone United States House of Representatives	Dear Mr./Ms. Stone:
secretary of state, for a state	The Honorable Joseph/Jane Stone Secretary of State State Capitol	Dear Mr./Madam Secretary:
senator, former (state or U.S.)	The Honorable Joseph/Jane Stone	Dear Senator Stone: Dear Mr./Ms. Stone:
senator, state	The Honorable Joseph/Jane Stone The State Senate State Capitol	Dear Senator Stone:
senator, U.S.	The Honorable Jane/Joseph Stone United States Senate	Dear Senator Stone:
speaker, U.S. House of Representatives	The Honorable Joseph/Jane Stone Speaker of the House of Representatives	Dear Mr./Madam Speaker:
territorial delegate to the U.S. House of Representatives	The Honorable Joseph/Jane Stone Delegate of _____ United States House of Representatives	Dear Mr./Ms. Stone
undersecretary, of cabinet department (applies to deputy and assistant secretaries also)	The Honorable Joseph/Jane Stone Undersecretary of the Department of _____	Dear Mr./Ms. Stone:

Table 9.   *(continued)*

Federal, State, and Local Government Officials

Federal, State, and Local Government Officials	Form of Address	Salutation
vice president, U.S.	The Vice President of the United States	Sir: My dear Mr. Vice President: Dear Mr. Vice President:
	or	*or*
	The Honorable Joseph Stone Vice President of the United States	Dear Mr. Vice President:

Military Ranks*	Branch of Service	Form of Address	Salutation
admiral	USCG/USN	ADM Lee Stone, USCG/USN	Dear Admiral Stone:
brigadier general	USAF	Brig Gen Lee Stone, USAF	Dear General Stone:
	USA	BG Lee Stone, USA	Dear General Stone:
	USMC	BGen Lee Stone, USMC	Dear General Stone:
captain	USAF/USMC	Capt Lee Stone, USAF/USMC	Dear Captain Stone:
	USA	CPT Lee Stone, USA	Dear Captain Stone:
	USCG/USN	CAPT Lee Stone, USCG/USN	Dear Captain Stone:
chief warrant officer	USAF/USA	CWO Lee Stone, USAF/USA	Dear Mr./Ms. Stone:
colonel	USAF/USMC	Col Lee Stone, USAF/USMC	Dear Colonel Stone:
	USA	COL Lee Stone, USA	Dear Colonel Stone:
commander	USCG/USN	CDR Lee Stone, USCG/USN	Dear Commander Stone:
ensign	USCG/USN	ENS Lee Stone, USCG/USN	Dear Ensign Stone: Dear Mr./Ms. Stone:
first lieutenant	USAF	1st Lt Lee Stone, USAF	Dear Lt. Stone:
	USA	1LT Lee Stone, USA	Dear Lt. Stone:
	USMC	1stLt Lee Stone, USMC	Dear Lt. Stone:
general	USAF/USMC	Gen Lee Stone, USAF/USMC	Dear General Stone:
	USA	GEN Lee Stone, USA	Dear General Stone:
lieutenant	USCG/USN	LT Lee Stone, USCG/USN	Dear Lt. Stone: Dear Mr./Ms. Stone:
lieutenant colonel	USAF	Lt Col Lee Stone USAF	Dear Colonel Stone:
	USA	LTC Lee Stone, USA	Dear Colonel Stone:
	USMC	LtCol Lee Stone, USMC	Dear Colonel Stone:

*These military ranks and their abbreviations are used with the names of military officers. The abbreviated rank is followed by the full name, a comma, and the appropriate abbreviation of the person's branch of service (USAF for United States Air Force, USA for United States Army, USCG for United States Coast Guard, USMC for United States Marine Corps, or USN for United States Navy). Example: ADM Lee Stone, USN. These forms of address apply to men and women, and the first name *Lee* is meant to cover both sexes. Subsequent pages give cadet/midshipman and enlisted ranks.

Table 9.   *(continued)*

Military Ranks	Branch of Service	Form of Address	Salutation
lieutenant commander	USCG/USN	LCDR Lee Stone, USCG/USN	Dear Commander Stone:
lieutenant general	USAF USA USMC	Lt Gen Lee Stone, USAF LTG Lee Stone, USA LtGen Lee Stone, USMC	Dear General Stone: Dear General Stone: Dear General Stone:
lieutenant (junior grade)	USCG/USN	LTJG Lee Stone, USCG/USN	Dear Lt. Stone: Dear Mr./Ms. Stone:
major	USAF/USMC USA	Maj Lee Stone, USAF/USMC MAJ Lee Stone, USA	Dear Major Stone: Dear Major Stone:
major general	USAF USA USMC	Maj Gen Lee Stone, USAF MG Lee Stone, USA MajGen Lee Stone, USMC	Dear General Stone: Dear General Stone: Dear General Stone:
rear admiral	USCG/USN	RADM Lee Stone, USCG/USN	Dear Admiral Stone:
second lieutenant	USAF USA USMC	2d Lt Lee Stone, USAF 2LT Lee Stone, USA 2dLt Lee Stone, USMC	Dear Lt. Stone: Dear Lt. Stone: Dear Lt. Stone:
vice admiral	USCG/USN	VADM Lee Stone, USCG/USN	Dear Admiral Stone:
warrant officer	USAF/USA	WO Lee Stone, USAF/USA	Dear Mr./Ms. Stone:

Cadets and Midshipmen

cadet		Cadet Lee Stone	Dear Cadet Stone: Dear Mr./Ms. Stone:
midshipman		Midshipman Lee Stone	Dear Midshipman Stone: Dear Mr./Ms. Stone:

Enlisted Personnel: A Representative Listing

airman	USAF	AMN Lee Stone, USAF	Dear Airman Stone:
airman basic	USAF	AB Lee Stone, USAF	Dear Airman Stone:
airman first class	USAF	A1C Lee Stone, USAF	Dear Airman Stone:
chief petty officer	USCG/USN	CPO Lee Stone, USCG/USN	Dear Mr./Ms. Stone:
corporal	USA	CPL Lee Stone, USA	Dear Corporal Stone:

Table 9.   *(continued)*

Military Ranks	Branch of Service	Form of Address	Salutation
gunnery sergeant	USMC	GySgt Lee Stone, USMC	Dear Sergeant Stone:
lance corporal	USMC	L/Cpl Lee Stone, USMC	Dear Corporal Stone:
master sergeant	USAF USA	MSGT Lee Stone, USAF MSG Lee Stone, USA	Dear Sergeant Stone: Dear Sergeant Stone:
petty officer	USCG/USN	PO Lee Stone, USCG/USN	Dear Mr./Ms. Stone:
private	USA USMC	PVT Lee Stone, USA Pvt Lee Stone, USMC	Dear Private Stone: Dear Private Stone:
private first class	USA	PFC Lee Stone, USA	Dear Private Stone:
seaman	USCG/USN	SN Lee Stone, USCG/USN	Dear Seaman Stone:
senior master sergeant	USAF	SMSGT Lee Stone, USAF	Dear Sergeant Stone:
sergeant	USAF USA	SGT Lee Stone, USAF SG Lee Stone, USA	Dear Sergeant Stone: Dear Sergeant Stone:
sergeant major (a title not a rank)	USA/USMC USA/USMC	SGM/Sgt.Maj. Lee Stone,	Dear Sergeant Major Stone:
specialist (as special- ist 4th class)	USA	SP4 Lee Stone, USA	Dear Specialist Stone:
staff sergeant	USAF USA	**SSGT** Lee Stone, USAF **SSG** Lee Stone, USA	Dear Sergeant Stone: Dear Sergeant Stone:
technical sergeant	USAF	**TSGT** Lee Stone, USAF	Dear Sergeant Stone:

Professions	Form of Address	Salutation
attorney	Mr./Ms. Joseph/Jane Stone Attorney-at-**Law** *or* Joseph/Jane Stone, Esq.	Dear Mr./Ms. Stone:
dentist	Joseph/Jane Stone, DDS	Dear Dr. Stone:
physician	Joseph/Jane Stone, MD	Dear Dr. Stone:
veterinarian	Joseph/Jane Stone, DVM	Dear Dr. Stone:

Titles and honorifics in signature blocks.   The only courtesy titles used before a writer's name in the typed signature block are *Ms.*, *Miss*, and *Mrs.* With a single exception (i.e., *Mrs.* plus the writer's husband's name), these courtesy titles, if used, must be enclosed in parentheses. They are never used in the written signature. Remember that *Mr.* is also never used in the typed or written signature.

typewritten signature	written signature
(Ms.) Jane Doe	Jane Doe
(Miss) Jane Doe	Jane Doe
(Mrs.) Jane Doe	Jane Doe
Mrs. John M. Doe	Jane Doe

If the writer holds an advanced degree such as MD, PhD, DVM, or DDS, the abbreviated form of the degree may be used in the typed and written signatures following the surname. The writer never uses *Professor* or *Doctor/Dr.* preceding the name.

typewritten signature	written signature
J. Robinson Smith, MD Chief of Surgery	J. Robinson Smith, MD
Nancy Y. Hanks, PhD Professor of Molecular Physics	Nancy Y. Hanks, PhD

Holders of *Esq.* may use it in the typewritten signature block but not in the written signature:

typewritten signature	written signature
Jane L. Smith, Esq.	Jane L. Smith

Holders of *The Honorable* never use the term themselves:

typewritten signature	written signature
John M. Sweeney Associate Justice	John M. Sweeney

Ministers may choose to use *The Reverend/The Rev.* before their names in the typewritten signature block; however, they never use it in the written signature:

typewritten signature	written signature
Francis S. O'Leary, SJ	Francis S. O'Leary, SJ
Jonathan K. Stein, DD	Jonathan K. Stein, DD
Eric C. Swenson Pastor	Eric C. Swenson
The Very Rev. Alexis I. Ivanov Rector	Alexis I. Ivanov

Government officials and military personnel never put their titles or rank designations before their full names in typed or written signatures. Titles and indicators of rank appear only in the typed portion of the block, one line below the writer's name:

typewritten signature	**written signature**
Edward M. Keene	Edward M. Keene
United States Senator	
Elizabeth A. Meaney	Elizabeth A. Meaney
United States Ambassador	
Lee A. Lawson	Lee A. Lawson
Captain, USA	

MEMORANDUM FORMAT

An interoffice memorandum, like a business letter, is a means of transmitting written information from one person, group, or office to another or others. Unlike a letter, however, a memorandum lacks an inside address, a salutation, and a complimentary close. Instead, a memorandum has the following headings: a "To" line on which you list the recipient or recipients; a "From" line on which you list the writer or writers; a date line on which you include the month, day, and year when the communication was written; and a subject line on which you type the main thrust of the message. The headings for these lines are printed at the top of the memorandum sheet. Ancillary data such as a telephone extension, a department name, or a "Copies to" indicator also may be included in the printed headings, depending on the policy of your company. The rest of the page is designated for the message. The typist's initials, lists of courtesy copy recipients, distribution lists, or attachment notations appear at the end of the message, if necessary. Should the memorandum contain sensitive material, the notation CONFIDENTIAL is typed in capital letters at the very top of the sheet above the main printed heading *Memorandum.*

Paper size and the appearance of the memorandum.   The most usual paper size is $8\frac{1}{2}''\times 11''$; however, the half size measuring $8\frac{1}{2}''\times 5\frac{1}{2}''$ may be used for very brief messages. Memos also may be typed on plain bond paper, but if this method is used you must head the sheet with the capitalized term MEMORANDUM followed on subsequent lines by capitalized TO, FROM, DATE, and SUBJECT headings punctuated by colons.

Some companies use colored memo paper especially for interoffice communications generated by chief executive and chief operating officers or by specific departments and divisions. Color choice, weight, size, and design of memorandum paper vary according to company policy.

Maintain appropriate margins so that the memorandum is balanced attractively on the page. One-inch margins are best for long memos, while $1\frac{1}{2}''$ margins work well with medium-length and shorter memos. Align your heading fill-ins so that they look neat and consistent. Some printed headings are themselves aligned to the right in order to facilitate typing the fill-ins:

TO:	Marketing Division
FROM:	Office of the President
DATE:	12/13/92
SUBJECT:	Dictionary Advertising Campaign

If all the printed headings have been so aligned, skip two spaces before typing the fill-ins. If the headings are aligned to the left instead, begin typing the fill-ins two spaces to the right of the longest heading (usually the subject heading) and block all other fill-ins with it:

TO:	Marketing Division
FROM:	Office of the President
DATE:	12/13/92
SUBJECT:	Dictionary Advertising Campaign

Regardless of the positioning of the printed heads, however, you must skip two spaces before beginning the fill-ins. Ensure that your fill-ins are aligned with the printed headings: they should appear neither above nor below the headings. Use your variable line spacer or ratchet release to achieve proper horizontal alignment.

The appearance of an interoffice memorandum is a tangible indicator of your skills and your attitude toward the company. Memos with ugly strikeovers, penned-in corrections, marginal runovers, poor spelling, bad grammar, unaligned headings, and crumpled paper edges reflect badly on you, your executive, and your entire department. Remember also to store your memo paper in its original container. Keep only a small quantity in your desk drawer; otherwise, the paper will deteriorate from exposure to dust and also may become crumpled along the edges.

The "To" line: content and styling.   The "To" line may contain a single name or several names. It also might include a departmental name or the collective designation "All Desks" with material to be distributed companywide. A courtesy title such as *Mr., Ms.,* or *Dr.* is generally omitted unless the recipient outranks the writer. If the memo has been addressed to several recipients one of whom requires use of a courtesy title, similar titles must be used with the names of the other recipients. You may use full names or initials and surnames in the "To" block. For instance, you might say *Jane C. King* or *J.C. King.* Follow the style dictated by the writer. The recipient's departmental affiliation may be included on a line under the name, depending on the size of the company and its policy:

TO:	Frank R. Richardson
	Polymer Research Division

With a memorandum directed to many individuals, type the asterisked word *Distribution** in the "To" line space. At the end of the message, skip two lines, repeat the word *Distribution**, skip two more lines, and list the recipients in a single-spaced flush left block, one name to a line, in alphabetical order by surname or in order of corporate rank. Use the latter order only when the memorandum has been directed to a group of high corporate officers. In a case like this, the chief executive officer's name would appear first on the list followed by the names of various vice presidents in order of rank within the company.

The "From" line: content and styling.   The "From" line may contain a single name or multiple names. It may indicate that the memo is from a particular office or department. The "From" line is styled just like the "To" line, except for the omission of a courtesy title with the writer's name: the writer's name may appear as a full form (John L. Lee) or in abbreviated form (J.L. Lee), but a courtesy title (such as "Mr. John L. Lee") is never used.

The date line.   You may abbreviate dates in memos to the all-numeric form such as 12/13/92 where 12 means December, 13 means the thirteenth day of the month, and 92 means 1992. The full form—December 13, 1992—is also correct. Use the style that the writer prefers.

The subject line.   The gist of the letter is encapsulated in the subject line, which should be short (one- liners are preferable from the reader's standpoint, and for subsequent filing purposes). The writer should dictate the subject line. Key words within the subject line may be capitalized initially or the entire line may be capitalized. Do not underscore the subject matter and do not punctuate the line with a period.

The message.   Skip three vertical line spaces from the last heading and its fill-in before beginning the message. Paragraphs may be blocked flush with the left margin or indented to the right by five or six spaces. Single-space the paragraphs internally, and use double spacing to separate the paragraphs from each other. (With very short memos you may double-space the entire message; however, you must indent the paragraphs by at least six spaces to set them off one from another.) Maintain adequate margins to the right, left, and bottom of the page. Some writers prefer to enumerate their paragraphs with Arabic or Roman numerals or with letters. Follow the style indicated by the writer. Displayed data such as long quotations, numerical lists within paragraphs, and tables should be set off from the body of the message by block indentations and double spacing at the top and the bottom of the displayed matter. Displayed quotations and lists should be single-spaced internally. Skip two lines between each unit of an enumeration.

Memorandum

TO   Janis Wilcox   FROM Arthur R. Lee   DATE 12/13/83

SUBJECT Memorandum Format

This is an example of a properly formatted full-page company memorandum featuring printed headings. Notice that the fill-ins have been horizontally aligned with the heads and that two spaces have been left between the last letter of each head and the first letter of each typewritten fill-in.

Since this is a rather long memo, we have set our margins at one inch. Had the memo been short, we might have chosen a 1½-inch or a 2-inch margin setting with double-spaced, indented paragraphs.

You ought to skip at least three vertical lines from the last heading to the first line of the message. This space may be increased with extremely short memos.

Handle displayed enumerations like this:

1. Skip two vertical lines between the text and the first item in the enumeration.

2. Block and indent the entire enumeration as we have done here.

3. Skip two lines between each item in the list, but maintain single spacing within each unit.

4. Skip two vertical lines between the last line of the last enumerated item and the first line of the continuing text so that the displayed material will be clearly set off from the rest of the message.

Use a blank continuation sheet matching the memorandum paper in size, weight, color, and texture if the message exceeds one page in length. Construct a heading for the continuation sheet or sheets that includes the name of the recipient, the page number, and the date styled as you have typed it on the first sheet.

Paragraphs in memoranda may be indented by five or six lines or they may be set flush with the left margin as we have done here. The flush left format is the easiest.

Include your initials at the end of the message, two vertical line spaces below the last line of text, if you wish. Copy recipients should be listed two lines below your initials or two lines below the last line of the message if no initials appear on the page.

Attachments are listed separately below the other notations or two lines below the last message line if no other notations appear on the page.

cc: Mary Allen
     Sandra Kendall

Attachment: Style Manual

Full-page Memorandum

Memorandum

TO   Editors   FROM Mary Roe *Mary*   DATE 12/13/91

SUBJECT   Editorial Department Meeting – New Product Development

There will be a meeting of all editors in my office on Monday, December 16, at 10:30 a.m. for the purpose of proposing and discussing new electronic and print products for the Reference Division in the coming year. Please come prepared to discuss your ideas in detail and defend them if necessary. A detailed agenda will be issued to you before the meeting.

Half-sheet Memorandum

MEMORANDUM

TO: All Desks - All Locations   FROM: John R. Doe

SUBJECT: Jean Roe   DATE: 12/13/83

I am pleased to announce the appointment of Jean D. Roe as Assistant Business Manager for the Reference Division. She will be responsible for many of the budget-related financial systems in place and for the development of new systems for project and quality control in print and electronic media. She will provide assistance in coordinating Reference Division data processing projects and other administrative services.

Jean has been an auditor with the Internal Audit Department of Houghton Mifflin Company since June, 1982, and has participated in audit programs for the School and Reference Divisions in Boston and in various regional offices. She brings to Houghton Mifflin her experience as a project manager in the Social Services Department for the Commonwealth of Massachusetts and three years' experience as a Senior Auditor and Senior Consultant for Arthur Young & Company. She has also worked as an accountant in the Boston office of Dun & Bradstreet.

Jean is a Certified Public Accountant in the Commonwealth of Massachusetts. She earned her B.A. in economics from Boston College and her M.B.A. from Harvard. She and her family reside in Wellesley.

I am sure that all of you will extend a most enthusiastic welcome to Jean as she joins the Reference Division at this very exciting time.

Memorandum on Blank Sheet

With a message exceeding one page, use a plain continuation sheet matching the printed memorandum page in color, texture, weight, and size. Margin settings and paragraph alignment must match the format on the first page. Skip at least six vertical line spaces from the top edge of the sheet before typing the heading. Either block the heading flush with the left margin or spread it across the page. If the heading on the first sheet reads "Distribution*" use the flush left format, and include only the page number and the date on the continuation sheet. If you have styled the date in numerals on the first sheet, use that styling on the continuation sheet. If you have written out the date on the first sheet, write it out on the continuation sheet.

Typist's initials.   Typist's initials, if included, are positioned two vertical line spaces beneath the last message line, flush with the left margin. Inclusion of these initials depends on company policy, the writer's wishes, and/or the typist's own preferences.

Copy recipients and distribution lists.   Copy recipients' names appear two vertical line spaces below the typist's initials (if included) or two lines below the last line of the message:

    cc: Kathryn K. Overton
          Michael I. Simms
          Theodore R. Thomas
          Laverne T. Udall

A distribution list for many recipients of copies is set up in much the same manner, with two spaces separating the distribution notation from the list itself:

    Distribution*

    Mary A. Brown
    Alice V. Collins
    Franklin B. Fields
    James W. Hay
    Leo V. Isaacson
    Mary W. Kay

With a memo destined for a single recipient, the writer usually retains a copy and sends the original to the intended recipient. With memos to multiple recipients, the writer usually retains the original and sends copies to all of the recipients. (Put a check by the name of each recipient before putting the memo in the envelope.)

Attachment notations.   If attachments accompany the memo, put a notation to this effect two lines below the last notation on the page or, if there are no other notations, put the attachment notation two lines below the last message line. Don't forget to staple or clip the attachments to the memorandum.

> Attachments: P & L Statement 1984
> OP Sales Estimates 1985

Envelopes.   If electronic mail is not being used, memorandums are generally routed to their recipients via unsealed, string-tied interoffice mailers. These envelopes have lines on which you write the recipient's name and intracompany location. With confidential memos, use a sealable manila envelope or a regular letterhead envelope with the word CONFIDENTIAL typed or hand-lettered in the top left corner, the recipient's name in the center, and the notation "Company Mail" or "Interoffice Mail" lettered or typed in the space where the postage ordinarily would have been affixed. Another way of indicating that the envelope is for interoffice delivery is to place an inked-in "X" mark where the postage ordinarily goes.

PRESS RELEASES

Companies issue press releases chiefly to help maintain a high public profile and thereby increase sales. For example, a press release might be issued to promote the launch of a new product or to announce markedly increased revenues, stock splits, or bigger dividends. Other stories might announce the appointment of a new chief executive officer or the installation of new members of the board of directors. The press release—just one component of a comprehensive public relations, advertising, and sales campaign—is a highly visible indicator of corporate style and substance, and as such it must be devoid of all errors, especially factual ones. Since you are often called upon to type and proofread press releases, your role in maintaining your company's public image is quite important. Let your company's outgoing publicity be a credit and not a deficit to its reputation.

Since a press release is really a news story, the writer constructs it with a view to immediate newsworthiness. That is, the writer follows journalistic style by putting the most important data in the first paragraph: Who did What? When was it done and Where? And Why was it done? Supporting data are then included in subsequent paragraphs arranged in order from the most important to the least important. In this way, the writer makes the news editor's life much easier, for the story can be pruned from the bottom depending on the space available in the publication in which it will appear, without inadvertent deletion of crucial facts. Similarly, a broadcast editor can cut all but the most salient facts for inclusion in a television or radio newscast.

Paper and format.   A press release is usually keyed on a special printed form headed *Press Release, News Release,* or *News from* (company). The

from

Houghton Mifflin Company One Beacon Street, Boston, Massachusetts 02108

Contact: Stephen O. Jaeger
          Senior Vice President
          Chief Financial Officer
          (617) 725-5017

October 23, 1990
For Immediate Release

**HOUGHTON MIFFLIN COMPANY
ANNOUNCES THIRD-QUARTER
GAINS IN SALES AND INCOME**

BOSTON -- Houghton Mifflin Company today reported gains in revenue and income

for the third quarter, ended September 30, 1990. Net sales were $178.8 million,

a 6.7% increase over last year's $167.5 million. Net income rose 7.8% to $26.8

million, or $1.88 per share, compared with $24.9 million, or $1.75 per share, in

1989.

For the nine months ended September 30, 1990, net sales were $345.0

million, a 7.3% increase over the $321.5 million recorded in 1989. Net income

for the nine months rose 8.9% to $26.3 million, or $1.84 per share, from $24.1

million, or $1.70 per share, a year ago. The 1990 nine-month results included a

nonrecurring net gain of $4.0 million, or $.17 per share after taxes.

Nader F. Darehshori, Chairman and Chief Executive Officer, said,

"Educational publishing segment sales rose 6% in the third quarter led by the

School Division where sales grew at a higher rate. Sales of elementary and

secondary school publications both achieved solid gains over last year's third

quarter. General publishing segment sales increased 12% primarily from sales by

international operations including Gollancz, which was purchased in the fourth

- more -

Press Release

- 2 -

quarter of last year. Trade & Reference Division sales equaled last year's strong third-quarter performance and Software Division sales were above 1989's third quarter.

Darehshori said, "Earnings for the third quarter were affected by lower than planned college textbook sales and increased editorial and plate expenses associated with the development of new publications for the school and college markets. School and college marketing costs also increased during the quarter. As expected, the Company's foreign subsidiaries continued to have a dilutive . effect in the third quarter.

"The results for 1990 reflect the major investment the Company is making in new publications to address future opportunities. The Company is introducing for 1991 new elementary school reading and social studies programs as well as expanded lists of secondary school and college publications which will have a positive impact in 1991 and future years."

Darehshori said, "The Trade & Reference Division is expected to achieve good fourth-quarter 1990 sales results, but the continuing high level of college and school publication development and selling costs related to 1991 textbook adoption opportunities is expected to contribute to a fourth-quarter seasonal loss that exceeds historical levels."

# # #

company's full name, address, and telephone/Telex number(s) are usually printed on the form as part of the heading along with memorandum-style subheadings such as

From: Sandee Martin
Contact: Laura Mason

in which the writer's name appears first followed by the public affairs person whom the editor might wish to contact for further information should a major story develop. These subheadings may be positioned in the top right or left corners of the first page. If the material is to be published or broadcast immediately, the phrase FOR IMMEDIATE RELEASE should be typed near the top edge of the first page in a conspicuous position relative to the heading and subheads.

The paper itself may be $8\frac{1}{2}'' \times 11''$ or it may be $8\frac{1}{2}'' \times 14''$ (legal). Double-space the text for easier editing later on. Allow right and left margins measuring $1''$ and a bottom margin of about $1\frac{1}{2}''$ to accommodate insertion of the continuation indicator *more*. Leave $2–2\frac{1}{2}''$ of white space from the bottom of the printed heading to the typewritten headline of the first page.

The headline.   The headline—a sentence or phrase focusing on the most important point of the story—is typed in capital letters centered on the page below the printed heading. Skip at least three and possibly four vertical line spaces from the headline to the first line of the story itself.

The story.   Begin the story with a flush left or indented date line (such as BOSTON, December 13—) in which the city name appears in capital letters followed by a comma, the month and the day, followed by a dash set tight or spaced with the day. Do not give the state's name unless your city's name is the same as those of several other cities. Begin typing the story right after the dash, on the same line, with no space or one space intervening between the dash and the first word of the running text:

```
BOSTON, December 13—John N. Kennedy, Chairman and Presi-
dent of FFF Air Lines, has announced a new super-saver fare
structure, effective immediately. Passengers will realize
savings of up to 30% on tickets. . . .
```

Indent each subsequent paragraph by at least five or six spaces to set it off from the next one. If the story exceeds one page, type the word *more* in lowercase letters at the bottom of the page, centered within the bottom margin space. Style this continuation indicator as -more- or (more), using hyphens or parentheses. Use blank continuation sheets matching the first sheet in size, color, texture, and weight. Maintain margins on the continuation sheet that match those on the first sheet, except at the top of the page. The heading of the continuation sheet should begin from four to six lines below the top edge. Number and caption the continuation sheet(s) as directed by the writer. The capitalized caption will contain a key word or words derived from the substance of the headline, followed by a dash and the page number set tight on one line, as FFF SUPER-SAVER—2.

The end.   Signal the end of the story by typing one of the following devices in the center of the last page about two or three vertical line spaces from the last line:

   # # # # *or* #### *or* ### *or* -30- *or* -end- *or* (END)

Proofreading.   Proofread the entire document line-for-line against the original. Check for typographical, grammatical, and factual errors. Query the executive if a fact appears to be inconsistent with other data or if you think it might be wrong. Then read the document again from beginning to end without looking at the original. Use the team proofreading approach for one last check: have a colleague read the original aloud while you read the final document.

CORPORATE REPORTS

Several kinds of reports are generated in business: memorandum reports, letter reports, and megareports (i.e., long complex documents sometimes encompassing hundreds of pages). These documents serve many needs and are directed to various readership levels inside and outside the company. A report might introduce and then analyze in detail a given market; discuss a particular business problem in depth and then offer a solution; lay out an annual or multiyear strategic plan; delve into a highly complicated legal or financial question; provide impetus for the research, development, and launch of a new product; or offer a stock/investment prospectus. Reports may be destined for staff, line management, top management, or outside clients. Some reports are general in content while others are highly technical. Your task is to organize and keyboard the draft materials into a logically ordered, consistently and neatly typed final product devoid of typographical and factual errors. You also may be requested to assist in producing tabular and graphic exhibits called *visual aids.* And of course the responsibility for proofreading, fact checking, duplication/printing, collation, binding, and distribution to the designated readership probably will be yours.

Although shorter reports are often dictated as memorandums, the longer ones are usually handwritten or typed as annotated drafts. In many cases a long report represents the input of a number of other executives besides yours. For instance, the summary in a new product report might have been written by your executive while the sales forecast might have been prepared by the sales director. The manufacturing cost estimates and production schedule might have been worked out by a manufacturing manager. The financials might have been prepared by a business manager or an accountant, with the advertising/promotion strategy having been developed by an advertising manager or an outside agency. Assuming that your executive is in charge of the entire document, you should be aware of some common pitfalls. Multiauthor reports usually abound in stylistic, spelling, and factual inconsistencies; hence, you should read the entire document from beginning to end and note all inconsistencies, errors, and unclear points before touching the keyboard. Tab them with self-sticking notes and then query the writer or writers responsible for the problematic points or sections. Check all major and subsidiary headings in the text to ensure consistency of style. Find out where the displayed tables and graphics are to appear: will they be scattered throughout the text (if so, room must be left for them) or will they be clustered together in an appendix? If possible, input the report into a word processor and store it on memory for easier final editing/correction.

The Memorandum Report

For a short (i.e., a two- to three-page) report intended for in-house distribution, use the company's printed memo paper and continuation sheets. Put the report title in the subject block and then follow the guidelines in this chapter regarding memorandum format. A typical memorandum report might be a monthly sales analysis for a product line in a given region or territory or a monthly departmental progress report with respect to on-line projects.

The Letter Report

A letter report might be used to convey information to various off-site managers or to the members of a board of directors. A letter report is just what the designation indicates: a letter to the recipient(s) that has been modified stylistically to include various headings and subheadings. The letter report is typed on corporate letterhead and continuation sheets matching the letterhead. We recommend the Block or the Modified Block Letter styles for such a report. These two styles lend themselves readily to graceful, balanced presentation of information, whether it be running text or displayed matter. In most cases the letter will be duplicated for many recipients. We therefore recommend that you save extra white space in the inside address block to accommodate inclusion of names and addresses varying markedly in length.

The following guidelines have been developed to assist you in typing the typically occurring heads and subheads in letter reports. Read the guidelines and then refer to the two-page Block facsimile of a letter report at the end of this subsection.

REPORT TITLE STYLED AS SUBJECT LINE
position: 3 vertical line spaces below salutation
             3 vertical line spaces above text or first main heading
             flush left
styling: capitalized
             underscored

MAIN HEADING
position: 3 vertical line spaces below what has gone before
             (i.e., title or text)
             3 vertical line spaces above what follows (i.e., text or
             another head)
             flush left
styling: capitalized

First-level Subhead
position: 3 vertical line spaces below what has gone before (i.e., text)
             3 vertical line spaces above what follows (i.e., text or
             another head)
             flush left
styling: capital and lowercased letters
             underscored

Sideheads.
position: flush left, run in with the text
styling: initially capitalized and then lowercased
             underscored
             punctuated with period (optional)

If the Modified Block Letter style is used, the secretary positions the
title/subject line, the main headings, and the first-level subheads in the
center of the page while maintaining the same vertical spacing as that
shown with the Block Letter. The sideheads are run in with the text.

Table 10.   **Corporate Report Typewriting Guide**

Margins

location	machine setting: unbound & top-bound
top/p.1	12 lines
top/p. 2ff.	6 lines
bottom/all pp.	6 lines
left & right/all pp.	12 spaces/elite
	10 spaces/pica
	machine setting: sidebound

Table 10.   *(continued)*

Margins

left/all pp.	18 spaces/elite 15 spaces/pica

Spacing

element of report	machine setting: unbound, top-bound, & sidebound
body of report	single or double
between paragraphs	if single-spaced paragraphs, double spacing to separate them; if double-spaced paragraphs, triple spacing to separate them
long quoted matter, displayed	single
enumerations, tables	single within units; double between units
footnotes	single
bibliography	single

Indention

element of report	machine setting: unbound, top-bound, sidebound
paragraphs	indented format: 5–6 spaces block format: no indents
long quoted matter, tables, lists	blocked 5–6 spaces right and left
footnotes	2–5 spaces, first line only
bibliography	no indent on first line; 2–5 spaces, runover lines

Pagination: unbound & top bound—numerals 3–6 lines from bottom center, each page; sidebound—numerals 3–6 lines from top of page or 3–6 lines from bottom and $\frac{1}{2}''$ to the right of center

element of report	kind of number
flyleaves	no pagination
title fly	lowercase Roman numeral i
title page	lowercase Roman numeral ii
front matter (i.e., letters of authorization/transmittal, acknowledgments, table of contents, lists of tables and graphics, preface, foreword, executive summary)	lowercase Roman numeral iii
first text page	Arabic numeral 1
subsequent text pages (i.e., body of report, appendix, footnotes listed separately, bibliography, index)	Arabic numeral 2 ff.

Houghton Mifflin Company

Two Park Street, Boston, Massachusetts 02108
(617) 725-5000   Cable HOUGHTON

Reference Division

December 13, 19--

Mr. Arthur R. Lacey
Lacey, Middleton & White
123 Beacon Street
City, US 98765

Dear Mr. Lacey:

THE TITLE OF THE LETTER REPORT STYLED AS A SUBJECT LINE

This is a facsimile of a letter report in which the title is styled in underscored
capital letters, flush left and three vertical line spaces from the salutation
and the first line of running text. Although it is not good form to underscore
the subject line in conventional business correspondence it is entirely correct to
do so in the letter report in order to set off the title clearly.

THE FIRST MAIN HEADING

The first main subject heading is also typed flush with the left margin but it is
not underscored. Use this format for all of the major headings in the writer's
text. Assuming that we have now reached a subheading, let us proceed to type
it three vertical line spaces below this paragraph.

The First-level Subhead

The first-level subhead, typewritten in capital and lowercase letters, is underscored and positioned three lines above the running text applicable to it. While
main headings correspond to the Roman numerals I, II, III, and so on in outlines,
first-level subheads correspond to the capital letters A, B, C, and so on, also
used therein.

The first sidehead. The sidehead, run in with the paragraph text to which it re-
lates, is initially capitalized and underscored as shown here. It may be
punctuated by a period but the inclusion of the period is not required. The sidehead in a letter report corresponds to the numerals 1, 2, 3, and so on, as used
in outlines.

Note that the spacing between paragraphs within major categories is double. Use
triple spacing between main and first-level headings only. If you decide to
use the Modified Block Letter style instead of the Block Style illustrated here,
you may center the subject line, the first main heading, and the first-level
subhead on the page.

Atlanta / Dallas / Geneva, Illinois / Hopewell, New Jersey / Palo Alto / London

Letter Report Forms

Page 2
Mr. Arthur R. Lacey
December 13, 19--

Since most letter reports will exceed one page, you should plan on using continuation sheets matching the letterhead in size, color, texture, and weight.
Of course, your margins on all subsequent sheets must match the ones you have
maintained on the letterhead.

THE SECOND MAIN HEADING

Many reports contain an Executive Summary (also called an Abstract) and lists
of conclusions and/or recommendations. Consider these sections important
enough to rate main headings as shown just above. The Executive Summary may
appear at the very beginning or at the end. The conclusions and/or recommendations almost always come at the end.

Another First-level Subhead

Displayed data such as tables or lists may be set within the running text or
grouped together in an Appendix. If the material is to be incorporated within the text, follow the guidelines given in the business correspondence section of this chapter for block indention of displayed data.

A second sidehead. The letter report concludes with a complimentary close and
a typewritten signature block, just as a conventional business letter does.
Follow the guidelines given in the business correspondence section of this
chapter.

If enclosures are to be included along with the report, annotate the report to
this effect as we have shown below.

Very truly yours,

Robin N. Brown
Corporate Counsel

RNB:ahs

Enclosures: Proxy Statement
             Agenda, Stockholders' Meeting
             Board of Directors' Meeting Schedule
             Agenda, Board of Directors' Meeting

The Megareport

By *megareport* we mean a lengthy, complex, formal document on a given subject or subjects intended for internal distribution or for an outside client. Its essential elements include a title page, an executive summary (also called an abstract), and pages of running text. Ancillary elements included or omitted depending on the content and purpose of the document, the writer's wishes, and/or company policy, are: a cover, a flyleaf or flyleaves, a title fly, letters of authorization/transmittal, a foreword, a preface, acknowledgments, a list of graphics and tables, a list of conclusions or recommendations, an appendix, footnotes, and a bibliography. Sometimes an index is included.

The report is typewritten on $8\frac{1}{2}'' \times 11''$ white bond paper that will withstand repeated handling. The pages should be typed with a view toward the planned method of binding: will it be stapled at the top left (a good method for shorter reports), or will it be sidebound (preferable for extremely long reports)? The prefatory sections (i.e., the letters of authorization/transmittal, the acknowledgments, the table of contents, the list of graphics and/or tables, the foreword and/or preface, and the executive summary) are paginated sequentially in lowercase Roman numerals (e.g., i, ii, iii, iv, v, and so on) centered on the page about three to six vertical line spaces from the bottom edge of the sheet. The body of the report and all appended materials are paginated sequentially in Arabic numerals positioned at the top right margin about one inch from the top edge of the sheet or about one inch from the bottom edge of the sheet flush with the right margin. The first page of the body of the report is unpaginated.

Select a cover for the report that will protect it over the long term and one that is appropriate for the overall length of it. A ring binder, for example, is particularly appropriate for a five-year plan running hundreds of pages in length. The cover ought to contain a gummed label bearing the title and perhaps the writer's name or the name of the company. The label should be neatly and clearly typed.

The flyleaf, title fly, and title page.   Formal reports often have a flyleaf—a blank page appearing at the very beginning. Sometimes a report may have two of these, one at the beginning and another at the end. Flyleaves protect the rest of the document and allow space for readers' comments. The title fly contains the capitalized title of the report, centered neatly on the page. The title page, on the other hand, contains the title plus the subtitle if there is one, the writer's name and corporate title, the writer's departmental affiliation, and the name of the firm. In a multiauthor report, the name of all the writers together with their corporate titles and departmental affiliations may be included on this page. If the report has been prepared for an outside client, the client's name and address also appear on the title page. Job numbers, purchase orders, or contract numbers are included as required by the individual company. The date on which the report was prepared must appear on the title page. If the report is a revision of an older work, that fact should be noted too, as "Revision A – 1992" or whatever. Sometimes key words reflecting the main topics discussed in the body of the report are appended to the title page for use in subject-coded computerized information retrieval systems. Type and spell the key words exactly as the author has written them.

Type the title in capital letters and the subtitle (if any) in capital and lowercase letters. Double-space the title and center it in the top third of the page. Add the writer's name and/or the name of the client plus any other necessary data in the bottom third of the page, positioned in such a way as to be attractively balanced. Use capital and lowercase letters for this material.

Letters of authorization and/or transmittal.   If official written authorization has been given to do a study (such as a market research survey or an engineering proposal for an outside client), the writer often includes a photocopy of that document in the front matter of the study. The photocopy should be clean with sharp contrast between typescript and paper. A letter of transmittal encapsulating the purpose, scope, and content of the study may be included if the report has been commissioned by an outside source. In effect, the letter of transmittal replies to the letter of authorization and says "Here is what you asked for." This letter should be typed on company letterhead and signed by the writer or the person having overall responsibility for the project. Ensure that the left margin of the letter is wide enough to accomodate side binding (i.e., allow a margin of $2\frac{1}{2}''$ on the left side in documents to be sidebound).

Acknowledgments page.   When other people have assisted the writer in preparing the report, a brief notation acknowledging their help, support, and work is the right way of showing one's appreciation and crediting their efforts. Acknowledgments of this type are included on a separate page, usually styled in one or two short, single-spaced paragraphs. The word ACKNOWLEDGMENTS is typed in capital letters three lines above the text. The text paragraphs are separated by double spacing. All of this material should be centered and balanced on the page.

Table of contents.   The table of contents presents at a glance an outline of the major and subsidiary topics covered in the report together with appropriate pagination. When compiling the table of contents, you should use the major and subsidiary headings found in the body of the report. If the writer has used Roman numerals and letters to introduce the headings, include them in the table of contents. If the writer has used an all-numeric system of signaling heads in the text, use these numbers in the table of contents. Word the headings in the table of contents exactly as they are worded in the text.

The table of contents is centered on the page with ample margins all around. Double-space between headings and subheads; single-space runover lines within these headings. Headings and page numbers must be horizontally and vertically aligned. Numbers, letters, or other devices introducing heads also must be so aligned. Use a continuation sheet for a table of contents exceeding one page, and head the continuation sheet "Table of Contents – Continued", or a variation thereof. This heading should be centered and typed in capital and lowercase letters near the top of the page. Remember, however, that the title for the first contents page must be styled in capital letters, as: TABLE OF CONTENTS. The use of leaders (horizontally typed periods) to link headings with their page numbers is optional. Leaders may be set tight (i.e., typed consecutively in a line with no intervening spaces) or spaced (i.e., typed consecutively in a line with one space between each period). Leaders must align vertically as illustrated in the table of contents facsimile on pages 214–215.

Don't try to type the table of contents until the body of the report has been typed in final form and approved by the writer or writers, because last-minute changes in the text affecting pagination may render your earlier efforts fruitless. Before typing the contents page you should check and recheck pagination, heading titles, and numerals. After the contents page has been typed, you should repeat this procedure. Have the writer check the material at least once before you release the document for duplication, printing, binding, and distribution.

List of graphics and tables.   The table of contents of a report containing few graphics and tables can be augmented with a short list of these features appearing at the end of the contents section. List the graphics in one section and the tables in another. Head the lists: LIST OF GRAPHICS and LIST OF TABLES. Include figure and table numbers, titles, and pagination. Reports incorporating many graphics and tables must include complete lists that are typed on separate pages and styled as above for both of these features. The format of these lists should match that of the contents page.

Foreword and/or preface.   A foreword or a preface or both may be included in a report. The foreword—written by someone other than the writer of the report itself—tells why the report was written. The preface—written by the author of the report itself—is a short statement regarding the scope and content of the study. These sections should be single-spaced on one page apiece, headed FOREWORD and PREFACE, respectively.

Executive summary.   An executive summary, sometimes called an abstract, appears on one page in the front matter. Composed of about 150 words, the executive summary encapsulates for busy readers the major issues, conclusions, and recommendations contained in the body of the report. It is also a useful device in constructing computerized report files.

Type the heading EXECUTIVE SUMMARY near the top of the page. Skip three lines and begin the summary. Single-space the paragraphs of the summary, but leave two spaces between each paragraph.

The text.   The text of the report may be double- or single-spaced. Follow the writer's instructions, or, if none are forthcoming, follow your company's typing guidelines. (Many companies prefer that reports be double-spaced so that readers can add comments more easily.) Maintain even, ample margins all around. For sidebound reports maintain a left margin of $2-2\frac{1}{2}''$. (See Table 10, Corporate Report Typewriting Guide, on page 205–206 of this subsection.) Ensure that the heads and subheads in the text have been typed exactly as the writer has indicated. Three heading systems are in common use today: freestanding headings, all-numeric headings, and Roman numeral/alphabet headings. Freestanding headings are those recommended for inclusion in the letter report:

MAIN HEADING IN CAPITAL LETTERS

First-level Subhead in Underscored Capitals and Lowercase

Run-in subhead underscored and initially capitalized.

Freestanding headings may be aligned flush with the left margin or centered on the page as explained in the section on letter reports. (Run-in tertiary heads are always set flush left.)

The all-numeric system, often employed in technical reports and proposals, features the use of decimals to signal the levels of the headings. Follow the company guidelines with regard to use of all-numeric headings.

1.0 FIRST MAIN SECTION
   1.1   FIRST MAIN SUBSECTION
   1.2 SECOND MAIN SUBSECTION
   1.3 THIRD MAIN SUBSECTION
      1.3.1   FIRST SUBUNIT
      1.3.2   SECOND SUBUNIT
      1.3.3   THIRD SUBUNIT
   1.4 FOURTH MAIN SUBSECTION
2.0 SECOND MAIN SECTION

The combined Roman numeral/alphabet system is basically the same as the general outline system followed by students when writing term papers:

I. MAIN HEADING
   A. Subheading
      1. Sub-subheading
      2. Sub-subheading

   B. Subheading
      1. <u>Sub-subheading</u>
         (a.) Most limited subcategory
         (b.) Most limited subcategory
      2. <u>Sub-subheading</u>

II. MAIN HEADING

Follow carefully the writer's directions when using this format. Remember that if you have a heading labeled A., 1., or (a.), you must have at least one other heading in the same set, as B., 2., or (b.). A heading in one set should never stand alone.

Some reports are really technical job proposals for outside clients. The body of a proposal usually includes some headings and subheadings excluded from non-technical business studies. They deserve brief mention here. The proposal begins with an introductory section in which the problem to be solved is defined, the objectives of the study are set forth, the proposed solution to the problem is described in steps or work phases, the resultant benefits to the client are given, and the capabilities of the contracting company are delineated. The introduction is followed by a technical operations plan—a detailed section explaining how the goals and objectives will be met and how the total program will be implemented step-by-step. Next comes the management plan detailing the project's organization—i.e., the number of personnel required, the on-going documentation to be generated (e.g., progress reports), and the quality control procedures to be maintained throughout the program. The report often concludes with the financials, a section outlining the forecast costs and fees. This basic format is augmented when necessary by other sections and subsections.

Many reports—technical and general—end with a list of conclusions and/or recommendations. These items should be listed in enumerated format. They should be block indented, single-spaced internally, and double-spaced between each other.

Appendix.   An appendix containing ancillary charts, graphs, illustrations, and tables may be included in the report. The appendix appears before any other back matter sections such as footnotes, a bibliography, a glossary, or an index. Introduce the appendix in capital letters; for example, a centered format:

APPENDIX
TRADE DIVISION FORECAST
VOLUME BY TITLE
1984–1985

The material appears on a separate page as shown above. Multiple appendices should be separately listed on a page as APPENDIX A, APPENDIX B, and so on. Some companies call this section a LIST OF EXHIBITS instead.

TABLE OF CONTENTS

(i)

TABLE OF CONTENTS - Continued

SECTION IV

EXHIBIT A

AVAILABLE INFORMATION

The Corporation is subject to the informational requirements of the Securities Exchange Act of 1934 and in accordance therewith files reports, proxy statements, and other information with the Securities and Exchange Commission (the "Commission"). Such reports, proxy statements, and other information filed by the Company can be inspected and copied at the public reference facilities maintained by the Commission at Room 1024, 450 Fifth Street, N.W., Washington, D.C. 20549 and at the Commission's regional offices at the following locations: Room 1028, 26 Federal Plaza, New York, New York 10278; Room 1228, Everett McKinley Dirkson Building, 219 South Dearborn Street, Chicago, Illinois 60604; and Suite 500, 5757 Wilshire Boulevard, Los Angeles, California 90036. Certain information filed by the Corporation with the Commission can be inspected at the Commission's regional office located at 150 Causeway Street, Boston, Massachusetts 02114. Copies of all the above-mentioned material can be obtained from the Public Reference Section of the Commission, Washington, D.C. 20549 at prescribed rates. In addition, such reports, proxy statements, and other information concerning the Corporation are available at the offices of the New York Stock Exchange, 1 Wall Street, New York, New York 10005. Additional updating information with respect to the securities covered hereby may be provided in the future to members of the Plan by means of appendices to the Prospectus.

INCORPORATION OF CERTAIN DOCUMENTS BY REFERENCE

Each of the following documents is incorporated by reference into this Prospectus:

(a)   The Corporation's Annual Report on Form 10-K for the year ended December 31, 19-- filed pursuant to Section 13 or 15(d) of the Securities Exchange Act of 1934.

(b)   The Plan's Annual Report on Form 11-K for the year ended December 31, 19-- filed pursuant to Section 13 or 15(d) of the Securities Exchange Act of 1934.

(c)   All other reports filed pursuant to Section 13 or 15(d) of the Securities Exchange Act of 1934 with respect to the Corporation and the Plan since the end of the fiscal year covered by the annual reports referred to in (a) and (b) above.

(d)   The Corporation's definitive Proxy Statement filed pursuant to Section 14 of the Securities Exchange Act of 1934 in connection with the latest Annual Meeting of Stock-holders of the Corporation and any definitive proxy state-ment so filed in connection with any subsequent Special Meeting of Stockholders.

The First Text Page of a Lengthy Report

SECTION I

XYZ CORPORATION
EMPLOYEES' SAVINGS AND THRIFT PLAN

1. <u>General</u>

The "XYZ Corporation Employees' Savings and Thrift Plan" (the "Plan")
has been established to encourage retirement savings by participating
employees ("Members") of the Corporation and of designated
subsidiaries and affiliates of the Corporation. Commencing January 1,
1984, such savings shall be effected by means of pre-tax salary
adjustment arrangements. The Corporation will also make matching
contributions to the Plan in an amount based upon certain savings by
Members. The Corporation also expects to make an additional
contribution to the Plan on behalf of each eligible Member based upon
its employee stock ownership tax credit. The amount of this
additional ESOP contribution is based upon the total combined
compensation of all eligible Members of the year. All of the
Corporation's matching and ESOP contributions will be invested in
Common Stock of the Corporation, and all or part of Members' savings
may be so invested. All contributions and savings will be held in
trust and invested by Bank of New England, N.A., Trustee of the Plan.
An "Employees' Savings and Thrift Plan Committee" (the "Committee"),
appointed by the Board of Directors of the Corporation, will supervise
and administer the Plan.

The Plan will form part of the Corporation's program for providing
competitive benefits for its employees. The operation of the Plan is
expected to encourage employees to make added provision, through
savings on a pre-tax basis, for their retirement income. It will also
encourage employees to participate in ownership of the Corporation's
Common Stock. The Board of Directors believes that the Plan will
provide an additional incentive to employees to contribute to the
continued success of the Corporation and will be in the best interests
of the Corporation and its stockholders.

The Plan is subject to the provisions of the Employee Retirement
Income Security Act of 1974, as amended ("ERISA"), including reporting
and disclosure obligations to Plan participants, fiduciary obligations
of Plan administrators, and minimum participation and vesting
requirements. The benefit insurance coverage established by Title IV
of ERISA does not provide protection for benefits payable under the
Plan, and the funding requirement under Title I or ERISA are also
inapplicable.

A summary of the Plan's provisions follows. This summary is qualified
in its entirety by reference to the text of the Plan which is appended
as Exhibit A hereto.

3

The First Main Section of a Lengthy Report with Flush-left Paragraphs

15. <u>Tax Consequences</u>

The Internal Revenue Service has ruled that the Plan qualifies as a
profit sharing plan under Section 401(a) of the Code. The Corporation
will submit the Plan, as amended, to the Internal Revenue Service to
obtain a determination as to whether the Plan, as amended, continues
to qualify under Section 401(a) of the Code, whether the provisions of
the Plan relating to salary adjustment contributions qualify under
Section 401(k) of the Code and whether the provisions of the Plan
relating to the employee stock ownership credit qualify under Section
409A of the Code. So long as the Plan so qualifies under the Code,
the Federal tax consequences to Members under present laws as
understood by the Corporation may be summarized as follows:

    (a)   Contributions made to the Plan by the Corporation on your
behalf pursuant to your salary adjustment election, and
any earnings on such amounts, are not includable in
your taxable income until such amounts are returned to
you either as a withdrawal or distribution. At that
time, the entire amount of your distribution in excess
of your pre-19-- after-tax contributions to the Plan is
subject to Federal income tax because none of this
money was previously taxed.

    (b)   Any earnings on your pre-19-- after-tax contributions
to the Plan are not taxable to you until returned to
you either as a withdrawal or distribution. Since your
after-tax contributions were subject to Federal
income tax when made, such contributions are not
subject to Federal income tax when distributed or
withdrawn.

    (c)   Corporation matching contributions and Corporation ESOP
contributions, and any earnings on such amounts, are not
taxable to you until distributed or withdrawn.

The tax deferral aspect of the Plan can result in some
important tax advantages for you.

    (1)   If you wait until you retire to receive funds out
of the Plan, your tax rate may be lower. Retired
persons generally--though not always--have lower
incomes than they had while working, so their tax
rates tend to be lower.

    (2)   If, upon retirement or other termination of
employment, you (or your beneficiary) receive a
lump sum distribution from the Plan and part or
all of such distribution is in the form of shares
of Common Stock instead of cash, a portion of the
tax (on net unrealized appreciation) may be
postponed until these shares are actually sold and

11

Headings and Subheadings in a Lengthy Report

SECTION IV

APPENDIX

The information in this Appendix will be updated from time
to time. Be sure to refer to the most current Appendix.

1. Current Administrative Information

     The present members of the Employees' Savings and Thrift Plan
Committee are John M. Roe, Jane T. Smith, Martin I. Miller, Joseph L.
Edge, Sally A. Harris, Leila B. Summers, and John T. Williams.

     Harry B. Selkirk and Lewis K. Callahan, Directors of the Corpora-
tion, are also directors of Bank of New England Corporation, the
parent company of Bank of New England, N. A., Trustee of the Plan.

2. Members of the Plan

     As of December 31, 19--, there were 999 employees partici-
pating in the Plan, out of a total number of approximately 1,600
employees eligible to participate. As of July 1, 19--, there
were 981 employees participating out of 1,500 eligible.

3. Fund A Minimum Rates

     The present minimum rates of interest for contributions to
Fund A during the following years are set forth below. These
rates are in each case guaranteed for five years:

                         19--   11.5%
                         19--   10.75%
                         19--   10%

4. Investment Performance

     (a) The table below shows values for shares of the Corpora-
tion's Common Stock in Fund B as of the indicated dates, which
are based upon the quoted New York Stock Exchange closing prices
for such shares at the indicated dates.

	Fund B Price per Share of Common Stock
Valuation Date	of the Corporation *
December 31, 19--	$11.750
December 31, 19--	$19.375
August 31, 19--	$22.500

*Adjusted for 2-for-1 split on July 3, 19--

18

Appendix Format

Footnotes and bibliographies.   Chapter One provides detailed guidelines to the proper styling of footnotes and bibliographies. Hence, the forthcoming paragraphs concentrate only on mechanical typewriting conventions for reference sources in a report. Keep in mind these general points when preparing footnotes to a long report:

1. Footnotes may appear at the bottom of the pages on which the quoted passages occur or they may be listed separately at the end of the report. Separate listing is the easiest from the typist's standpoint.

2. Footnotes are signaled within the running text by raised Arabic numerals positioned just after the quoted passage with no space intervening. Type the raised numeral after the final quotation mark:

```
". . .indicates an instability in an otherwise static
market."¹⁰
```

3. Number the footnotes consecutively throughout the report if they are to be listed together at the end. If the report is particularly long with many major sections in which the notes have been listed on the pages where the quoted matter is found, renumber them with the start of each new section. Be sure to check and recheck the numerals for proper sequence.

4. The first line of a footnote is indented from three to six lines and runover lines are aligned flush with the left margin. The footnote is introduced by a raised numeral keyed to the appropriate quoted text passage with one space intervening, or it may be introduced by the numeral and a period all aligned on the same line as the note itself. The latter method makes for easier typing. Footnotes may be single-spaced internally, with double spacing separating them from one another. They should be double-spaced internally with triple spacing separating them from one another if the report is to be published in typeset form. Examples:

```
¹⁰ Thomas J. Peters and Robert H. Waterman, Jr., In
Search of Excellence: Lessons from America's Best-Run
Companies (New York: Harper & Row, 1982), p. 8.
```

or with aligned numerals:

```
10.   Thomas J. Peters and Robert H. Waterman, Jr., In
Search of Excellence: Lessons from America's Best-Run
Companies (New York: Harper & Row, 1982), p. 8.
```

The bibliography lists alphabetically the sources used by the writer. Chapter One provides specific style guidelines for bibliographies from the standpoint of business English. The forthcoming paragraphs focus solely on points of typing style. Remember these points when typing a bibliography (note that the entries are ordered alphabetically by author surname):

1. The bibliography, entitled WORKS CITED or BIBLIOGRAPHY, appears on a separate page in the back matter.

2. The bibliography is hanging-indented: the first line of each entry is set flush left with runovers indented by five or six spaces.

3. Bibliography entries, like footnotes, are unnumbered.

4. Bibliography entries, like footnotes, may be single-spaced internally with double spacing separating them from one another, or they may be double-spaced internally with triple spacing separating them from one another. Use the latter approach if the report is to be typeset for outside publication. Examples:

```
Katzan, Harry Jr. Office Automation: A Manager's Guide.
     New York:  AMACOM, 1982.

Peters, Thomas J. and Robert H. Waterman, Jr. In Search
     of Excellence: Lessons from America's Best-Run Compa-
     nies. New York:  Harper & Row, 1982.
```

Index.   You may be asked to type an index for a very long, detailed study. The index lists alphabetically all major and subsidiary topics covered in the report along with applicable page numbers. An index is developed by reading through the text and circling all major and subsidiary headings plus all key words in the report. Each circled item is written on a 3" × 5" card together with the page number. The cards are ordered alphabetically and the page numbers and subjects rechecked. The writer then constructs from the cards a draft index. (Note: Software for compiling an index on computer is available. This section, however, presumes that the manual method will be employed.)

The main components of an index are main entries, subentries, sub-subentries, and cross-entries. A main entry is a prime subject category usually corresponding to a main heading in the text. A main entry includes a heading and often (but not always) a page number. It is typed flush with the left margin:

```
Input systems
   for computers, 22, 53-63
   optical character recognition
      for, 16
Input/output units, 53-63
```

In the example, *Input systems* and *Input/output units* are main entries. Note that the first word of the main entry is initially capitalized, while the other words are lowercased unless they are proper nouns, proper adjectives, or trademarks. Main entries are alphabetically ordered by the first key word.

A subentry represents a topic of secondary importance. It appears under the main entry with which it is associated. Subentries, ordered alphabetically by the first key word, are indented by three spaces. Subentries, like main entries, are composed of headings and page numbers. Subentries are lowercased throughout unless they contain proper nouns, proper adjectives, or trademarks. In the previously shown example, *for computers* and *optical character recognition for* are subentries.

A sub-subentry is a topic of tertiary importance. It appears under the subentry with which it is associated:

Communications, 80–108
   electronic mail systems for, 80–90,
      100–101
         Telex in, 91–92

In the example, *Telex* (a proper noun) is the sub-subentry under *electronic mail systems*. The alphabetically ordered sub-subentries, indented by three spaces, are usually lowercased unless they contain proper nouns, proper adjectives, or trademarks.

Cross-entries direct the reader from one point in the index to another related point where more information is to be found:

Diskettes. <u>See also</u> Floppy disks.
   in word processing systems, 42–81.
In the example, <u>See also</u> Floppy disks is a cross-entry. When the reader turns to the main entry *Floppy disks*, more information is at hand:

Floppy disks (diskettes), 22–32
   microdiskette, 25–32
   minidiskette, 23–24
   standard, 22

Cross-entries are introduced by the underscored and initially capitalized words <u>See also</u> followed by the main entry to which the reader is referred in initial capital letters (i.e., Floppy disks), followed by a period.

Two commonly used index formats are the indented and the run-in. The writer should indicate which of the two indexing formats is to be used. The indented format (used in our earlier examples) is preferable, for it provides quicker information retrieval. Note that each entry is typed on a separate line:

Disk storage media, 85–95
   operating systems on, 96
   software on, 94
   in word processing systems, 42, 82–90

The run-in format occupies less page space but is more difficult for the reader to use since all subentries are run in together:

Disk storage media: 85–95;
   operating systems on, 96;
   software on, 94; in word
   processing systems, 42,
   82–90

An index features minimal punctuation. Follow these guidelines for punctuating index entries:

1. Use a comma between an entry and any term(s) modifying it and between an entry and the page number relating to it:

   Disk storage media, 85–95
      in word processing systems, 42, 82–90
   Disks, standard, 22–24

2. Use a semicolon to separate entries only in the run-in index:

   Disk storage media: 85–95;
      operating systems on, 96;
   . . . .

3. Use a colon after a main entry just before its pagination only in the run-in index:

   Disk storage media: 85–95;
   . . . .

4. Terminate a cross-entry with a period; do not use periods elsewhere:

   See also CRT.

Tables, graphics, and other visual aids.   All visual aids should be titled either in capital letters or in capital and lowercase letters, and sequentially numbered: FIGURE 1, FIGURE 2; TABLE 1, TABLE 2, and so on. Titles may be centered or positioned flush left. Select one style and stick to it for the sake of consistency.

Word processors with graphics capabilities have alleviated most of the drudgery in preparing tabular and graphic exhibits. However, you must have a feel for the length of the table as it will appear in typewritten form and the approximate number of character spaces to be allowed between columns so that you can instruct the machine properly. In general, six character spaces are allowed between columns, especially in tables that are to be typed horizontally. Tables involving more than four columns are generally set up horizontally—that is, the standard page is flipped on its side. The title of the table should appear at the top (i.e., along what used to be the left margin of the vertical sheet) and the end of the table should appear at the bottom (i.e., along what used to be the right margin of the vertical sheet). In this way, the tabular data will face outside and not toward the gutter of the bound report.

Tabular entries and subentries can be capitalized in their entirety, capitalized and lowercased by key word, initially capitalized, or lowercased in their entirety. Main headings are usually capitalized in their entirety as shown in the next example. Once you have selected a style, stick to it throughout all of the tables for the sake of consistency:

TOTAL NET SALES
MANUFACTURING COSTS
ROYALTY EXPENSES
TOTAL COST OF SALES
  % of net
EXPENSES
  Editorial
  Plate
  Sales
  Advertising
  Fulfillment
  Administration

In the previous example, the capitalized items are considered main entries and the indented, capitalized and lowercased entries are considered secondary to the main entries. Secondary entries can be indented as shown here or set flush with the left margin. Choose one style and adhere to it.

Numerical data in tables must be aligned to the right, as:

UNIT SALES TO DATE
12,700
34,000
 6,000
  765

Tabular entries consisting of numerals and symbols such as plus and minus signs, percentage signs, or dollar signs must be aligned vertically. Decimal points also must be so aligned:

$800,000.00	−14 points	45.9%
4,000.98	−12 points	6.4%
55,896.00	−33 points	28.0%
564.34	+12 points	60.2%

Avoid the use of vertical and horizontal rules in tables constructed on conventional machines: while the horizontal rules can be done easily on the machine, the vertical ones will have to be drawn in by hand, and hand-drawn rules often look messy.

If the table exceeds one page in length, type a continued heading in capital and lowercase letters, as: "Table 3, continued" and center it on the page. Continue typing the tabular data, using the same tabbing and margins as those on the first sheet. Maintain consistent entry and subentry style.

   Displayed lists are useful especially in executive summaries and in sections detailing conclusions and/or recommendations, for the displayed matter is clearly visible to the busy reader. Use of the lowercase *o* followed by one space and the text is a neat way of presenting important data (a spaced period also can be used in this manner to highlight significant data):

o Generating business information
o Analyzing business information
o Transmitting/distributing business information

Sometimes the writer will include pie charts and graphs to illustrate points made in the body of the report. These should be roughed out by the writer and then submitted to the company's special media department for professional production. In a company lacking such a support department you may be called on to assist the writer in preparing these visual aids. If so, you'll need the following materials: press-on or contact tone sheets, rules, and letters (available in a graphic arts supply store); T-square, ruler, and compass; nonrepro blue pencil or pen; designer's fine-line black pen; rubber cement or a glue stick; art gum; scissors; artist's knife (sharp, triangular blade); graph paper; and hard-finish drawing paper. Graphs are usually laid out as rectangles on an average scale of 4:3 or 7:4. The title may appear at the top or bottom entirely in capitals or in capital and lowercase letters. Choose one style and stick to it. Position the labels and key lines horizontally on the page for easy reading. You can typewrite the title, labels, and key lines or you can use the press-on letters available in art supply houses. If you use the press-on letters (or numbers) be sure to choose a size compatible with the overall size of the graph. Letters that are too large look horsey and detract from the visual impact of the illustration. With line graphs you can ink in the lines by hand or you can use the press-on rules available in art stores. The press-on rules come on rolls. Using the nonrepro blue pencil or pen and a ruler, draw in the lines of the graph. Using the artist's knife, cut the press-on rules to fit the outline of the graphed matter. Pull off the backing and affix the rules where appropriate. With bar graphs, you will need press-on tone sheets showing, for instance, dark areas, striped areas, or dotted areas. Many different styles and designs are available. Using the nonrepro pencil or pen and a ruler, measure and construct the various bars called for. Using the artist's knife and the ruler, cut the tone sheets to fit the various bars, peel off the backing, and affix the tones to the graph. You also can shade the bars by hand, but hand shading does not look as professional as the tone sheet shading. Ensure that there is a color/tone separation of at least 30% between different shadings and tints in the graph; otherwise the shadings and tints will all look alike when reproduced in black-and-white. The press-on sheets usually contain color separation percentages.

The pie (or circle) chart is a useful way of depicting percentages, say, of corporate growth or market shares. Use a compass fitted with a nonrepro blue pencil to construct the circle. Then use the compass to mark off sectors in degrees corresponding to the desired percentages. Typically used percentage values of a circle are these:

360°	=	100%
180°	=	50%
90°	=	25%
36°	=	10%
18°	=	5%
3.6°	=	1%

Cut the press-on tone sheets to fit the marked-off sectors of the circle and then affix them to the chart. Use press-on letters and numbers to label the sectors. If the color/tone contrast between the parts of the circle and the labels is adequate you can insert the labels within the circle itself. But if the contrast is inadequate or if space is tight, you should put the labels outside the circle and use press-on key lines or arrows to connect the labels with the applicable sectors of the circle.

How to make an overhead. Before attempting to make an overhead audiovisual, also called a *transparency,* make sure that the brand you plan to use is appropriate for the copying machine you have at hand. The packaging for the transparencies will list the machines and model numbers in which that brand of transparency can be used. For example, some copiers require transparencies to bear a white sensing strip. Additionally, you must determine which way the white strip should face when you load the tray; loading the transparencies the wrong way may result in the machine becoming jammed.

Once you have read the instructions for the brand of transparency you are using, you are ready to begin. Follow these procedures:

1. Load the transparencies properly on top of a moderate base of paper in the paper tray.

2. Secure the paper tray.

3. Set the machine for one copy.

4. Place the document that is to be made into a transparency on the glass in the correct image area for $8\frac{1}{2}$" × 11" paper.

5. Close the cover.

6. Activate the machine.

7. Always allow for one transparency to be processed through the copier and dropped into the output tray before activating the machine again.

8. Delete imaged areas with perchloroethylene (tetrachloroethylene) or the suggested solution for the particular brand if corrections must be made. New data may be added with a grease pencil or solvent marker.

Transparencies are made of plastic film, and therefore will not perform with the same high reliability as plain paper. The toner image cannot penetrate into the transparent film, so be careful not to scratch the finished transparency. If the copier jams more than twice during a single job, the problem is probably with the machine. In these cases, a repairperson should be called. Should the copier become jammed, find the defective transparency (look carefully on the drum if it is nowhere else to be found) and remove it. If you cannot find the transparency, *do not operate the copier* until a repairperson has serviced the machine.

You may notice a thin oily coating on the transparency. This is normal and will eventually wear off. You can remove it by gently wiping both sides of the transparency with a dry tissue or by moistening the tissue with rubbing alcohol. You should note that this oily coating contains silicone which can cause irritation to your eyes if contact is made. Should this happen, flush your eyes thoroughly with clean water.

One other point: before attempting to make the transparency you should ensure that the chart, table, or other information to be displayed has been typed or drawn in such a way as to fit the screen size of the audiovisual machine (overhead projector) to be used. Cardboard mats similar to the ones used in picture frames are available in various sizes keyed to the projectors; a common size is $7\frac{1}{2}''\times 10''$. Using a nonrepro blue pencil, you can draw this measure around the material to be reproduced, thus ensuring inclusion of all data.

MAKING INVISIBLE CORRECTIONS IN YOUR DOCUMENTS

All of us make occasional typographical errors, and writers often wish to reword their communications after seeing them in typewritten form. Minor errors are easily corrected in most instances but rewordings often require complete retypes. Documents input into word processing memory are easily edited and corrected with no sign of the changes visible on the final printouts, but this is not necessarily the case with material typed on conventional equipment. The truly professional typist knows how to get the most out of the correction products currently available so as to produce perfect documents.

In the 1990s it would be ridiculous to include in a discussion of correction products the use of the knife and the eraser when so many better materials are on the market. The knife pits and cuts the paper and the eraser digs into the surface of the paper, damaging its texture and resulting in distorted retyped characters. Smudges also can occur due to the effort generated in attempting such corrections. Secretaries now rely on self-correcting typewriter ribbons, correction fluid, correction strips, tabs, and tapes. A brief summary of these materials follows.

Tackless lift-off correction tabs are particularly desirable with film typewriter ribbons. When an error has been made you simply backspace to it, insert the correction tab with the coated side placed down directly onto the error, retype the incorrect character, and then remove the tab. The error has been "lifted off." You then backspace and type the correct character. The correction is invisible.

Self-correcting film typewriter ribbons work on the same principle as the lift-off tabs, but you must depress a special correction key in order to backspace to the error. You restrike the last incorrect character to delete it. The self-correcting film ribbon with a lift-off tape removes the error. You then proceed to type the correct character. The correction is invisible.

Correction fluid employs fast-drying enamel in white or in blended color tones that is gently brushed over an error to render it invisible. Shake the bottle vigorously before attempting to apply the fluid. Test the consistency of the fluid by putting a tiny dot of it onto a piece of scratch paper. If the liquid is too thick, add some thinner and reshake. You also might consider cleaning the little brush with thinner to remove globs of thick, partially dried fluid. Test the fluid consistency again. Thick application of correcting fluid results in distorted characters, obliterations, peel-off characters, damaged paper, and, over time, a build-up of dried shards within the workings of your typewriter. When making the correction, roll the paper bail forward and the carriage to the far left or right for easier access to the error. Put a tiny dot of fluid onto each incorrect character. Correct each character one at a time for best results. Do not attack an entire word, a whole line, or several characters all at once like a floor painter. Allow the fluid to dry for 8–10 seconds before retyping. Typing onto wet fluid will cause very dark distorted characters. Special correction fluid for use on photocopies is also available.

Chalk-coated correction papers are also handy, but the corrections that they make are not permanent. After a certain period of time the chalk will flake off, the original error will show up, and the correction site will look like a strikeover. Chalk-coated correction papers can be used for drafts and documents having short-term shelf lives. You backspace to the error, insert the paper chalk-side down onto the error, restrike the error, remove the paper, backspace, and type the correct character.

Self-adhesive correction tapes are available in one- and two-line widths. You pull off the desired length of tape, cut it, remove the backing strip, and affix the tape to the page, thereby covering the error or errors. The tape is useful only in documents destined for typesetters. Avoid using it on documents to be photocopied, for the stripping marks will show through on the photocopies. Never use the tape on an outgoing original.

4

Sending Business Documents: Conventional and Electronic Mail

CONVENTIONAL MAIL

INTRODUCTION TO CONVENTIONAL MAIL

Just as the telephone and computer terminal are communication lifelines in business and industry today, so too is the mail. But written correspondence, unlike sophisticated electronic devices, is relatively inexpensive and technologically uncomplicated. In addition, conventional mail is the most private medium and the one least likely to be monitored or tampered with, without your knowledge. In today's very competitive domestic and multinational workplace, security of communications is a factor to be reckoned with as we have seen from the highly publicized activities of computer hackers and telephone eavesdroppers.

Although the expression "conventional mail" may sound somewhat less entrancing than descriptors for its more exotic electronic counterparts, its importance in keeping business moving cannot be overemphasized. The mail may be conventional in form or method of delivery, but it is often far from conventional in import or impact. The descriptions that follow are not intended to cover every possible working environment or situation. The volume and type of incoming and outgoing mail are directly proportional to the nature of the business and the executive's position within that business, and the procedures established for your office should be arrived at only after consultation with your employer.

INCOMING MAIL

Sorting and Opening Procedures

Some office functions still cannot be relegated completely to automation. Sorting and slicing open the mail are prime examples, not to mention reading, annotating, and evaluating the contents. The forthcoming subsections discuss these and other manual activities.

229

Initial sort.   Separate the letters from the periodicals and packages. With the envelopes still unopened, sort the letters into piles containing correspondence marked PERSONAL, first-class mail, bills and statements, and mass mailings (also known as *direct mail* and typically recognizable by their preprinted mailing labels). The categories in the initial sort will vary, depending on the nature of the business you're in. If you organize the mail on a daily basis, you will soon spot an emerging pattern. Define your own groupings and sort accordingly. Eventually you will become proficient enough to omit this step and sort and slice at the same time. Note that the initial sort should help you in the next stages: opening and reading. Out of respect to the writer and your employer, open no mail marked PERSONAL or CONFIDENTIAL. If you open something like this inadvertently, simply say so (an initialed notation on the envelope should suffice), and take measures to prevent it from happening again. That is, look at all envelopes carefully before opening them.

Opening.   For slicing open the envelopes, the stiletto-style openers are preferable. The more functional-looking a letter opener is, the longer it will remain on one's desk. However, if one's opener does sprout legs and march off, one can use the long blade on a Swiss Army knife. A sharp knife like this cuts through strapping tape and packaging better than scissors. An artist's knife is also handy for slicing through well wrapped parcels. Although automatic opening machines are available, you must receive a high volume of mail to justify the expense of buying one. Furthermore, in the time required to feed the letters through the device, they could have been opened manually. A simple cost-benefit analysis will determine whether an automatic opener is a necessity. Whatever method is used, care should be taken not to slice through the contents of the envelope.

During the sort, you may find accumulations of junk mail. Junk mail should be set aside and discarded later after it has been evaluated. If you have found that your employer does not wish to receive mail from certain organizations, request that his or her name be removed from their mailing lists. Before doing so, however, get permission from your employer.

Correspondence categories.   Before reading the opened letters, you should have created files corresponding to the general nature of your daily mail. This is where the emerging patterns mentioned earlier come in. Many offices can get away with file categories identical to those in the initial sort. Other offices may need to create narrower subcategories to handle mail during conventions, crises, and at any other times that mail flows in at flood level. These categories and the date on which the mail was delivered are written on the tab at the top of the file folders, thus precluding the need for stamping each piece with the date on which it was received. You may only need to make a special date notation on an item when there is a large time lag between the date on which the letter was written and the date on which it was received or if it is an invitation for a function already held the night before. However, if you prefer to stamp each piece with date and time, a variety of devices are available. They range from rubber stamps that imprint "Received" in a box large enough to accommodate the date and time of receipt written in by hand or adjustable daters that stamp the date and time, to automatic dating machines. Your own needs will dictate your choice. You may thumb through any periodicals, catalogues, lengthy advertising packets, or media kits you receive and annotate them as described below. Open packages that are not marked "confidential" or "personal." Stack all bulky items neatly alongside your employer's in-box.

Reading, Annotating, and Digesting

At this point, you've got your mail sliced open and the files ready. Now comes the fun: the reading. Ideally, your employer should handle each piece of mail only once, lest he or she—and you—become unnecessarily saddled with excessive paperwork. In this single shot, the letter should be read and a decision passed on it: Does it get filed? Answered? Or is further research required? Here are some techniques that may be useful to you in helping your employer act on each piece of incoming correspondence in an expeditious manner.

Reading and highlighting.   Read the letter and annotate the gist of the message. Some letters must be read in their entirety in order to avoid overlooking good information. On occasion, usable information is found at the end of the letter or on page three of a four-pager. It's unfair to expect your employer to plow through the fluff to get to the pertinent material; that's your responsibility. Once you hit the main point in the letter, you must call attention to it. Use removable self-sticking notes. They are neat and easy to use, and they come in a variety of sizes. Mark pages and passages with them; write your remarks and references on them. When making notations directly on letters and journals (and only you can decide which ones they are), use nonrepro blue pens. They now come in felt tip, far preferable to conventional graphite. Notations made in nonrepro blue are invisible when photocopied.

Affixing envelopes and enclosures to the letters.   Just as you must check the outside of the envelope for PERSONAL or CONFIDENTIAL notations, so should you examine the letter itself for the return address. If a letter arrives without the correspondent's return address, attach the envelope to it even if the address does not appear thereon. Remember, you can never give too much information; neglecting to clip an envelope to a piece of correspondence is tantamount to withholding information. And always affix enclosures to the letter. If enclosures are referred to in the letter but have not been included with it, make a notation to this effect in the margin or on a self-sticking note, and then—if necessary and appropriate—call the correspondent and request the enclosures. This can be a frustrating task, but it will make *you* more careful about your own out-going mailings and their enclosures.

Handling hate mail.   Any section dealing with incoming mail would be incomplete without a frank discussion of hate mail. Hate mail, or poison-pen letters, often have the same effect on their readers as pathological or obscene telephone calls have on their recipients. If you ever feel endan-gered by the contents of a particular letter or parcel, do not hesitate to call your company's security guard, the police, or the Postal Inspection Ser-vice. Laws proscribe such abuse of the mail system just as other statutes forbid obscene and obnoxious telephone calls.

Maintaining a mail log.   Some offices require maintenance of a log in which the receipt of important pieces of mail is recorded. A mail log allows you to refer again to basic data about a letter without pulling it from the file. A typical log records the date and time of receipt, the date of the letter itself, the name and affiliation of the correspondent, the nature of the letter, the name of the addressee, and the nature and date of the final disposition. If filing space is limited, use of a mail log precludes the need to save originals. (Nowadays, such records can be stored in your computer system.) It also may be advisable to keep a log as a record of outgoing mail, especially with mass mailings.

Submitting the mail.   The final step in the processing of incoming mail is submission of the sorted stack of files to your employer. Always put the most important folder(s) on top of the stack.

OUTGOING MAIL

Proofreading
The typewriting and formatting of business letters are discussed in Chap-ter Three. However, the final proofreading before signature and mailing is important enough to be discussed again here. You don't have to be in publishing to be a picky proofreader: the truly professional secretary scru-tinizes all outgoing correspondence for correct spelling and good syntax as well as for the presence of strikeovers. Your goal is to compose or tran-scribe a letter calling attention to itself because of its correct format, substantive content, and original ideas—not because of a typographical error or an incorrect use of an honorific with a recipient's name. Remem-ber that all outgoing letters represent your employer and the corporation to others. The better you make them look, the better you will look, too.

Signature
Letters, contracts, checks, or forms in need of signing may be submitted to the executive in several ways. Place all such paperwork in a file folder

labeled "To Be Signed," indicate on each piece where the signature and date are to appear (use a self-sticking note), and submit the folder for signing at the executive's convenience. It is preferable to submit a stack of documents all at one time rather than seeking signatures several times throughout the day. However, a letter, contract, or form sometimes must get out posthaste, and you will not be able to wait until you've amassed numerous documents. That's when a clipboard comes in handy. A clipboard allows your employer to sign a letter in the absence of desk space, e.g., while sitting at a word processing terminal or in a reading chair. Another advantage of using a clipboard is that your employer need not be concerned with smudging the document. This technique works especially well for one-page letters.

A large volume of outgoing mail may justify the use of an Autopen, an automatic signature machine that reproduces original signatures. Though it is preferable to a rubber-stamp signature facsimile, it is extremely expensive. If you sign letters on your employer's behalf, it is customary to follow the employer's signature with a slash and your own initials. Sending out an unsigned letter indicates carelessness on your part. Furthermore, such a letter is technically invalid. Even though most offices recognize that slips like this do occur and treat an unsigned letter as genuine, the practice of posting such letters should be avoided.

Enclosures

If enclosures are to be included in an outgoing letter, type the standard notation *Enc.*, or one of the other conventional forms of it, flush left below the signature line. When sending two or more items, indicate the number and type it next to the enclosure notation. (See Chapter Three for specific stylings of enclosure notations.) It is also useful to itemize the enclosures and include a brief description of each one as a way of avoiding omissions. Overlooking enclosures is, at the least, annoying to the addressee and an embarrassment to you. Spare yourself some blushes: when proofreading a letter, you might want to attach a self-sticking note to the edge of the letter and jot down a list of the required enclosures if you haven't already itemized them in the enclosure notation itself.

Courtesy Copies

The abbreviated notation *cc* deserves initial comment because its changing meaning is a direct reflection of the impact of the technological revolution occurring in the workplace today. As we all know, the photocopy machine is now a permanent fixture in most offices, thus making carbon paper and pressure-sensitive copy books virtually obsolete. A question repeatedly asked is: If *cc* stands for *carbon copy*, shouldn't the notation be changed to *Xc* for *Xerox copy* so as to reflect modern trends? The abbreviation *cc* now also stands for *courtesy copy*, thereby covering photocopies, carbons, and pressure-sensitive copies. The meaning of the notation is not the prime issue, though; its page placement is. The copy notation typically appears below the enclosure notation (if any), flush left, and a few lines below the signature. (See Chapter Three for specific guidelines regarding the styling of copy notations, illustrated by typewritten facsimiles.) When sending copies to more than one recipient, put a check mark next to the name of each person to whom you are mailing the material.

With blind copies, the notation *bcc* appears only on the copy and not on the original. Placement of this abbreviation can vary. The typed *bcc* notation is traditionally positioned flush left with the upper or lower margin of the page. Another option is to write the abbreviation in nonrepro blue at the lower left margin, just below any *cc* or enclosure notations. Subsequent photocopies made from the file copy will not bear the *bcc* notation, about which you may not wish the recipient to know.

File copies.   Don't forget to retain copies for your files. Depending on the set-up of your filing system and the space available, put a copy of the letter in the alphabetical file of the correspondent's name or company, in the subject file if the letter is topical, or in the chronological file. The chronological file is a sequential file of all letters emanating from the office, and it serves as a journal or diary of business. Having letters arranged in this fashion will be convenient if your employer's memoirs are ever written. However, the immediate, short-term reason for maintaining a sequential correspondence file is retention of evidence of business transactions. Often the letters can be discarded once a transaction has been completed and a record of request is no longer needed; therefore, it is important to review regularly the contents of the chronological file. The amount of space available and the historical importance of the letters themselves dictate whether or not this approach is appropriate for your office. It also helps if your organization has archives or other ample storage facilities.

Outgoing Mail Log

If your filing system is solid, sensible, and spacious, then a mail log may not be necessary. However, if you do keep an incoming mail log, you may want to keep an outgoing log to make your records more meaningful and complete. Data to be included in an outgoing mail log are the date of issue, the name and address of the recipient, a description of the material sent, the method of dispatch (class of mail service, telegram, courier, etc.), and the description and date of any subsequent follow-up activity.

Envelope Selection and Folding

Standard letterhead.   Letters should be folded and inserted according to the kind of envelope selected. Standard letterhead and half-size, memo-style stationery are folded into traditional thirds. If you're mailing multiple sheets of the same size, attach everything together and insert them into the proper envelopes so that when the letter is open and unfolded, the text will be right side up. If you're sending several different-sized sheets, fasten everything together so that when the letter is removed from the envelope the pages, clippings, or other enclosures will not scatter. (See Chapter Three for detailed information on envelope sizes and applications.)

Envelopes and mailers made of glossy paper have been known to shed their stamps before reaching the intended recipients—a situation having several undesirable effects: the letters may be returned to you for postage, thus delaying delivery, or they may be delivered to the addressee with postage due. If you have a large mailing and a problem such as this develops, notify your post office. Mail handlers will look for the problematic pieces and will help you to rectify the difficulty.

Oversized mailers.   When including a letter with a larger item, you have several options. You can fold and insert the letter into its matching envelope and pack it with the enclosure in a larger mailer. Or you can put both letter and enclosure into a single large envelope. If you choose not to fold them, use a piece of corrugated cardboard to prevent damage in transit. Use padded mailers for books, small manuscripts, press kits, files, or similar materials. The mailers cushioned with plastic bubbles or Styrofoam are preferable to those lined with lint because they are neater and lighter. However, the bubble-lined bags are more costly than the ones filled with lint. It is more economical to maintain an ongoing supply of the bubble-lined bags in several sizes for use only with particularly important mailings. The cheaper shipping bags or large manila envelopes can be used for less important oversized pieces.

Specialized envelopes.   Offices issuing a lot of international mail may wish to use the commercially available overseas airmail envelopes that are lighter than standard office envelopes. A rubber stamp can be used to customize them. Window envelopes, often used in mass mailings, require careful insertion of letters. If the recipient's name and address do not appear through the window, then the time you have saved by not addressing the envelope separately will have been wasted. Some letterhead stationery has a line indicating where to fold the page so that the recipient's name and address will show through the window. Generally, though, the procedure is to fan-fold the sheet in thirds with the inside address outside on the top, as opposed to folding it so that the top third folds over the bottom third with the address block on the inside. Allow about one fourth to one eighth of an inch between the edge of the window and the address to prevent blocking any part of the address. (See also the section on envelopes in Chapter Three.)

Addressing

The United States Postal Service has modernized its operations with automated scanning and sorting devices that improve dissemination of the mail. To get the most from these mail processing advancements, consider the post office's needs when addressing envelopes:

1. Use envelopes no smaller than $3\frac{1}{2}''\times 5''$ and not exceeding $6\frac{1}{8}''\times 11\frac{1}{2}''$.

2. Center the address and single-space each line flush with the left edge of the line above it. This is called *blocking*. Do not indent the lines of the address.

3. Avoid the slanted address styling. Typewrite the lines parallel to the top and bottom edges of the envelope.

4. Include all information within this block in this fashion (or in one of the other ways described in Chapter Three:
   SUN GUARDIAN CITY BUREAU
   Lee Smith
   Ninth Floor
   1000 Jonesville Avenue
   City, ST 12345

Note that attention references, suite numbers, and other nonaddress information should appear within the address block, not set apart from it. The Zip Code should appear on the same line as the city and state. (See Chapter Three for details regarding automated mail handling and addressing envelopes for automation.)

Special-handling, eyes-only, and other such notations are typed in uppercase letters below the postage line and above the top address line, one third of the way in from the right or left edge of the envelope. The name of a foreign country should appear in capitals as the last line of the address block. (Follow these fundamental guidelines also when addressing mailing labels for larger containers. Since the label can loosen from the mailer, you ought to secure it with a label cover or tape.) The return address should appear in the upper left corner or on the obverse of the envelope. Be neat and precise. Include the name of the person posting the item, his or her suite or mail stop number, department, and any other information that will ensure the parcel's safe return to sender in the event it is refused or returned by the addressee.

Make certain that the degree of color contrast between the envelope or mailing label and the typed address is sharp enough to be detected by optical character scanners. Contrast is not a problem with standard-colored stationery (white, ecru, or manila) and with single-use film typewriter ribbons. However, if the mailer is of a color that reduces contrast or if your fabric typewriter ribbon is worn, you may inadvertently obstruct the mail's distribution.

Number 6¾ Envelope

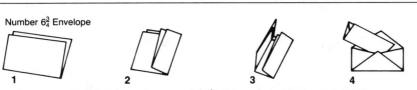

1   **2**   **3**   **4**

1. Fold the bottom half of the stationery to within $\frac{1}{2}''$ of the top edge. Crease it. 2. Fold the stationery from right to left, a bit more than one third of the width. Crease it. 3. Fold from left to right, allowing a $\frac{1}{2}''$ margin at the right. Crease it. 4. Insert the last folded side into the envelope first.

Number 10 Envelope

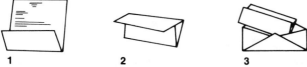

1   **2**   **3**

1. Fold the lower third of the stationery. Crease it. 2. Fold the stationery from the top down, allowing a $\frac{1}{2}''$ margin from the edge of the first fold. Crease it again. 3. Insert the last folded side into the envelope first.

Window Envelope

1   **2**   **3**

1. Fold the bottom third of the letter. Crease it. 2. Fan-fold the upper section of the letter back to the edge of the first fold so that the inside address will be on the outside and not on the inside. Crease it. 3. Insert the stationery so that the inside address is clearly visible through the window ($\frac{1}{4}''$ margins needed).

NOTE: Some printed letterhead intended exclusively for window applications is marked to indicate placement of the inside address. Printed fold lines are often included.

Folding and Inserting Stationery into Envelopes

Sealing

There are a half dozen ways to seal a mailing container: saliva, sponge, Scotch tape, staples, strapping tape, and string. A sponge or transparent tape may be used if the quantity of the letters is excessive or if the glue is especially evil-tasting. Large numbers of outgoing envelopes can be

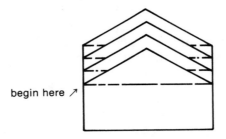

begin here ↗

Sponge-sealing of Many Envelopes

moistened all at once by stacking them with their flaps open, glue side facing you, one behind the other, with the glue strips touching but not overlapping. Pass a wet sponge over the glue strips all at one time. Then, working from the top envelope, fold the flaps down one by one. For mailing bags, staples work well, as does strapping tape, especially the kind reinforced with strands of fiber. Boxes should be sealed with strapping tape and tied with string. Make sure that you have not left loose edges on the parcel that will jam up the post office's equipment.

POSTING THE MAIL

Presorting

From deposit to delivery, a letter passes through about twelve steps at the post office. By sharing the sorting workload yourself, you may obtain reduced postal rates and faster delivery. If you generate a consistently high volume of first-class letters (or a minimum of 500 pieces per mailing), presorting them yourself can save you a substantial amount of money on postage (at present, 17%).

The mail is initially sorted by Zip Code from low-numbered zones to high and each piece of mail must bear this code. When a Zip Code has been omitted or when an incorrect Zip Code appears on a parcel, mail room or postal employees must look it up or correct the error. And that's not their job; it's yours. A Zip Code directory should be part of a professional secretary's desk library. It contains the codes of course, as well as other pertinent mailing information such as the standard two-letter state abbreviations. Zip Code directories can be purchased from the post office. With the advent of the expanded nine-digit Zip Code called *Zip + 4*, directories of all the codes have become real necessities. The additional digits in Zip + 4 allow the Postal Service to process much more mail with greater speed and efficiency. The program is intended to eliminate all manual mail sorting. (See Chapter Three for more information regarding Zip + 4 and its use on envelopes.) Letters going to the same post office (i.e., letters bearing the same five digits in the Zip Code) should be bundled together. Mail destined for one major city (i.e., mail whose Zip Codes share the same first three digits) also ought to be bound together.

Postage for presorted mail must be paid by postage meter, permit imprint, or precanceled stamps. For mailings exceeding fifty pieces, a postage meter and/or envelopes preprinted with your permit number are preferable. If you use precanceled stamps, affix them with a roller or a wet sponge. If presorted letters have not been stamped with precanceled stamps having the printed notation "presorted first-class mail," the letters must be annotated by hand. If your office does not meet the minimum mail volume to qualify for the presort postage rate, you can still hasten the mail's delivery by separating it into broad categories (i.e., local, intrastate, interstate, and international) and by arranging the pieces from low to high Zip Codes. Separating the mail by other classes (second, third, and fourth) and by Zip Code within those classes also will speed delivery.

Stamping

You have several options for stamping outgoing mail. These include postage meters, imprints, and manual methods—all discussed in the forthcoming paragraphs. But regardless of the method chosen, you should have at hand an accurate postage scale and lists of the current postage rates applicable to the classes of mail service that your office uses if it lacks a mail room.

Postage meters.   Postage meters apply postage in any amount (you set the denominations) directly onto an envelope fed into the machine or onto a label then affixed to the parcel. Postage meters may be purchased from the manufacturer or leased and licensed from the United States Postal Service, which also sells the postage and sets the descending register to reflect the amount of postage purchased. Each time the meter is used the descending register, which keeps a current tab on the balance of postage remaining in the meter, is reduced by the denomination of postage affixed to the piece of mail. The ascending register then increases by that amount, thus reflecting the amount of postage used. If an incorrect unit of postage has been printed on the envelope or on a label or if the envelope or label has been in some way defaced after having been endowed with metered postage, a partial refund (and in some cases, a full one) can be obtained from the post office. However, you must bring the unusable pieces of mail to the post office and complete some forms within one year of the date appearing on the metered postage in order to obtain the refund.

One major benefit of a meter is that the postmarked dated item requires no further cancellation at the post office, thus bypassing another processing activity and thereby expediting delivery. Remember, though, that five or more pieces of metered mail must be bundled together; otherwise they will be processed and canceled in the usual fashion. Postage meters also allow for customized postmarks. And, of course, meters are faster than manual affixation of stamps.

Permit Imprints.   Permit imprints allow an organization to print postage directly onto envelopes or post cards. Generally, the organization's return address is also printed at the same time in the upper left corner on the face of the envelope, on the obverse, or in the address block on a self-addressed stamped return envelope. Permit imprints are popular with mass mailing programs and are used in all classes of service (first through fourth). Regardless of class, permit-imprinted mail must be sorted by the sender, an extra activity that can neutralize the benefits and conveniences afforded by preprinted permit postage.

Other stamping methods.   Another stamping method includes the use of commercial postage stamp dispensers that require neither lease nor license. One such hand-held gadget called a Postafix holds a roll of stamps. A press of the hand dispenses the postage, one stamp at a time. If you have a uniform stack of envelopes or cards, you can speed matters by fanning the upper right edge with one hand and stamping them with the other. Stamps in roll form or in sheets also can be applied rapidly without a special device. Tear off a manageable number of stamps, moisten the first one while it is still attached to the rest of the section, apply it to the letter, and then tear it at the perforation.

MAIL CLASSIFICATIONS

You should be familiar with four classifications of mail: first, second, third, and fourth. To improve your service, clearly label your mail according to its appropriate classification. Mail classifications are discussed in the next few paragraphs.

First-class.   First-class mail includes letters and materials sealed against postal inspection: handwritten and typed correspondence, post cards, bills, statements, and invoices. First-class mail can be insured. Priority mail is first-class mail weighing from 12 ounces to 70 pounds. Priority is a class of mail, not a special-handling service. It receives the same treatment as first-class parcels weighing under 12 ounces. Do not use priority if you expect some sort of preferential service.

Second-class.   Unsealed second-class mail is used for posting periodicals such as newspapers, journals, and subscription forms. Because second-class mail is the cheapest, organizations must obtain a special permit to mail items at this rate.

Third-class.   Third-class mail is most frequently used by direct-mail purveyors but it is available to anyone. Essentially, mail that need not go first class, that is not considered a periodical, and that weighs under one pound is third class. Since third-class mail may be opened for postal inspection, the parcels should be wrapped and sealed with this in mind. Third-class mail can be insured.

Fourth-class.   Fourth-class mail, also called parcel post, consists of pieces weighing one pound or more that are not required to be sent first class and are not classifiable as second class. No correspondence, unless it is an invoice or a statement, may be enclosed with a fourth-class parcel; first-class postage must be paid on all such enclosures. Fourth-class mail can be insured. Specific dimensions, rate structures, and other periodically changing data can be obtained from your local post office. The

United States Postal Service provides detailed mailing information available free upon request.

SPECIAL SERVICES

Registered Mail
Registered Mail is used to protect highly important, often irreplaceable domestic first-class mail. A receipt is issued by the accepting post office, a card is returned to you when delivery has been made, a record of delivery is maintained at the originating and destination post offices, and the mail is monitored through all the steps in between. If the item is lost or spoiled, the post office will award restitution to the sender. The receipt issued for the cost of registered service shows the name of the recipient and the date of delivery. You may specify "restricted delivery": the piece will be delivered only to the person you've designated. Registered mail will be forwarded if the addressee has submitted a change of address notice to the post office, and the post office will report the new address to you, should you request that information.

Certified Mail
Certified mail is used when the sender of an article with no intrinsic value wishes to have proof of mailing and delivery. No receipt is issued unless you request one, so you need not bring outgoing certified mail to the post office in person; it can be dispatched with ordinary items in a collection box. For an additional fee, restricted delivery and return receipts are available for certified mailings. The major differences between certified mail and registered mail are cost and speed. Because of the human resources spent monitoring registered mail, the cost is greater and the delivery process is slower than for certified mail. Essentially, registered mail should be used for protection of extremely valuable materials.

Special Delivery Mail
Although special delivery mail will receive special handling at the destination post office, it will probably be shipped from the originating post office with the regular post. This service is available only on classes first, third, and fourth. Special delivery mail is supposed to be delivered to the addressee the day it arrives at the destination post office, even on Sundays and holidays. However, to ensure immediate—and overnight—delivery, consider the United States Postal Service's Express Mail or the services of one of its private-sector competitors.

Express Mail
Advantages of using Express Mail include insurance against loss or damage at no additional cost and the convenience of using a postage meter or

stamps. Express mail is more than just next-day delivery, although that feature is by far the best known. Express Mail service includes:

1. Same-day airport service: the parcel is posted from an airport mail facility and must be claimed by the addressee at the destination airport mail facility.

2. Airport to addressee: the parcel is shipped from an airport mail facility but is delivered directly to the addressee by the post office.

3. Office to airport: your parcel is picked up at your office by the post office, but the recipient must claim it at the destination airport mail facility.

4. Pick-up and delivery: the post office picks up and delivers the parcel, door-to-door.

5. Next-day service: a more accurate appellation would be "next-business-day delivery." Post—or have your letter picked up—prior to 5:00 p.m. (the earlier the better), and it will arrive no later than 3:00 p.m. the following business day.

6. International Express Mail: an overseas mailing will arrive at its destination in three days. Many major cities now offer this service.

Extra charges are added for collections from your office, and pick-up arrangements generally require a service contract between your organization and the United States Postal Service. Check with your post office to determine which services are offered there and which options would be best for your needs.

Mailgrams
The Mailgram provides another form of next-business-day delivery. The difference between it and Express Mail is that the Mailgram is transmitted electronically, not physically. To send one or several, call Western Union and read your message, or use a Telex if your office is so equipped. Remember to have a confirmation copy sent to you. There is an additional fee for such a copy, but surely you will want a file copy and an opportunity to check the message for any errors in transcription or transmission, in which case Western Union will send, at no additional cost to you, revised Mailgrams. Mailgrams have many uses, from amending information in a social announcement or invitation to issuing a product recall. (See also the section of this chapter on electronic mail where Mailgrams are further discussed.)

COD
With COD (collect on delivery) mail, the cost of purchased goods and the cost of mailing the goods are absorbed by the addressee. The maximum

collectible COD payment is $600.00. The COD charges also include insurance against nonpayment, damage, or loss. For an additional fee you can be notified of nondelivery before the package is returned to you. First-, third- and fourth-class mail can be sent by COD. Some private-sector carriers also deliver COD packages.

PRIVATE-SECTOR CARRIERS

Private shipping, delivery, and courier companies offer services that rival those of the United States Postal Service and challenge its erstwhile monopoly on mail delivery. In some instances, these operations feature services that the post office does not provide. Most private carriers will establish an account providing for regular billing and will supply you with preprinted mailing forms. The urgency of your mailings and your own budgetary concerns will affect your choice of mailing methods.

Local messengers.   Local messenger services offer same-day service within your city. They will collect a parcel from your office and deliver it across town, often within the same hour. Of course, the cost can be high compared with the cost of posting the same parcel through the United States mail. However, the impact of a hand-delivered letter often offsets the expense. Many lobbyists and politicians distribute their "media advisories" (as press releases are now known) via messenger because hand-delivered items are usually treated with higher priority in the recipients' offices. Check the messenger's references carefully.

Couriers.   Courier services, like local messengers, provide rapid surface deliveries to nearby metropolitan locations. Check your local Yellow Pages for specific information.

Bus parcel.   Bus parcel service is more economical than air package delivery. Services and companies offering these services vary throughout the continental United States. Common options include door-to-door pick-up and delivery, and terminal-to-terminal pick-up and delivery wherein the parcel is taken to the bus depot by the sender and claimed at the destination bus terminal by the addressee. This second option may be combined with the services of a local messenger, who can claim delivery at the destination depot and deliver it to the appropriate office. Before sending parcels, packages, and pouches in this fashion, it is wise to check on the security measures taken at each bus terminal.

United Parcel Service.   United Parcel Service (UPS), serving intrastate and interstate destinations, is one of the Postal Service's prime competitors. The advantages of using UPS are virtually no damage or loss, fast service, and low rates. A package shipped by UPS can be taken to a UPS office or picked up at your office by a UPS driver. If you choose to have it collected from your place of business, you can call UPS to arrange for pick-up the next day. No matter how many package collections a UPS driver makes from your office each week, a one-time weekly pick-up surcharge is added to the shipping fee. If you use UPS often, it is a good idea to arrange for a driver to come by your office the same time each day, thus precluding a telephone call and a day's wait for parcel pick-up.

Air couriers.   Air courier services function as air freight forwarders. Parcels are taken to local offices or collected from yours and are shipped by regularly scheduled commercial carriers or by the courier's own fleet of planes. Federal Express and Airborne are among the better known air courier companies; major commercial airlines such as United have also entered the air courier market. (See the Electronic Mail section of this chapter for information regarding air courier use of electronic mail technology.)

SPECIAL MAILING PROBLEMS

Military Mailings
Letters, packages, and other parcels destined for Army, Air Force, or Fleet Post Offices overseas are sent to the nearest domestic gateway city where they are pouched and airmailed to their destinations. Overseas government mail is treated in a similar manner. Parcel Airlift (PAL) mail is flown from the city of origin to the point of embarkation. Space Available Mail (SAM) is transported via regular parcel post (i.e., via surface mail) to the gateway city. Both PAL and SAM mail are assessed postage for service from the point of origin to the point of overseas embarkation (the United States gateway city). PAL costs more than SAM because you pay a fee for air service plus the regular parcel post rate. (See Chapter Three for specific instructions regarding the methods of addressing military mail.)

Overseas Customs Data

Incoming mail.   Incoming international mail is first shipped to United States Customs for inspection. Pieces not requiring duty payments are turned over to the Postal Service and are then delivered to the addressee. Parcels requiring payment of import tariffs are issued mail-entry forms stating the duty due. They are returned to the post office, which then delivers them and collects the fees. You may challenge the duty assessed on any international parcel if you believe the customs fee to be incorrect. This is done in one of two ways. Pay the duty and lodge your protest by sending a copy of the mail-entry form affixed to the package along with a covering letter to the customs office listed on the form. The import duty originally charged will be reviewed and a refund issued, if deemed proper. Or you may refuse the parcel and submit a letter to the holding post office objecting to the import duty levied. The original assessment will be reexamined by customs.

Freight.   International freight shipments either clear customs at the initial port of entry or travel to another customs port for clearance. You are responsible for arranging clearance of international freight coming to your office. There are at least two ways to do so. For example, a freight forwarder will, for a fee, arrange clearance and forward your parcel to you. Or you may name an unpaid agent to act on your behalf. The agent must have in hand a letter addressed to the attention of the officer in charge of customs stating that the bearer of the letter is acting for you.

Express.   Express shipments arriving from foreign nations are generally cleared at customs by the express carrier and then are delivered to you.

Forwarding

The best way to redirect mail is to place over the old address a label bearing the forwarding address and conforming to standard scannable format. That's how the post office does it when they've been informed of a change in address. For misdirected letters, you may cross out the incorrect address and write the correct one directly on the envelope. However, forwarding a piece of mail in this way reduces the likelihood of its being electronically scanned, thus delaying its delivery. It would be ideal both for you and for the post office if no mail had to be forwarded in this fashion. There are several ways to inform correspondents of address changes:

1. The post office provides free change-of-address kits. They're fine if you've only a handful of people to alert.

2. You can have announcements of your imminent move printed. In addition to the new address, include the effective moving date and new telephone numbers, if they also will change.

3. Preprinted Rolodex cards are a special courtesy; you may want to send them to clients and customers in addition to change-of-address notification cards.

4. And don't forget to notify your old post office and the new one, too.

TROUBLESHOOTING AND REVIEW

Incoming Mail: Recapitulation

1. Unless you are told otherwise, do not open items marked PERSONAL or CONFIDENTIAL.

2. Suspicious-looking parcels and letters should be brought to your employer's attention and to the attention of your company's security officer. If need be, contact the police and/or the Postal Inspection Service. This kind of mail includes suspected letter or package bombs and written threats.

3. If a letter and/or its envelope bear no return address, clip both items together before submitting them to your employer.

4. Maintain accurate correspondence files or mail logs. Few things are less professional than having to request from the sender a copy of a letter to your employer because it has been misfiled, discarded, or otherwise lost.

Outgoing Mail: Recapitulation

1. Inspect all outgoing letters. Are words broken into their proper syllables at the ends of lines? Do verbs agree with their subjects? Are margins neat? Take the time to retype any correspondence in which the answer to any of the above questions is "no." Sending out a letter that you know contains errors or inaccuracies is a sign of laziness. One such slip can—and often will—lead to another. Soon you will have lowered your standards and will have compromised the integrity and efficiency of your office, an unfortunate situation that can become a way of life. If you find yourself in this situation and cannot seem to reverse it, ask yourself several questions: Is the problem from within or without? Is it endogenous, or is it beyond my control? Get assistance if you need it.

2. Be sure that all required signatures are in place; that enclosures, attachments, and other referenced items have been included; that courtesy copies have been duly noted and posted; that file copies have been made; and that the mail logs are updated. Ensure that letters are inserted into their proper envelopes. Another symptom of unprofessionalism is mixing up letters or other items and their envelopes or containers.

3. The envelope or address label should always be typed. Remember to style all address information in block format.

4. Sharp contrast between the mailer and the address information is a requirement for faster mail processing.

5. There is not much hope for a parcel whose mailing label has fallen off unless the return address appears directly on the mailer (in which case the parcel will be returned to you). Tape labels to containers or use mailing label holders for added security.

6. Envelopes with weak glue should be sealed with tape.

7. Clearly note the desired class of service on all outgoing mail. With distinctive air mail or green-edge first-class envelopes, further desig nation of class is unnecessary.

8. Use a postal scale and current rate charts to determine proper postage. When in doubt of the proper rate, call your post office or private carrier. Answers to usual and unusual questions can be obtained over the telephone, in person, or from brochures.

9. Whether you use the United States Postal Service or a private carrier, consider time, expense, and indemnity. Why send a parcel by overnight air when bus parcel achieves the same result and is less costly?

10. Investigate the reliability of the company to which you plan to entrust your mail. What recourse will you have in the event of delay, spoilage, or loss?

11. Mail early in the day to reduce delivery time by almost one full day.

ELECTRONIC MAIL SYSTEMS

INTRODUCTION TO ELECTRONIC MAIL

The trend in office automation today is toward total integration of corpo-rate facilities via communications to and from relatively low-cost user workstations. These workstations can provide users with integrated capa-bilities such as word processing and printing, electronic filing and retrieval, graphics, and electronic mail. What *is* electronic mail? We define *electronic mail* as written messages transmitted and received elec-tronically between terminals linked by telephone lines or microwave relays. Electronic mail allows users to transmit information such as memos and letters, graphics, reports, or spreadsheets from one worksta-tion terminal to another—whether the terminals be situated within one company or sited within several different companies, whether the termi-nals be located within the United States or found in various other coun-tries of the world. Electronic mail also allows the user to transmit and receive mail fast. No doubt there have been times when you and your employer have waited for the arrival of and worried about the fate of an important piece of mail: Where *is* it? Frantic telephone calls. It's in the mail. But *where*? They don't know where. Well, put a tracer on it. They still can't find it. If they *don't* find it by tomorrow, we'll be dead in the water. Does that scenario ring a bell? With the global reach of today's business, the timely delivery of accurate messages has become an abso-lute necessity.

A truly flexible, broad-spectrum electronic mail system permits and expedites fast, accurate communication among individuals, groups, departments, and corporations from the types of workstations described earlier. With electronic mail, you can create (i.e., "write"), edit, transmit, read, and print your own mail. Conversely, you can answer your incoming mail, forward messages to other people using the system, request that return receipts be sent to your terminal, and file the mail. If your employer has such a system, he or she can do all of this, and you too can use the system. When you key in your outgoing message it is transmitted *at once* —there is no delay involving mail pickup and delivery—and the recipient of the message can read that message right away or at a later, more convenient time (an additional advantage from the standpoint of workflow and time management).

Just to give you a concrete idea of the capabilities of electronic mail, we cite here the major features of Customizable Electronic Mail as described on page III–4 of the book *Digital's Office Solutions* (Concord, MA: Digital Equipment Corporation, 1984):

Mail Preparation	—Create, Edit, Send
Mail Reception	—Read, Answer, Forward, Print, Delete
Mail Filing	—File, Search File, Read List, Print List
Mail Distribution	—Send To, Carbon Copies, Mailing Lists
Mail Utilities	—Index of Messages

If you examine carefully these features and their resultant capabilities, you will see right away that five features fulfill sixteen tasks, ten of which (i.e., Edit, Send, Answer, Forward, Delete, File, Search File, Carbon Copies, Mailing Lists, and Index of Messages) either eradicate secretarial tasks altogether or markedly reduce them. For instance, the Edit capability disposes of drafts and redrafts. Send bypasses the fold-insert-into-envelope-affix-stamp operation. Answer enables the executive to respond to a letter or memo directly without intervention of the dictation-transcription-read-correct-edit operations. File and Search File virtually eliminate one of the tasks most disliked by secretaries. And once you yourself have been freed up from mundane chores such as filing, you will have more time to devote to other, more enjoyable and challenging responsibilities.

We have seen, then, that electronic mail combines the speed of a telephone call with the permanency and impact of a letter, and at the same time liberates the secretary from the drudgery of the past. Other advantages of electronic mail stem from the ability of most equipment to operate unattended, thus eliminating "telephone tag" (people leaving telephone messages in response to previous messages but never reaching one another) and allowing overnight operation when transmission charges are lower. (An ancillary advantage to overnight transmission and unattended reception of messages is, of course, the fact that an executive returning late from a trip need not go into the office on the way home in order to obtain accumulated messages or call you for an update on the messages. The executive can, with proper equipment, dial into the mail system from any location at any time and receive the messages.)

Types of Computer-based Mail Systems (CBMS)

Basically, this form of electronic mail involves the use of computers to store and transmit messages. Written messages are transmitted to and retrieved from in-boxes and out-boxes within a computer system. The boxes aren't physical objects, but are instead special computer files earmarked for messages. Physically, a CBMS can be based either on a central computer serving as a repository for all the messages, or on a network of computers automatically transmitting messages to each other through the telephone lines, a data network, or a local area network. The next illustration shows the difference between a central computer system and a network system. If you are using a network, your computer should take care of all the details of message transmission and reception. If you are accessing a central computer using an office computer as a terminal, your office computer may be able to handle everything automatically. Otherwise, you will have to handle the details of making the connection with the computer. But in terms of how the system functions, the user may not be able to tell the difference between a centralized system and a network. Functionally, electronic mail systems can be grouped into stand-alone, integrated, and public systems. These are discussed in the next sections.

Stand-alone and Integrated Electronic Mail Systems

A stand-alone electronic mail system is really a computer that handles electronic mail and does nothing else. At the minimum, it should be able to receive messages automatically for later retrieval either from directly connected terminals or from remote sites with auto-answer modems through which the computer can answer the telephone. The integrated electronic mail system combines the mail features with word processing and other capabilities.

Almost any electronic mail system will include these features:

1. **Append**   The system will allow you to attach pre-prepared documents to the bottom of an electronic mail message.

2. **Directory**   The system can supply a list of its users. On public systems the directory may be intentionally restrictive.

3. **Distribution**   The system can send the same message to a prestored list of recipients.

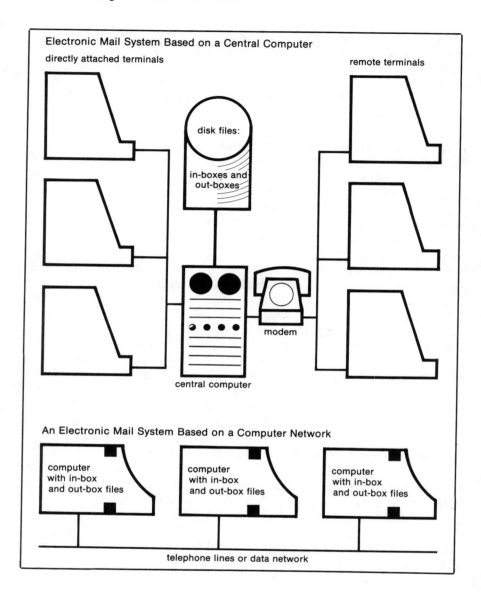

Electronic Mail System Based on a Central Computer

directly attached terminals

remote terminals

disk files:

in-boxes and out-boxes

modem

central computer

An Electronic Mail System Based on a Computer Network

computer with in-box and out-box files

computer with in-box and out-box files

computer with in-box and out-box files

telephone lines or data network

An electronic mail system based on a central computer (top) can be compared with a bulletin board on which people post and remove messages. The computer's files serve as the repository for all messages, and users can get to them through terminals attached to the system, or by calling in from remote terminals. Ther terminals themselves may be computers. An electronic mail system based on a computer network (bottom) can be compared with a private Telex network. The computers transmit messages to each other through the telephone lines or over a data network. The two methods overlap, since central computer systems also may exchange mail with computers in other offices.

4. **Editing** Text can be edited off-line prior to transmission.

5. **Gateway services** You can send Telex, E-COM, or Mailgram messages through the system.

6. **Message status** The system can list the headers of incoming messages and the status of outgoing messages, i.e., whether or not they have been transmitted.

7. **Registered mail** The system sends you a confirmation when the recipient reads the message.

8. **Reply requested** After you read a message, the system requires that you type a response, which immediately goes to the sender's mailbox.

9. **Security provisions** Access can be restricted by passwords, by the encryption of messages, or by both.

10. **Store and forward** The system can store a message for delivery at a later date.

Public Systems

A number of organizations offer public subscription electronic mail systems. These are stand-alone systems open for public use. You can exchange messages with any other subscriber, transmitting outgoing messages to the recipient's mailbox and downloading any messages you find in your own mailbox. Services like these are offered as an extra option by several packet switching networks such as Telenet and Tymnet, data service companies like The Source and CompuServe, communications carriers like MCI Communications Corporation, and specialized electronic mail companies. The gateway services offered by some Telex carriers are similar. Prices vary widely, as do service options. The mail system offered by The Source, for instance, requires that you first sign onto The Source, usually through one of the packet switching networks. To send a letter you then type MAIL SEND. The system will ask for the recipient's account name and then the subject. These items, plus the date and time, will form the header of the message. You then type or upload the text of the message, concluding with the .SEND command (pronounced dot-send). The message is immediately copied into the recipient's in-box. To check your in-box, you type the command MAILCK. If any mail is present the system tells you, and then you can read your mail with the command MAIL READ. (MAIL SCAN will cause the system to list out just the message headers.)

Data Networks

Computer-based message systems (CBMS) often employ local area networks and packet switching networks in message transmission.

Local Area Network (LAN).   A LAN is a network of computers that communicate with each other through direct wiring rather than over telephone lines. A LAN can be a system allowing the participating computers to use one another's disk files and printers automatically (as with the Xerox Ethernet or with the Datapoint ARC network), or it can be just a pathway for sending messages.

Packet switching networks.   The number of nationwide data networks is growing. Although some of them use other switching techniques, *packet switching network* has become a generic term for them. Subscribers attach their computers directly to the network, and anyone can reach that computer as long as he or she has access to the network. You can usually access the network through a local telephone number. After the connection has been established, the network usually asks for a terminal identifier so that it can add special features (such as filler characters after a carriage return) to the data stream required by some terminals. Then you type in the code identifier of the computer you wish to reach. If that computer accepts your call, thereafter you will be able to act as though you were attached directly to the computer, and the packet switching network will become "invisible." The average cost for connect time is currently $6.00 an hour, regardless of distance. Most connections between a terminal and a computer are made collect.

FACSIMILE MACHINES

A fax machine is basically a copier that scans a full-page document and transmits a signal to a second copier, which reproduces the document on another piece of paper. Whatever is on the page will be transmitted whether it is a typed or handwritten message, a drawing, a signed legal document, or the executive's doodles. Delivery is possible within minutes between any two points served by telephone. The fax machine has become an indispensable communications medium in today's business place.

Types of Hardware

Fax machines from different makers were previously incompatible. But in 1976 the Consultative Committee on International Telegraph and Telephone (CCITT) established transmission standards allowing compatibility between brands. The standards divide fax machines into the four groups described here.

Group I.   These machines (which have almost vanished from the market) use analog signaling techniques that require 6 minutes to transmit a page with a resolution of 96 by 96 lines per inch. They can transmit shades of gray. Also included are many older units manufactured before the

Houghton Mifflin Company

One Beacon Street, Boston, Massachusetts 02108   Trade & Reference Division
(617) 725-5000   Cable HOUGHTON

REFERENCE DEPARTMENT

FAX COVER SHEET

DATE: ___10/08/91___

TO: ___Christina Warner___

COMPANY: ___Artech Graphics___

FAX NUMBER: ___(101) 222-3333___

FROM: ___Andrew Granville___

NUMBER OF PAGES BEING TRANSMITTED (INCLUDING COVER SHEET): ___5___

MESSAGE: ___Here is the production schedule for the first quarter of___
___1992, as we discussed at last week's meeting.___

___If you have any questions, please don't hesitate to let me know.___

FAX Cover Sheet

CCITT standards were established, for which compatibility should not be assumed.

Group II.   These machines use analog techniques to transmit a page in 3 minutes with a resolution of 96 by 96 lines per inch. The principal difference over Group I is higher speed and the use of FM instead of AM modulation. Some cannot transmit shades of gray.

Group III.   These machines use digital techniques to transmit a page with a resolution of about 200 by 200 lines per inch. They do not transmit shades of gray. Transmitting at 9,600 baud, a Group III machine can send the 200,000 bits usually required to "describe" a page in about 20 seconds. (*Baud* is a unit of data transmission speed, usually equal to one bit per second.) These machines usually come with a step-down modem that automatically switches to a lower speed if the line is too noisy due to background static caused by poor connections or other problems. The average transmission speed you can expect in the United States is 8,000 bits per second, but it is much lower over some foreign telephone systems.

Group IV.   These machines are the most advanced models currently marketed. They use transmission speeds of 56,000 baud and offer a resolution of 400 by 400 lines per inch. Laser printers with similar features should not be confused with Group IV fax machines.

Features

Most machines have the option of transmitting at higher speeds (4 minutes for Group I; 2 minutes for Group II) with less resolution. Group III and Group II machines often have the ability to communicate with machines of a lower group. Other possible features and options are:

1. **Polling**   You can leave the machine overnight with material in it, and someone can call in and trigger the machine to start transmitting. It will answer the telephone and hang up automatically.

2. **Automatic receiving**   You can set the machine in a similar manner to receive any incoming documents automatically.

3. **Activity reports**   The machine can print out a list of the transmissions and receptions that it performed on a given day.

4. **Sender ID**   As a sort of "postmark," the machine can print the telephone number or code name of the message sender, plus possibly the date, time, and page count across the top or bottom of the page.

5. **Local copy**   The machine can be used as if it were an office photocopier.

6. **Computer printer**   Although the coding used by Group III machines is not the same as ASCII (American Standard Code for Information Interchange) or any other data communications code, some machines have the ability to receive ASCII and function as if they were computer printers. The transmission of a Group III machine can also be stored in a computer just as any other digital data can be.

Facsimile Services

A number of organizations now offer various facsimile transmission services. Usually you have to bring your documents to their offices, but high-volume customers may be given their own fax machines by the service provider.

INTELPOST.   A service of the US Postal Service and several foreign postal services, INTELPOST allows you to transmit documents from or to the INTELPOST center in Chicago, Houston, New York, San Francisco, or

Washington, DC; to or from a post office in a foreign city, where it then can be forwarded by regular mail or special delivery or left for counter pickup. At this writing INTELPOST connects to points in Argentina, Canada, France, Hong Kong, the Netherlands, the United Kingdom, and West Germany. The cost is $10.00 for the first page and $6.00 for each additional page. Special delivery and other services are extra. You can submit your document to the nearest INTELPOST center over the counter, by Express Mail, or through a Group III fax machine.

Data carriers.   Several data carriers offer their subscribers various value-added facsimile services. Fax transmissions can be recorded for later retransmission, converted from one CCITT standard to another, or broadcast to multiple receivers. Messages also can be received through Telex or data terminal machines and retransmitted by facsimile machines and vice versa. The vendors include ITT World Communications (Secaucus, NJ) and Graphnet Incorporated (Englewood, NJ).

THE TELEX NETWORK

As the descendant of the original Morse Code telegraph, the Telex network spans the globe. There are about 200,000 subscribers in North America and 1.5 million in the rest of the world. Using a standard keyboard printer often called a Teletype or teleprinter and a dial-up arrangement similar to that of the telephone system, a subscriber can print out a message on any other subscriber's machine.

The Telex network is heavily relied on in Europe where language barriers limit the usefulness of long-distance telephone calls. The Telex network is also important to organizations dealing in international trade, if only because time differentials make it difficult to reach people by telephone. The drawbacks of Telex are slow and noisy operation, absence of lowercase letters, and relatively inferior print quality compared with most computer printers. In most countries the local Telex network is operated by the postal authorities. In the United States the Telex network was formerly a monopoly of Western Union, which carried all domestic traffic except in a few major cities. But Western Union was not allowed to handle overseas traffic and such messages were routed through any of several other companies called International Record Carriers (IRCs). Then in 1981 the government deregulated the industry. As a result, Western Union can now connect you directly to an overseas number and the IRCs can set up their own domestic Telex networks. Since the government requires that the networks interconnect, you can get through to anyone regardless of network affiliation. Some of the IRCs having their own Telex networks are: FTC Communications Incorporated, Graphnet Incorporated, Global Communications, TRT Telecommunications Corporation, Comsat Corporation, and CCI. In 1989 Western Union was acquired by AT&T.

Operating pointers.   Careful study of the instructions provided by Western Union or your international record carrier (IRC) is required before you can use the Telex network successfully. But basically, Telex machines are not very mysterious. They are just remotely connected electric typewriters with dial-up mechanisms. The only thing you might not immediately understand is the answer-back mechanism and the tape reader-puncher.

The answer-back mechanism is a metal cylinder with studs, similar to the one that you might find in a music box. When you push the HERE IS key, the cylinder revolves and causes the machine to send the characters encoded by the studs. This is your machine's answer-back message, and is listed with your number in the Telex directory. Pushing WRU (Who Are You) causes the machine at the other end to transmit its own answer-back. Usually you begin a message with an exchange of answer-backs. This ability to identify positively both parties has allowed Telex messages to serve as legal contracts in many countries. The paper tape mechanism allows you to code the message onto tape while the machine is off-line. The tape is fed into the tape reader and transmitted after the connection is made. This device allows you to save on connect charges since you cannot type as fast as the machine's transmission speed—slow as it may seem.

Gateway Services

A recent trend has been for the Telex carriers to enable subscribers to use office computers in place of Telex machines. Many IRC subscribers do this, and the Western Union gateway service is called EasyLink. All you have to do is rig your office computer for communication through a modem and dial into the Telex carrier's central computer (usually through a toll-free number). When the connection has been made, you then have full access to the resources of the Telex network. Incoming messages can be stored within the central computer for later retrieval, with the computer supplying your answer-back. Or the incoming message can be forwarded to you real-time through a telephone call to an electronic mail system in your office.

Teletex

In Europe where greater reliance is placed on the Telex network, the Teletex standard has been developed to combine the idea of Teletex with the advantages offered by the computer revolution. Teletex is not a physical network, but rather a standard that allows properly equipped and programmed office computers to send and receive messages automatically as though they were advanced Telex machines. The standard involves a transmission speed of 2,400 baud through whatever connections are available. Teletex allows lowercase letters, with the text formatted to look like a standard business letter. It also allows interconnection to the Telex network.

Hybrid Services ("Time Sensitive Mail")

A number of services combine electronic mail with some other form of delivery. This field, too, has seen the emergence of competition and a proliferation of services.

Domestic telegrams.   A domestic telegram is basically a Telex message sent to someone without a Telex machine. A Western Union clerk telephones the recipient and reads the text, and then the printed copy is forwarded by mail if requested. Delivery by messenger is available in most cities for an extra charge. You can send a telegram directly from your Telex machine or through your local Western Union office. Attempted delivery is guaranteed within two hours for telephone-delivered telegrams and five hours for hand-delivered telegrams. Domestic telegrams cannot be considered cost-effective if there is any hope of getting through with a long-distance telephone call. But telegram notification is often required in legal contracts.

Cablegrams.   International telegrams (Cablegrams) are similar to domestic telegrams except that they are handled at the receiving end in whatever manner is standard in the local country. Cablegrams can be sent from a Telex terminal, or through a Western Union office or an IRC offering Cablegram service. Either way, the charge is based on the number of words in the message, with a minimum of seven words. Since the charge per word can be more than 30¢, it is important that anyone who regularly writes Cablegrams understand the word-count rules.

Information on word-count rules is available from your Cablegram carrier, but the basic rule is that any word in any language that can be found in a dictionary counts as one word, to a maximum of fifteen letters. Code words count as one word for every five letters, as do combinations of letters and numbers, and numbers by themselves. Every space counts as a new word, so that names like *De La Garza* would be counted as three words, and should be written *DeLaGarza*. Short words can be combined (*tobe* instead of *to be*), but such combinations count as code words and the five-letter rule applies. Do not use the characters $#&%¢ in Cablegrams, since they are not used overseas. Other punctuation marks can be used but they count as one word each, with certain exceptions. Every word in the recipient's address is counted except for the destination country and any routing symbol. Therefore, it pays to use one-word cable addresses. These can be found on company letterhead or from the most recent edition of *Marconi's International Register*, available in libraries. Cable addresses should not be confused with Telex answer-backs.

If the first word in the Cablegram is LT, then it becomes a letter telegram

telegram. A letter telegram costs up to 50% less and will be delivered the next business day in the receiving city (or whatever is standard). Some countries will not accept LTs, and code words cannot be used. The minimum length is twenty-two words. Other Cablegram options include prepaid responses, night delivery, delivery by mail, telephone or Telex, notification of delivery, and the inclusion of a list of alternate addresses.

Mailgrams.   A joint venture of Western Union and the Postal Service, Mailgrams are Telex messages sent to the Telex-equipped post office nearest the recipient, where the message is removed from the machine and delivered as mail. Mailgrams sent during business hours should be delivered the next day. Mailgrams sent early in the morning may be delivered the same day. They can be sent from a Telex terminal or by calling Western Union. There is a maximum length of seven pages. Confirmation copies are available at an extra cost. Mailgrams may also be sent to a few foreign countries, including Canada and the United Kingdom.

E-COM.   A service designed for high-volume mailers, E-COM allows you to transmit letters to one of twenty-five specially equipped serving post offices (SPOs), where they will be printed out and mailed in distinctive blue-and-white envelopes. They will be delivered within two days, provided that they have been addressed to the area served by that SPO. The letters can be unique messages to individual addresses, a common message to a list of addresses, or a mix of common and unique text for each addressee. However, you must have at least 200 letters to use the service. Your equipment and software also must be certified as workable by the Post Office, you must pay a yearly fee, and you must set up a trust fund with the post office that will be debited as you make each mailing. In conjunction with electronic mail, E-COM is particularly attractive if your company has high-volume mailings such as these: communications to shareholders, financial and legal announcements, price-change notifications, broad-spectrum sales promotions, sales bulletins, product maintenance/recall bulletins, credit collections, subscription renewals, invoices, fund-raising campaign material, and surveys or polls.

Index